WIFE, INC.

CRITICAL CULTURAL COMMUNICATION

GENERAL EDITORS: Jonathan Gray, Aswin Punathambekar, Nina Huntemann
FOUNDING EDITORS: Sarah Banet-Weiser and Kent A. Ono

Wife, Inc.

The Business of Marriage in the Twenty-First Century

Suzanne Leonard

NEW YORK UNIVERSITY PRESS

New York

NEW YORK UNIVERSITY PRESS
New York
www.nyupress.org

References to Internet websites (URLs) were accurate at the time of writing. Neither the author nor New York University Press is responsible for URLs that may have expired or changed since the manuscript was prepared.

Library of Congress Cataloging-in-Publication Data
Names: Leonard, Suzanne, author.
Title: Wife, Inc. : the business of marriage in the twenty-first century / Suzanne Leonard.
Description: New York : New York University Press, [2018] | Series: Critical cultural communication | Includes bibliographical references and index.
Identifiers: LCCN 2017037993 | ISBN 9781479874507 (cl : alk. paper)
Subjects: LCSH: Marriage—United States—History—21st century. | Wives—United States. | Marriage in popular culture.
Classification: LCC HQ536 .L46 2018 | DDC 306.810973—dc23
LC record available at https://lccn.loc.gov/2017037993

New York University Press books are printed on acid-free paper, and their binding materials are chosen for strength and durability. We strive to use environmentally responsible suppliers and materials to the greatest extent possible in publishing our books.

Manufactured in the United States of America

10 9 8 7 6 5 4 3 2 1

Also available as an ebook

For Alan

To passions and aspirations, past, present, and those to come

CONTENTS

Introduction

The Wife Industry

The premise of FYI's *Married at First Sight* (2014–) was stark but simple: agreeing to leave matrimonial decisions up to so-called science, the show's six principals acquiesced to marrying a stranger, sight unseen. Relying on metrics such as in-depth personality profiles, attractiveness rating scales, and home visits—or what the show repeatedly termed "sophisticated instruments"—*Married at First Sight*'s experts (a psychologist, a sexologist, a sociologist, and a spiritual adviser) selected mates from the show's contestants. As implied, prospective spouses literally meet at the altar. Rationalizing her appearance on the show, one participant argued that dating is difficult because etiquette has changed. People use text messages or online communication, she lamented, losing that face-to-face connection. "It's a serious experiment," confirmed sociologist Dr. Pepper Schwartz. "This might be an antidote to a chaotic dating system that is really tiring people out." Performing an end run around the vagaries of choice and intent, as well as sparing participants the awkwardness of failed first dates, *Married at First Sight* is perhaps the answer for time-crunched professionals weary of dysfunctional dating climates: in short, the show models how one might outsource the process of finding the "one."

Married at First Sight provides apt introduction to *Wife, Inc.*, thanks to its reliance on heuristics of efficiency, a supposedly scientific approach to coupling, and a relentless emphasis on the work that participants must undertake to establish their marriages as legitimate. After a month of marriage, spouses decide if they wanted to continue or abandon the arrangement. The show, I assert, is a reminder that American marriage culture has been radically reenvisioned in the twenty-first century, an alteration we can credit in part to the notion that marriage is the sort of business that must be gotten down to, much like one might decide it is time to secure a full-time job or purchase a house. Orchestrating a rationalized system for the procurement of a mate, *Married at First Sight* elevates an individual's readiness for marriage into the sole reason that she or he should undertake the commitment. In *Wifey 101: Everything I Got Wrong after Meeting Mr. Right*, the female counterpart in one of the only two couples to have succeeded in operationalizing *Married at First Sight*'s promises of marital longevity (despite the show's five-seasons-and-counting run) matter-of-factly asserts that a successful marriage needs no more than time, effort, and a will to succeed. Writing about her decision to agree to a "scientifically arranged, legally binding blind marriage," author Jamie Otis divulges that post-wedding there was still more work to be done: "If I wanted my marriage to last, I had to learn to be a good wife and even better in-law quickly and efficiently."[1]

Theorizing the rationalized understandings of marriage newly embedded in the cultural fabric of twenty-first century America, *Wife, Inc.* attempts to untangle them via an in-depth analysis of female media culture. Specifically, it attends to popular television, film, and literature, as well as mass-market news, women's magazines, new media, and advice culture in order to understand these developments. While the systems I reference involve both men and women, the position of women vis-à-vis marital cultures is the more pronounced of the two, particularly as the term "wife" has gained increased traction. Though the prevalence of the moniker might suggest otherwise, for women especially, the institution of marriage has changed dramatically in the past forty years. For one, the inequities with respect to labor, economics, and domesticity that once bespoke women's disadvantage have given way to a host of social upheavals and liberal progress. The sort of second-class citizen designation that wives once faced—a positionality that helped to ignite a feminist critique of the marital institution during both the first and second waves—has receded in a postfeminist era where women's gains are widely touted. Understandings of the need for equality in both the home and in professional spaces have been largely mainstreamed though not, of course, necessarily realized. As a result, nowadays it feels downright anachronistic to suggest that a woman's sexual needs could only be met in marriage, that men are necessary for procreation, or that women must do the lion's share of the emotional, domestic, or physical work it takes to support a functioning household. Both romantic and practical,

American marriages are widely understood to be based on equal partnership, economic solvency, and romantic love, renegotiations that have benefited women in particular.

Part of what is so shocking about *Married at First Sight* is that it appears to ignore these advances and suggest instead that marriage is a decision best left to experts, a seemingly antiquated notion that calls on histories of matchmakers and arranged marriages. Similarly retrograde about the show's premise is that ours is a culture schooled on the belief that marriage should be a choice, rhetoric now as entrenched in the gay marriage movement as it is indebted to postfeminist conceptualizations of female individualism. At the same time, the fact that a series of attractive twenty- and thirtysomethings would sacrifice this near-sacred right to choose their partners based on love and literally marry the person that a set of strangers has selected for them because they are so eager to get to the experience would seem to counteract the widespread perception that women's dependency on marriage has sharply declined. Publications as run-of-the-mill as *Cosmopolitan* have not been afraid to suggest that marriage is no longer as important a commitment as it once was. The cheekily titled "I Do, or Do I?" which ran in August 2013 surveys a host of marital experts and young women, reaching the conclusion that women are "delaying marriage or, increasingly, not getting married at all at a rate that is only accelerating." The article suggests that women are "ambivalent about marriage in their twenties,"[2] an observation that echoes demographic data. According to a 2014 Pew Center report, 20 percent of adults older than twenty-five (about forty-two million people) have never married, a figure that sharply contrasts data from the 1960s when only 9 percent of Americans fell into this category. Support and confirmation for these recent statistics can also be found in the reality that men and women wait longer to marry than they once did: the average age for a first marriage is twenty-seven for women and twenty-nine for men.[3]

This data appears to corroborate the widely held belief that marriage is less socially relevant, less necessary, and less common than ever. According to the 2010 census, only 20 percent of American households consisted of a married heterosexual couple with children, statistics underpinned by realities like rising cohabitation rates, increasing ages for first marriages, what was then the lack of gay marriage as an option in

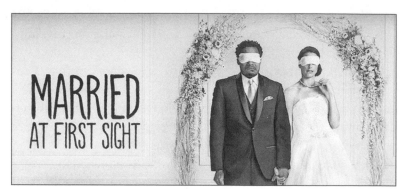

Figure I.1. *Married at First Sight* uses tongue-in-cheek humor to promote its practice of marrying willing strangers.

many states, and the mainstreaming of the notion that marriage is no longer a necessary precursor to reproduction. These dwindling numbers have not, however, lessened the stronghold that marriage occupies in the symbolic imaginary, nor do they indicate an obviation of the capacious interest in and energy that surrounds the institution. As historian Stephanie Coontz wrote in 2013, "Rumors of the death of marriage are greatly exaggerated. People are not giving up on marriage. They are simply waiting longer to tie the knot."[4] The perception that marriage no longer matters is also hard to maintain if one makes even a cursory foray into the discourse of popular American media, and particularly if one looks at the role of heterosexual women in those spaces. In fact, wives dominate the terms and concerns of twenty-first-century female popular culture: courting eagerly, marrying lavishly, and divorcing scandalously. More specifically, wives write memoirs and advice books, start businesses based on wifedom, and star in fictional and reality television shows that centralize their position as wives. Rather than slide into oblivion, the wife has morphed into postfeminist media culture's most favored icon, one endlessly utilized to frame discussions of female life cycles. In this milieu, the wife is at once historically diminished while also more important than ever.

It is the contention of *Wife, Inc.* that wifedom and marriage remain the preferred modalities for postfeminist media to investigate, prescribe, and proscribe female life cycles. Differently put, depictions of wives are the foremost way in which American culture currently negotiates norms of femininity. In part, this dominance of marriage culture arises from its seemingly obvious role as a step on the path to maturity, adulthood, and reproductive futurity. Consider the backbone of any conventional love story: love and romance lead to marriage and children. With the advent of gay marriage as a national right (although one that is admittedly more precarious under the Trump administration), marital trajectories have, if anything, only become more ineluctably etched in the popular consciousness. Marriage persists as the preferred teleology that structures not simply individual lives, books, films, or television shows, but also entire genres such as chick lit, romantic comedy, and reality dating shows. As Stephanie Harzewski details in her study of chick lit, despite the fact that the genre often imparts a "sociologically realistic commentary on the tenuousness of the marital bond and the romantic wedding's failure to assure long-term fulfillment . . . wedlock still signifies a developmental endpoint of sorts; dating is teleological in intent."[5] This disconnect begs a question: why is marriage at once so sidelined, and yet simultaneously so prominent in female media cultures? One explanation has been offered by Angela McRobbie, who contends that increased focus is directed toward marriage's cultural profile precisely because the financial incentives have diminished:

> Great effort is invested in this task of maintaining and consolidating masculine hegemony for the very reason that there are forces that appear to threaten its dominance. Thus the paraphernalia of marriage culture assumes much visibility within popular culture at the very moment when its necessity is being put into question. If for women in the West survival itself, and the well-being of children, no longer rests on finding a male partner who will be a breadwinner, then the significance of marriage is much reduced. . . . This is the case of what is no longer economically central becoming, for this very reason, culturally necessary.

McRobbie hypothesizes that a renewed "celebration of marriage culture and all its trimmings" is an attempt to "ensure that orderliness prevails in a context of change and movement."[6]

For evidence of marriage's continued status as culturally though not economically necessary, we might reference the glutted cottage industry that is wifely media. From speculative re-creations that imagine the

Figure I.2. Julie Pennell's *The Young Wives Club* is one of many "wife" books that dot the roster.

wives of historical husbands (*The Paris Wife*, *American Wife*, *The Aviator's Wife*, *The Wives of Los Alamos*), to fictionalized novels that use the word in their title as a marketing hook (*The Senator's Wife*, *The 19th Wife*, *The Tiger's Wife*, *The Lost Wife*, *Husband and Wife*, *A Reliable Wife*, *Wife 22*, *The Invisible Wife*, *The Silent Wife*, *How to Be a Good Wife*, *The Secret Wife*, *The Zookeeper's Wife*, *The Millionaire's Wife*, *The Young Wives Club*, *My Husband's Wife*), to television programs touting her nomenclature (*Wife Swap*, *Desperate Housewives*, *The Real Housewives*, *The Good Wife*, *Sister Wives*, *Army Wives*, *Trophy Wife*, *The Astronaut Wives Club*, *American Housewife*), wives are quite frankly an overexposed lot. In this list, I deliberately include only materials that use the term "wife" in their titles. While these offerings do very different work, much of which will be parsed out in this study, one clear beginning point for analysis is simply to recognize and acknowledge the wife's rise to cultural prominence in contemporary mediated milieus.

Marriage: Then and Now

One of the most important underpinnings of this study is its understanding of marriage as a shifting cultural institution that has had unique implications for women in particular. Perhaps the most predominant transformation in marriage in Western cultures was its movement "from obedience to intimacy" whereby "love conquered marriage"— both taglines in Stephanie Coontz's opus *Marriage, a History*. As Coontz explains, through much of history, marriage was defined as a political and economic institution in which it served much as government and markets do today, namely, by organizing the "production and distribution of goods and people."[7] While marriage was a prominent social regulator of affect and economies alike, this function began to shift in the late eighteenth century when the notion that people might choose partners on the basis of personal affection began to proliferate as a cultural ideal. Belief in free choice and marriage for love in turn prompted what Coontz terms the "male breadwinner love marriage," whereby wives were expected to serve as nurturing homemakers and men as cultural providers. This ideal nevertheless had little economic viability except among the bourgeoisie until roughly the 1950s, which we now understand as an anomalous period wherein a middle-class family could thrive on the earnings of a single provider. This period, and the rigid gender roles that it concretized, nevertheless occupies a commanding position in the American cultural imaginary.

Marriage norms underwent another seismic revolution in the 1970s, a transition that is particularly germane to Coontz's account and to my study as well. In 2005, Coontz claimed that "the relations between men and women have changed more in the last thirty years than they did in the previous three thousand." She elaborates:

> In less than twenty years, the whole legal, political, and economic context of marriage was transformed. By the end of the 1970s women had access to legal rights, education, birth control, and decent jobs. Suddenly divorce was easy to get. At the same time, traditional family arrangements became more difficult to sustain in the new economy. And new sexual mores, growing tolerance for out-of-wedlock births, and rising aspirations for self-fulfillment changed the cultural milieu in which people made decisions about their personal relationships. During the 1980s and 1990s, all these changes came together to irrevocably transform the role of marriage in society at large and in people's personal lives.[8]

Coontz's statement refers obliquely to what is popularly understood as the women's liberation movement, which made women's equality in arenas like health care, education, and politics not merely a rallying cry but also a centerpiece of political organizing. As these reforms came about so, too, did a popular renegotiation of the ideals of domesticity and reimaginings of the marital commitment, such that mutuality and shared labor earned prominence as desirable facets of marriage. Women's economic and financial independence gained traction and visibility at the same time that the image of the male breadwinner was afforded less purchase. Women were thought to need marriage less for financial stability and more in order to stake a claim on emotional fulfillment.

Shifting understandings of marriage also politicized its importance. Both first- and second-wave feminists decried the institution as propagating unfair gender schemas, whereby men could access women's bodies, property, and labor without censure. In the 1960s and 1970s this critique was essentially taken to the streets, localizable in a wide range of activist, theoretical, and mainstream interventions. From the 1969 hex on the Bridal Fair that a radical feminist group staged outside Madison Square Garden; to the writings of activist feminists who claimed that the abolition of marriage was necessary because women's free labor in the home sabotaged their demands for equal pay outside of it; to myriad articles in mainstream magazines about the lot of dissatisfied housewives; to films and television shows featuring single, separated, or divorced women; and finally to fiction considering new sexual arrangements, the process of scrutinizing heterosexual marriage was something of a cause célèbre during this period. It is instructive to compare these critiques of marriage to the reassuring tone that Coontz adopts when describing the nature of American marriage in the 1980s and 1990s. In Coontz's rendering, the utopian dream of good jobs for women, as well as access to education, birth control, and divorce, made it possible for the populace to "make decisions" in accordance with requirements for "self-fulfillment."[9] This statement quite notably shares a number of assumptions that have come to define postfeminism, understandings that also shape the context for and realities of my study. For one, the statement does not account for economic inequality—many women do not have access to "decent jobs" and never did. Further, it evidences belief in a teleology of progress regarding issues that were classically cast as "women's," such as education and birth control, including a resolute investment in the power of the individual to make decisions. Elspeth Probyn helpfully named the postfeminist investment in individual choice "choiceoisie," a term she uses to refer to this tendency to frame all decisions in terms of the personal. Probyn quarrels with this idealization, arguing that "at a material level the great majority of women still have very little to choose from and that all these representations that fill the air with alluring options are but ideological manifestations."[10] The concept of personal choice has nevertheless become the most seminal ethos in renderings of the cultural politics of marriage.

As Coontz's description suggests, a resounding drumbeat in the 1980s, 1990s, and early 2000s was the articulation that marriage functioned primarily as a privatized commitment that benignly attempted to ensure happiness among its practitioners. These attributions rested in large part on the idea of marriage's pliability. One of the most celebratory positions emerged in the work of sociologist Anthony Giddens, whose landmark 1992 study *The Transformation of Intimacy: Sexuality, Love and Eroticism in Modern Societies* expounded on the belief that emancipatory potential lay in the realization of romantic love, thanks to a new emotional order wherein sexual relationships could be understood as mimicking the principles of a participatory democracy. Observing how feminists as well as everyday women not specifically connected to the movement demanded equality and reciprocity in relationships, Giddens argued that these ideals were realized in what he termed the "pure relationship," a highly utopian form defined by flexible terms of both entry and exit. According to Giddens, the pure relationship is entered into for its own sake and subject to dissolution on these same terms. Giddens differentiates between the pure relationship and marriage, although the experiences are frequently indistinguishable. He writes, "Love used to be tied to sexuality, for most of the sexually 'normal' population, through marriage; but now the two are connected more and more via the pure relationship. Marriage—for many, but by no means all groups in the population—has veered increasingly towards the form of a pure relationship."[11] The idea that marriage was not a shackle but instead a worthwhile and even emancipatory commitment represented a significant shift from the 1970s, when marriage's restrictive strictures invited significant backlash.

The 1980s and 1990s also witnessed a profound cultural emphasis on the importance of making marriages work, both for the sake of the primary parties and for their offspring. In addition to noting that these two decades witnessed a skyrocketing rise in the number of marriage counselors, historian Kristin Celello cites a 1987 *Newsweek* cover story titled "How to Stay Married" that applauded the virtues of "working" on one's relationship. Similar perspectives blanketed women's media. In 1980 the popular women's magazine *Mademoiselle* declared "nuptial madness" and in 1991 *Ladies' Home Journal* saw a "return to commitment."[12] Celebrations of the institution of marriage and discussions of its benefits even had a trickle-down effect on academic inquiry. Sociologist Wendy Langford argues that while some researchers did attempt to address questions of power in their work on marriage, "by the 1990s, however, prominent social theorists were again constructing the sexual couple as progressive and humane—claiming, moreover, that partly in response to feminism, love relationships are becoming more equal and more negotiable than ever before." While this rosy egalitarian vision is comforting, Langford's 1999 study suggests that it nevertheless did not hold up to scientific scrutiny. After interviewing women involved in long-term romantic relationships, Langford concluded that visions of democratic love mostly serve to mystify the actual conditions of women's lives, leading women to channel energies "into the reproduction of a social order characterized by gendered polarization, alienation and hierarchies of power, while we at once articulate the discourse of egalitarian couplehood."[13] Langford's findings also appear to confirm Shere Hite's much-lambasted 1988 study, published as *Women and Love: A Cultural Revolution in Progress*, where she argued that postfeminist women were still profoundly disappointed in their attempts to realize equal partnerships with their spouses.[14]

These congratulatory views of marriage as a free commitment and the dismissal of any views to the contrary helped to ensure that during the 1980s, 1990s, and early 2000s marriage held a relatively diminished position as an institution worthy of political critique. "Marriage used to be considered both natural and socially necessary. Now its naturalness is in question, and only right-wing public moralists regard marriage as a social obligation. Legally and ideologically, marriage is today the most private of practices and a matter of individual happiness and fulfillment," wrote cultural theorist David Shumway in 2003.[15] The belief that marriage was a privatized commitment responsible parties entered into and exited freely from without government interference or intrusion also shares a strong affinity with what we now think of as neoliberalism. Neoliberal attitudes permeate almost all reaches of public and private life and prioritize the belief that people are actualized agents who should act in their own self-interest, exercise free choice, and accept personal responsibility for their decisions and behaviors. Marriage's newfound status as a private commitment that was both the right *and* the responsibility of individual actors is a viewpoint highly consistent with neoliberal norms. I will soon address the impact that debates about gay marriage had on these formulations, but it is instructive to note how myopically heterosexist the discourse of marriage was during the late twentieth and early twenty-first centuries. Proclamations of marriage's emancipatory potential pointedly turned a blind eye to the fact that entire swaths of the population were not legally allowed to wed. Likewise, it is difficult to cast marriage as a commitment in which the state had no part when in fact same-sex couples desiring to marry acutely felt the weight of state intervention and prohibition, and did so until 2015 when gay marriage was legalized across the nation.

Neoliberal framings of marriage nevertheless occupy a foundational presence in this study, because the belief that finding, securing, and sustaining a marriage is a matter best left to individual agency is a sustaining cultural ideal. Scholars of neoliberalism, and particularly Wendy Brown, note that one of its hallmarks is the "casting [of] every human endeavor and activity in entrepreneurial terms." She continues, "It formulates everything in terms of capital investment and appreciation (including and especially humans themselves), whether a teenager building a resume for college, a twenty-something seeking a mate, a working mother returning to school, or a corporation buying carbon offsets." For my purposes, it is the "twenty-something seeking a mate" that provides the most illustrative example of how neoliberalism influences the organization of the social order. If, as Brown explains, neoliberalism converts subjects into "entrepreneurs of their own needs and desires who consume or invest in these goods,"[16] then *Wife, Inc.* posits that twenty-first-century wives not only fit snugly within that categorization but also in many ways exemplify it. As I will argue throughout this book, securing the title of wife is often a gesture of self-interest that requires deft entrepreneurial maneuvers. Though marriage enjoyed a sanitized, relatively conflict-free cultural profile from the 1980s to the early 2000s, I argue that this perch has shifted in the past ten years. The transition can be attributed to a number of factors including the intensification of neoliberal ideals, a diminished belief in the power of relationships to grant participants unrestricted emotional fulfillment, and finally, and perhaps most saliently, the economic insecurities that intensified during and subsequent to the great recession and the profound economic stratification that the recession both highlighted and exacerbated. In the wake of these shifts, I contend that wifedom is newly professionalized as an occupation in its own right and that the regulatory and affective investments that characterize contemporary labor relations also ground American wifedom. These reformulations have implications for current marital climates and for the socioeconomic order writ large.

Marriage and Class Stratification

Demographic data from the period in which this study concentrates suggests that marriage occupies new ground as a cultural status symbol. The fact that marital status serves as a barometer of financial security is a crucial observation I wish to reiterate, in addition to emphasizing the reality that marriage cultures sit on the foundation of the country's increasingly bifurcated class systems. According to a 2010 study released by the Pew Center, a new "marriage gap" in the United States is increasingly aligned with a growing education and income gap. As the study concluded, "Marriage, while declining among all groups, remains the norm for adults with a college education and good income but is now markedly less prevalent among those on the lower rungs of the socio-economic ladder."[17] Lowering marital numbers speak trenchantly to what is really a profoundly deterministic gap between wealthy Americans and those who are struggling. As W. Bradford Wilcox, director of the National Marriage Project at the University of Virginia, and author of a report titled "When Marriage Disappears: The Retreat from Marriage in Middle America" explained in 2011, "The roots of this growing marriage divide are economic (the postindustrial economy favors the college educated), cultural (less educated Americans are abandoning a marriage mindset even as college-educated Americans take up this mindset) and legal (less educated Americans seem particularly gun shy about marrying in a world where no-fault divorce is the law of the land)."[18]

Importantly, lowered marriage rates testify to the realities and impacts of socioeconomic distress, insofar as economic security is often seen as a precursor to marriage. As a 2014 Pew report confirmed, "For young adults who want to get married, financial security is a significant hurdle. Compared with their older counterparts, young adults who have never been married are more likely to cite financial security as the main reason for not being currently married."[19] Participants generally wait until they occupy stable financial positions to wed. As such, marriage is often a culminating act of economic achievement, a position that many Americans never reach. Failure to marry is in this respect not a matter of desiring to abandon the institution but rather a capitulation to a stark economic reality. "It's not that people don't want to marry. Most never-married Americans say they still aspire to marriage, but many of them see it as something grand and out of reach," claimed an *Atlantic* cover story in 2013.[20] Moreover, when class and education intersect with race, we see the deep historical entrenchment of these patterns. The lack of education and jobs for black men has, for instance, long contributed to their declining marital prospects.[21] This lack of eligible black men for women to marry has in turn been a consistent source of anxiety in female popular culture, which I address in chapter 1 of this study. These conversations remind us of the classist and racist history of the marital institution, its ties to wealth accumulation and consolidation, and the ways marriage refracts through and reifies class and racial hierarchies.

The correlation between economic security and marital viability is a particularly pressing problem for Americans with scant education and few marketable skills. Lessening numbers of marriages and the rise of single-parent households have been correlated with poverty, which has dire effects not only on living conditions but even on lifespan. A landmark 2015 study from Princeton economists found "a marked increase in the all-cause mortality of middle-aged white non-Hispanic men and women in the United States between 1999 and 2013. This change reversed decades of progress in mortality and was unique to the United States; no other rich country saw a similar turnaround."[22] While there are a variety of potential causes for rising mortality rates, the authors speculate that financial stress likely plays a significant role since economic pressures take a toll on health and longevity. This complicated commingling of economics, education, marital patterns, and life expectancy have in many ways been mystified by the rhetoric of choice, personal desire, and individuality that have overlaid discussions of marriage in the popular consciousness since the 1980s. These cherished American ideals of self-agency and personal responsibility have nevertheless been put under enormous stress as a result of the global economic recession and the resulting wage stagnation, joblessness, and debt that persisted in its wake. Relatedly, losses in myriad industries that once catered to less-educated Americans and the growth of low-paid service-sector employment have contributed to a growing sense of class determinism, a sentiment that Donald Trump blatantly tapped into during his 2016 presidential campaign.

Part of what my study aims to emphasize is that marital patterns have substantial economic, social, and political implications and that media products geared toward women in many ways support and even encourage economic division. The most profound trend affecting marriage patterns in the 2010s is that college-educated men and women are more likely to get married and stay married whereas those without a degree are less likely to embark on the commitment. In this way, marriage can newly be thought of as a luxury good, a status object that is unavailable to large swaths of Americans.[23] "Getting married is a way to show family and friends that you have a successful personal life. . . . It's like the ultimate merit badge," sociologist and public policy analyst Andrew Cherlin observed in 2010.[24]

Cherlin's sentiments echo recent accounts of national marriage patterns. According to June Carbone and Naomi Cahn, the authors of the aptly titled 2014 book *Marriage Markets: How Inequality Is Remaking the American Family*, "College graduates still largely forge lasting relationships and they typically will do so with one another, but they hedge their bets by delaying marriage and childbearing until they have a better idea of where they (and the partners to whom they commit) are likely to end up—concentrating elite advantage in the process as overwhelming numbers of them raise their children in financially secure, two-parent families."[25] Educated people of means tend to marry people in similar demographics and subsequently raise advantaged children who carry on in the same economic stratum, a reality that testifies to the persistence of economic stratification. "Of all the causes behind growing income inequality, in the long run this development may prove one of the most significant and also one of the hardest to counter," claimed a 2015 article titled "The Marriages of Power Couples Reinforce Economic Inequality."[26]

Educational and economic underpinnings situate and determine Americans' marital prospects as well as their financial futures. Marriage is an out-of-reach commitment for many low- and middle-income Americans, and exclusion from the institution limits prospects for class mobility. As Carbone and Cahn assert, "If there is any chart underlying this book, it is the one showing that divorce and non-marital births have become markers of class." Arguing that among the middle and lower classes, numbers of "marriageable men"—defined as men who are financially stable and solvent—are in decline compared to larger pools of marriageable women, the authors observe that many women of similar class and educational background choose singlehood and/or to parent alone. In fact, 50 percent of births to women without college degrees are out of wedlock. "In the middle and the bottom, there are more competent and stable women seeking to pair with a shrinking pool of reliable men. What we are watching as the shift in marriage markets rewrites family scripts and increases gender distrust is the re-creation of class—of harder edged boundaries that separate the winners and the losers in the new American economy," posit Carbone and Cahn.[27] The authors contrast these findings with the reality that elite women are now the most likely group to marry. The article "Getting Married Later Is Great for College-Educated Women" notes that "financially, college-educated women benefit the most from marrying later. Women who marry later make more money per year than women who marry young."[28] In total, the research reveals the existence of a marriage differential split along the fault lines of class. Economically disadvantaged classes choose to delay marriage as they struggle to find work and/or resist making long-term commitments. On the other hand, the more affluent classes find their marriage numbers stabilizing and even rising. Many of the media texts I survey in this book in turn assume the sort of confidence and economic security that are in fact the lot of educated women. Female media culture both features and addresses itself to this demographic stratum.

Wife, Inc. stresses the recognition that, as the bluntly titled *New York Times* article "Marriage Is for Rich People" asserts, marriage exists as a signal of privilege, and bespeaks a deep class divide: "The concentration of marriage among the richest Americans is amplifying the increase in income inequality."[29] Marriage in the contemporary period serves as a social and economic regulator and also forecasts a return to the sort of classist underpinnings that historically organized the institution. Taking seriously the fact that marriage has increasingly become the province of affluent and well-educated women, *Wife, Inc.* looks at how such understandings are normalized and endorsed by popular culture products. It urges, above all, that we pay attention to the marital commitment's increasingly more exclusionary status and female popular culture's circulation of understandings and attitudes that perpetuate this exclusivity.

Gay Marriage and Affective Reimaginings

When I began this project, I was convinced that debates about gay marriage would be salient to my analysis. To be sure, the marriage equality movement and its attendant discourses have helped to crystalize the issues under consideration in this book, conversations that serve as reminders of the pivotal role that marriage plays in mediating the private citizen's relationship to her nation. While I have argued that the 1980s and 1990s largely saw a turn to neoliberal understandings wherein marriage was considered merely a personal choice, that choice existed only for people whose marriages followed traditional gender scripts. The gay marriage debate in some ways pointed out the fallacy that lay at the heart of personalized understandings of marriage. By refusing to allow Americans who identified as gay or lesbian to marry each other, the nation in effect illustrated that the concept of personal choice was itself a mirage and a marker of heterosexual privilege. Far from a matter merely of choice, marriage is a mediator of a host of rights and privileges, which have implications that span everything from inheritance rights to childcare arrangements to visitation privileges in health-care settings. As sociologist Jaye Cee Whitehead wrote in 2011, "The vast expansion of the government over the past century has embedded marriage into all areas where the state and the individual intersect, from tax obligations to disability benefits to health care decisions to family law."[30] Gay marriage's elevation and visibility on the American landscape dismantled cultural myopia about marriage since these conversations so often foreground the marital institution's connection to governmentality and regimes of citizenship.

Oddly, the landmark 2015 Supreme Court decision that legalized gay marriage across the nation in some ways reinstated the mythos of personal choice against which activists fought so hard. Ideals of intimacy as a cherished, individualized commitment as well as advocacy against discrimination and inequality were used in arguments in favor of legalization, and had a strong influence on the court's stated decision in the *Obergefell vs. Hodges* case. "The right to personal choice regarding marriage is inherent in the concept of individual autonomy," wrote Justice Kennedy in the majority opinion. "No union is more profound than marriage, for it embodies the highest ideals of love, fidelity, devotion, sacrifice, and family. In forming a marital union, two people become something greater than once they were."[31] This optimistic language in many ways coheres with commonplace understandings of the salience of romantic love and its place as a centerpiece of human experience. At the same time, these discussions risk stigmatizing relations that fall outside the parameters of marriage, and sidestep recognition of the sort of economic benefits that accrue to the married. As J. Jack Halberstam noted in the years before legalization, "Gay marriage will do very little for queer people currently living in poverty while it has definite tax benefits for the middle class and very rich."[32] Reinstating marriage in the popular consciousness as a commitment to which almost all people can legally claim right further enhances the treasured image of marriage as a democratic ideal while its economic consequences persist unchallenged.[33]

In opposition to popular conceptualizations of marriage as a liberatory and emancipatory commitment that exists as an apotheosis of love, family, and sexual and romantic partnership, *Wife, Inc.* argues that a more pragmatic ethos circulates in contemporary mediated milieus and has direct bearing on female publics. At every juncture, I urge that we consider the imbrication of class structures with marital futures. At the same time, the book isolates the ways that popular culture educates women on the necessity of attending to the pressures of the marriage market and helps them develop strategies and skills that further their economic and social prospects. It thinks about disciplinary mechanisms that are in some ways less obvious than laws and looks to sites that acknowledge the marital commitment as exclusionary and hierarchical. Often, these sites school audiences on how to negotiate tight economies, be they in terms of time, age, or reproductive agendas.

Marriage's framing in this way is consistent with what Catherine Rottenberg has termed "neoliberal feminism," whereby feminist ideas are reformulated so that their main objective seems to be the maximization of female happiness. As Rottenberg explains, the feminist subject "accepts full responsibility for her own well-being and self-care, which is increasingly predicated on crafting a felicitous work-life balance based on a cost-benefit calculus."[34] Whereas Rottenberg concerns herself primarily with discourse focused on the work-life balance, my investigation takes us back in time in terms of the path that typically leads to marriage, asking how one finds and attracts a life partner, properly prepares for wifedom, and then executes these commitments in agentic (and often profitable) ways. Expectations for female entrepreneurialism in the realm of matrimony disrupt rosy pictorials of nuptial bliss and suggest that notions of pragmatism and self-interest likewise drive affective economies. I do not, of course, mean to suggest that individual women do not enter the commitment for stated reasons of love, intimate partnership, and child rearing. Likewise, many of the real-life women I survey via their memoirs, interviews, and appearances on reality television proclaim belief in these prized ideals. This study nevertheless argues that twenty-first-century female media culture is undergirded by a structure of feeling that is decidedly less misty-eyed in its estimation of the behaviors and postures that women must adopt in order to realize marital aspirations.

As alluded to earlier, I attribute this shift to a number of factors, most powerfully the nation's increasing class divide. It also bears acknowledging that what was once a winking or knowing postfeminist posture—evident particularly in romantic comedies, chick lit, and female-centered television drama—has hardened in recent years into a more brittle and even cynical vision. As economic pressures mount on all but the most affluent Americans, it is difficult to separate any institution from its financial exigencies, no less one as imbricated in the social, political, and cultural order as is marriage. In these difficult times, it feels shortsighted to look to marriage or to any individual relationship as one that can produce complete emotional fulfillment. And even if one relationship could, it is fundamentally misguided to think that personal relationships exist in a realm divorced from economic calculations. (It is perhaps no accident that marriage's depoliticization took place largely in an era of national prosperity and prior to the altering events of September 11, 2001.) Though I am in fact quite personally distressed by the turn in female media culture that this book documents, the fact that women might now approach marriage as a vehicle to reap a host of personal, economic, and status rewards looks in many ways merely like good planning. What troubles me is that these strategies are designed by and for the most affluent Americans. That marriage occupies a seminal place in the ranks of the divisive winner-take-all mind-set perpetuated by neoliberalism is less a surprise, perhaps, than its continued and significant participation in the process of reordering the nation's economic and affective futures. This dominance goes surprisingly unchallenged, even by those who consider economic inequality to be a top national priority. Marriage provides access not only to money but also to an emotional order coveted by many. Women and men alike are in this sense becoming priced out of love.

Admittedly, many marriages fail and many that succeed in name fail to live up to vaunted promises of idealized marital mythology. However, if marriage at the very least heralds a vision of secure partnership, lasting commitment, and sustained emotional and financial support, the reality that this commitment is out of reach for an increasing majority of Americans seems a depressing admission that emotional regimes are in their own ways as bifurcated and unjust as our current class systems.

Marriage as Entrepreneurship

In concert with these cultural patterns, *Wife, Inc.* situates twenty-first-century marriage much like any other occupational success. To achieve the status of wife, women must conceive of themselves as "assertive, entrepreneurial actors,"[35] a sensibility that has obvious and direct ties to both postfeminism and neoliberalism. If "the entrepreneur is the neoliberal subject *par excellence*,"[36] this book suggests that the entrepreneurial marital laborer puts her work in service of herself. Put slightly differently, *Wife, Inc.* offers the centralizing observation that twenty-first-century wifedom is newly imbricated in neoliberal conceptualizations of labor and professionalism whereby "finding and building relationships is cast as a professional, rational, quasi-scientific affair."[37] Contemporary wifedom, I argue, requires a set of labors steeped in the logics of professional cultures, in sync with the rhythms and ethos of the occupational sphere.

Whereas the role of the wife has typically been thought of in terms of the domestic, feminist scholars have long highlighted a false division between public and private existences, understandings that typically cloistered women in spaces that were considered apart from political realities. One of the foremost objectives of this thought revolution was to refute claims that women lacked a sphere of influence outside the home and to diagram, instead, how their power was deployed across myriad spaces. One division feminists sought to trouble, for instance, was the split between "family and factory," to quote literary scholar Nancy Armstrong.[38] My project continues that effort, though instead of recognizing the inherent politics of the domestic, it urges that we consider an identity once thought of in purely domestic terms—the wife—as a figure who belongs more to the realm of the factory than she does the home. Specifically, I argue that twenty-first-century American wifedom is emblematic of the identity formations actively encouraged by postfeminist entrepreneurial regimes. As if to recall marriage's origins in Western society when it was principally an economic arrangement, wifedom is once again an incentivized role.

Wife, Inc. is particularly concerned with investigating the work of wifedom as it occurs in public spaces, where it borrows flagrantly from the logics of the workplace. Whereas classic feminist arguments insisted that domestic labor performed under the auspices of nurturing and care also be recognized as work, *Wife, Inc.* posits that in the twenty-first century becoming—and remaining—a wife requires laboring in realms that are decidedly nondomestic in nature. Specifically, this volume examines how the work of wifedom occurs online, on reality television, in memoirs, in the spaces of social media, and on the campaign trail, and argues that fitness for wifedom requires women to adopt postures that nominate them as marriageable. In turn, wives leverage this identity in order to market themselves, their businesses, and their families. Conceptualizing wifedom as a role that one must agitate for and continually labor on behalf of, *Wife, Inc.* deliberately proceeds chronologically though the "wife cycle," pursuing an arc that follows women as they date, prepare to wed, and toil as wives. More specifically, the earliest chapters in this book analyze the capabilities and aptitudes required of modern women wishing to be wives ("wannabe wives" and "almost wives"). The book then follows with an examination of the realms where one can most readily instrumentalize and monetize one's wifedom ("housewives," "real wives," and "political wives"). While differing pressures attend each of these categories, a common theme of this book is that corporate logics circumscribe the wife's role, turning her into a business manager who must publicly manage her wifely brand.

The trends I record here accord with recent cultural developments that emphasize the monetization of intimate bonds. The increasingly transactional nature of intimate relationships has been studied by economist Viviana A. Zelizer, who notes that our discomfort over political marriages (a topic I tackle in this book's final chapter) stems from its appearing to mix "economic rationality" with "intimate ties." It is common, she acknowledges, to harbor suspicion toward "intimate economic relations," particularly thanks to our tendency to doubt the compatibility of economic calculations with interpersonal solidarity. This discomfort cannot obviate the fact that, as Zelizer says, "money cohabits regularly with intimacy, and even sustains it."[39] While Zelizer is keen to atomize the way in which exchanges take place in the domestic sphere, *Wife, Inc.* instead takes as its focus how the modern stages of wifedom incorporate rationalized calculations in their public presences. These organizations are propagated and sustained by current marital climates, which tend to emphasize the necessity of applying professional logics to the processes of matrimony and whose traces can best be found in contemporary media cultures. Rather than analyze how economic calculations impinge on wifely duties, this study examines how wifely identities are commonly deployed in media cultures through the framework of professionalism.

This newly reimagined conceptualization of wifedom draws on long-standing historical currents wherein marriage served primarily as a financial transaction. At the same time, *Wife, Inc.* interrogates affective climates and belief systems that clearly draw inspiration from feminist ideals of self-sufficiency and economic achievement. This hybridization—as well as the cultural fascination it generates—was on easy display in 2015 with the publication of Wednesday Martin's ethnography *The Primates of Park Avenue*. Training a supposed anthropological lens on the privileged denizens of the upper reaches of New York City's elite, Martin revealed that a number of women in her circle received a "wife bonus" from their husbands, "an annual payout related to a husband's earnings and a spouse's social (and implied sexual) performance."[40] While the claim was largely debunked, the idea that women would earn a yearly bonus for exceptional wifely performance such as getting their children into exclusive private schools or sagely maintaining a household budget calls directly on the sort of currents this book is tracing. Though admittedly extreme, the idea that women marry for financial as well as social gain, and do so with recourse to the logics, operations, and even temporality of the professional sphere (e.g., the "yearly bonus") is a through line in this study.

While occupying and claiming wifedom as a profitable status role has a number of benefits, I do not mean to minimize its considerable risk. "If our capacities for intimacy are most regularly exercised in the pursuit of competitive professional profit, we face the prospect of being unable to appreciate the benefits of intimacy for unprofitable purposes," Melissa Gregg cautions.[41] At the risk of sounding fatalistic, it appears that contemporary women lack the affective space for unprofitable intimacies. This reality is particularly salient if we conceive of finding a partner and even producing children as gestures circumscribed by the exigencies of time, age, and money. In a 2009 article on how relationship advice is deployed in women's magazines, Rosalind Gill refers to the fact that women must enact "intimate self-surveillance" involving intense monitoring of one's feelings, desires, and attitudes as well as those of a partner.[42] I suspect that intense emotional scrutiny has been rerouted outward in the era on which this book focuses: nowadays, internal emotional states matter less than proper external emotional displays. Put differently, while *Wife, Inc.* takes up the question of how women manage emotions, this conversation occurs primarily in the context of disciplining emotions and performing them suitably—that is, in order to attract a compatible partner. Happiness, confidence, and a willingness to be ready for love, as well as to work hard for it, are the mandated affective orders for the subjects of this book, issues I address specifically in chapters 1 and 2. Emotions also take center stage on reality programming, where participants must confess or even manufacture emotions in order to sell products and/or ensure continued employment, as I detail in chapters 3 and 4. As the somewhat bloodless political animals that I survey in chapter 5 make explicit, having or expressing emotions for their own sake rather than in service of some larger manipulation seems a quaint and even anachronistic ideal.

The Stages of Wifedom

Wife, Inc. presents a trajectory that attempts to mimic the life cycle of the wife in a contemporary climate saturated by neoliberal feminism. It begins with an investigation of the first phase embarked on by the marital laborer—negotiating the marital market. Women who desire marriage as well as those seeking guidance on how to ensure that their chances remain viable are often the target of female media culture's attention and advice. Hence, their position serves as an instructive beginning point for analysis. "Enterprising Wives: Dating as Labor in Hard Times" commences with an overview of the counsel offered by the now-infamous Princeton Mom, who urged female coeds to find a husband before they left college. Taking seriously the sort of marriage scarcity models that impel such advice and relatedly the recession-inspired worry that educated, high-status women will no longer have suitable men to marry, the chapter examines marital strategies that twenty-first-century popular culture offers women. Specifically, the chapter argues that in dire marital economies, the wannabe wife must build her brand, be a self-starter, and expect a high level of competition for what are increasingly understood to be scarce resources.

To test this premise, chapter 1 focuses most centrally on the idea of the marriage market and identifies online dating as a cultural formation that is particularly suited to and evocative of the operations and protocols that constitute current marital economies. As I argue, online dating requires a set of strategies steeped in brand culture and is widely recognized by female media culture as a laboring effort. Economic logics of professionalization inform online dating norms, which in turn cohere with the sociological reality that marriage occupies an increasingly exclusionary space in American contexts. By surveying studies about online dating, memoirs and firsthand accounts, and advice tracts, the chapter concludes that contemporary dating formulations normalize efficiency, encourage quantifiable self-assessments, and guide users to atomize their personalities. Online dating norms operationalize the perception that some users are "fitter" than others for the process and tend to reward daters who master a set of affective performances. For women especially, these requirements involve presenting an easygoing, everyday persona; being optimistic and uncomplicated; and not attending too closely to their own desires. Relatedly, online dating is an endeavor bound in a larger nexus that encourages women to present themselves as nested firmly within consumer culture and to communicate their personalities via product preferences. Chapter 1 begins to undertake the class analysis that this study proposes, arguing that online dating practices locate marriage as yet another commodity that those with sufficient time and money may most readily procure.

Continuing apace with the project of following the wife's trajectory, chapter 2 examines how wedding- and marriage-themed television disciplines women, encouraging that they work both physically and emotionally in order to prove their suitability as marital subjects. The analysis begins with an identification of the reality dating show as a place where intimate norms and specifically the process of dating and coupling are most readily on display in contemporary media. Reality offerings sync with and make manifest logics of choice, competition, and emotional and physical management, all of which comprise contemporary dating and marital cultures. Beginning with the reality dating franchise *The Bachelor*, where emotional openness and a sense of being "ready" to fall in love exist as hallmark requirements, the chapter proceeds to investigate the hierarchical organizations that structure wedding-themed reality television. These shows court, feature, and tend to appeal to affluent constituencies, an observation epitomized by Patti Stanger's *Millionaire Matchmaker* franchise, one that self-identifies as catering to the needs and desires of the most elite Americans. Stanger favors daters who are resilient and responsible, who demonstrate a willingness to be flexible, fix their appearance, and do the necessary psychological work of getting themselves ready to embark on relationships. Choice, individual empowerment, and personal responsibility underpin Stanger's presentation of the marital market, and she witheringly holds men and women, gay and straight, alike accountable when they refuse to properly prepare for love. Both *The Bachelor* and *Millionaire Matchmaker*, I argue, translate online dating's focus on efficiency, selectivity, and instrumentality into representational contexts and remind us how exclusionary marriage markets can be.

Chapter 2 then turns to "bad bride" television in order to illustrate how failing at wifely requirements in turn subjects one to the disciplinary mechanisms of the media machine, and documents how female popular culture shames brides who do not appropriately self-regulate. In particular, the long-running *Bridezillas* reminds viewers that its featured women are not worthy of the weddings they have, or the marriages on which they will soon embark. I trace this judgment to a class bias insofar as *Bridezillas* not only exhibits a troubling tendency to humiliate brides who act inappropriately but also suggests that brides from lower-class backgrounds do not deserve a posh wedding because they cannot behave in a manner befitting an elegant event. The chapter contrasts these unflattering representations with those offered by series such as *Bridal Bootcamp, Bulging Brides,* and *Shedding for the Wedding,* where brides subject themselves to multiple forms of surveillance and attempt extreme body modification. The chapter concludes with a brief section on reality weddings, offerings that underline and applaud the work that goes into preparing oneself to be a proper bride. In total, the chapter highlights the persistence and prevalence of bridal labor and reaffirms the extent to which postfeminist neoliberal entrepreneurialism inflects the bridal industry.

Chapter 3 represents a turning point for *Wife, Inc.* as well as for the cultural history of wifedom. By taking as its focus the housewife, the chapter examines how a figure once so intrinsically associated with domesticity became a public icon on which postfeminist debates center. Specifically, the chapter twins the observation that the housewife reemerged in twenty-first-century media culture with the recognition that she is a stand-in for all that is considered feminine in this era. One need only scan any televisual roster to find confirmation of the housewife's perch, where she sits atop and serves as the most high-profile form of wifedom in contemporary America. In order to understand and unpack this representational dominance, the chapter commences by revisiting some classic texts and conversations about the 1950s housewife, pinpointing her historical importance and lasting appeal. Despite the widely held notion that the housewife is defined by her separation from monetized economies, this section reinstitutes work, labor, professionalism, and economics as salient concepts for any discussion of the housewife.

Reading the housewife in this register anchors my assessment of and explanation for her comeback in the twenty-first century and provides a lens to examine her tongue-in-cheek reintroduction via ABC's *Desperate Housewives.* I argue that this much-debated show birthed a new conceptualization of the term "housewife," one in line with postfeminism's characteristic irony and postmodernist formulations of linguistic slippage, where the housewife is no longer a woman who lacks paid employment outside the home. Rather, the term serves as a placeholder for a set of popular culture conversations, interests, and concerns. The housewife's reappearance on the cultural stage re-galvanized long-standing controversies involving women, fueling all-too-familiar questions and debates, particularly over the much-rehearsed tug-of-war between stay-at-home versus working mothers. The housewife in the twenty-first century is therefore less an identity than a convenient opportunity, presenting a way for popular culture to remind women about the facets of femininity it considers the most salient.

To illustrate specifically how the term "housewife" came to ground logics of productivity and branding in media-driven economies, chapter 3 concludes with an analysis of the Bravo network's mega-franchise *The Real Housewives*. Wifedom in this context signals a focus on affluent women who rehearse predictable emotional conflicts (many of which center on female homosociality) as they in turn transact to launch personal brands and products. The franchise's representational dominance nevertheless confirms the importance of class in the current marital climate. Giving voice to only the most privileged subjects, the show exposes that contemporary wifedom has very little to do with marriage and very much to do with the monetization of femininity. In these new economic and emotional orders, a profitable endeavor might involve a girls' weekend in Cabo, where the impeccably dressed on-screen participants gossip, bicker, booze, and provide tabloid fodder. While non-domestic, non-caretaking endeavors would seem to be far removed from the cultural meanings of the classic 1950s housewife, the chapter attempts to link them by arguing that both are located in recognizable economies of affect and femininity. By rendering her daily activities profitable, the housewife is the aspirational everywoman.

Building on the themes of the previous chapter, chapter 4 addresses the explosion of wives across reality programming. This chapter examines the glut of wifely programming on reality television primarily in terms of the niche appeal wives lend to their respective networks, focusing on Bravo, VH1, and TLC as case studies. Reality wives in many ways work for their networks, publicizing these networks' interests as well as segmenting their intended audiences. The economic, racial, and status profiles of the shows and the networks on which they appear constitute a key heuristic for understanding the contours of the sort of work that reality wives perform. I carry over a conversation about Bravo's flagship *Real Housewives* franchise from the previous chapter, but with more of an eye toward the housewives' participation in concretizing Bravo's network identity as one keenly attuned to the wants and preferences of up-scale, brand-conscious, social media–savvy audiences. This conversation also focalizes *The Real Housewives of Atlanta*, Bravo's top-grossing show, in order to clarify further the sort of diversification from which Bravo has so handsomely profited.

Bravo has undeniably been a progenitor of the wives brand, one that VH1 adopts and adapts on *Basketball Wives*, *Football Wives*, *Basketball Wives LA*, and *Mob Wives*. These programs carry on Bravo's tradition of showcasing acrimonious female relationships yet speak back to its rather myopic focus on whiteness and affluence. Focusing primarily on *Basketball Wives* and *Mob Wives*, the chapter suggests that VH1 puts patriarchy at the center of its investigations and offers a female perspective on what have historically been male-dominated realms. These shows also give voice to the struggles of women of color, although their violent and at times physical confrontations have drawn criticism. As these shows illustrate, women's bodies do the work of making affective injuries visible, labor ultimately put in service of confirming VH1's brand identity as a network whose offerings and stars are gratuitously sensationalized.

The chapter ends with a brief discussion of TLC's wifely program-ming, illustrating how even a network known for its exaggerated and oversized portrayals of family life employs the same logics of wifedom this book has been tracing. Specifically, this section examines *Sister Wives*, *Extreme Cougar Wives*, and *My Five Wives*, examining how logics of supply and demand inform their content. In total, chapter 4 empha-sizes the observation that reality wives receive compensation for negoti-ating romantic and affective bonds on camera and for feeling and acting in accordance with audience and network mandates.

Wife, Inc.'s final chapter, "Good Wives: Public Infidelity and the Na-tional Politics of Spousehood," takes up the question of the political wife, one who has long been thought to trouble the supposed separation be-tween home and work. The chapter begins by highlighting that the figure of the political wife has enjoyed rather dubious distinction in twenty-first-century media culture. Specifically, thanks to a stream of adultery scandals featuring male politicians, the specter of the betrayed wife has fomented a rash of media commentary and inspired an array of televi-sion texts. Focusing on real-life political wives and their paratexts, as well as their fictional counterparts in television series such as *The Good*

Wife, Scandal, and *House of Cards,* this chapter argues that the wronged wife has been wrenched from her image as victim and instead reimagined in the post-Clinton era as a figurehead with her own ambitions and goals. Because their experiences foreground marriage as an act of visible labor that in many ways benefits them as much as their spouses, political wives—both in practice and in mediated representation—have opened up a space in which to talk about marriage as a platform for female achievement and professionalism. As such, they provide unique insight into marriage's laboring function.

This chapter offers a meditation on how political wives are typically circumscribed by careerism, pragmatism, and calculating determination. An initial section looks at the echoes of and intersections between Hillary Clinton, Huma Abedin, and *The Good Wife's* Alicia Florrick, arguing that the overlaps prove telling insofar as they reveal that women willing to use their wifedom for political gain are also hampered by their connections—and implied likeness to—flawed men. The chapter continues through an investigation of wifely memoirs written by Jenny Sanford, Elizabeth Edwards, Dina Matos McGreevey, and Gayle Haggard in order to suggest that they provide insight into the job of public wifedom, highlighting both its perils and its rewards. The chapter's final sections consider the deliberate instrumentalization of marriage by fictional women, including Alicia Florrick, *Scandal's* Mellie Grant, and *House of Cards'* Claire Underwood, as well as Huma Abedin, whose ill-fated union with former congressman Anthony Weiner reverberated throughout the national stage and to a particularly unexpected extent during the final weeks of Hillary Clinton's presidential run, leading up to her ultimate defeat. In total, the chapter argues that the political wife's secondary status vis-à-vis her husband has given way to a compromised resilience. Though often advancing an exacting political agenda in her own right, her wifely status can at times be as much a hindrance as an asset.

It is the contention of *Wife, Inc.* that wifedom continues to serve as the structuring conceptualization of the American woman's life, a rather surprising development that sits uncomfortably alongside the fact that marriage is roundly considered an institution in decline. Despite widely touted shifts in American marriage patterns, marital femininity continues to underpin the debates that consume popular women's media. By illustrating how corporate logics underpin these conversations, *Wife, Inc.* confirms the neoliberal mandates of postfeminist media culture and illustrates the effort they exert to shape the concerns, anxieties, and ambitions of female audiences. Exploring how traditional views of feminine behavior and identity are being reformulated according to the requirements of the professional sphere, *Wife, Inc.* argues that such alterations have contributed in myriad ways to marriage's increasingly exclusionary status. This phenomenon has both economic and affective implications for the American female imaginary, which I explore in the following pages in the hopes that doing so will serve a liberating function for women and men alike.

1

Enterprising Wives

Dating as Labor in Hard Times

People have said to me, "Oh, well, love just happens." No, it
doesn't. Nothing just happens. . . . If this is what you want
you have to go after it, you have to pursue it and you have to
do so methodically and smartly. You have to plan for your
personal happiness just the way you plan for your professional happiness, why would you ever think otherwise?
—Susan Patton

In the spring of 2013, Princeton alum Susan Patton published a letter in
the campus newspaper, the *Daily Princetonian*, explicitly addressed to
the "daughters I never had."[1] In a plea to Princeton female undergraduates, Patton urged her (implicitly heterosexual) readers to find a husband
while on campus, noting that their chances of finding a suitable mate
postgraduation were likely to plummet. As she asserted, "Smart women
can't (shouldn't) marry men who aren't at least their intellectual equal.
As Princeton women, we have almost priced ourselves out of the market.
Simply put, there is a very limited population of men who are as smart
or smarter than we are. And I say again—you will never again be sur-
rounded by this concentration of men who are worthy of you." With a
language of entitlement masked as empowerment, Patton positions her
audience as deserving good mates, men whose accomplishments and
earning potential are on par with what theirs promises to be. Yet, Patton's
underlying ethos is also, baldly, a law of diminishing returns. Even in the
brief four-year stint that constitutes most college experiences at Princeton, she warns, time is short. As Patton writes, "So, by the time you are a
senior, you basically have only the men in your own class to choose from,
and frankly, they now have four classes of women to choose from."[2] For
women (though not for men) time on the marital clock runs out quickly.[3]

As with many trend pieces that pertain to the terms of heterosexual femininity in twenty-first-century America, Patton's incendiary advice sparked a national conversation, much of which took place via social media. She was accused of elitism and misogyny, of being out of touch and—considering her own status as a divorcee—hypocritical. Alternatively, she was credited with affording young women a brand of refreshing honesty that was uniquely cognizant of the requirements of modern marriage. Because marriage advice attentive to current trends remains an endless source of American cultural fasciation, the 650-word letter also predictably earned Patton a contract with the prestigious publisher Simon and Schuster, which resulted in a 2014 book titled *Marry Smart: Advice for Finding THE ONE.*[4] The paperback, released in 2015, featured a subtle title change, perhaps meant to particularize Patton's message; it is called *Marry by Choice, Not by Chance: Advice for Finding the Right One at the Right Time.*[5] Patton's letter was nevertheless hardly original since it advocated an accomplishment that has for decades winkingly been termed the "MRS degree." Patton's letter likewise carried the self-righteous tone of much postfeminist backlash rhetoric since she positioned herself as bravely advancing a mind-set wherein aspiring to marriage and motherhood pushes back against feminism's perceived strictures.

More unremarked upon, however, and the premise that will organize this chapter, is Patton's unabashed participation in a marriage zeitgeist steeped in neoliberal mind-sets that demand agility, self-reliance, and a start-up business mentality. Perhaps best captured by the term "entrepreneurialism," aspiring wives must demonstrate a cutthroat and clear-eyed willingness to appraise their own value in a competitive marketplace and leverage their best assets in service of attaining their goal. Patton admits as much: her basic premise is less that Princeton's female undergraduates *must* marry and rear children but that, if they wish to do so, they bear sole responsibility for maximizing their chances and are roundly to blame if they do not. Roughly put, she offers a neoliberal formulation of the marriage market decidedly in line with the sort of hyper-individualist positioning that dominates free market capitalism, one whose logics have come to define postfeminist womanhood in an entrepreneurial age. It is no accident, in turn, that Patton obliquely references another book making waves in American cultural discourse

Figure 1.1. Susan Patton brandishes *Marry Smart*, a warning to all young women who dare to wait too long to secure a high-earning husband.

during the same period—Sheryl Sandberg's *Lean In: Women, Work, and the Will to Lead*, a handbook for female success in the workplace that encourages women to approach their own career advancement with a propensity to self-advocate, take risks, and negotiate from a perceived position of power.[6] Patton begins her piece, "Forget about having it all, or not having it all, leaning in or leaning out—here's what you really need to know that nobody is telling you."[7] Despite this disavowal, Patton and Sandberg similarly conceptualize marriage as deserving of intense calculation. "I truly believe that the single most important career decision that a woman makes is whether she will have a life partner and who that partner is," Sandberg writes in *Lean In*.[8] These twin proclamations about marriage, both of which foreground women's responsibility for maximizing marital opportunities, provide apt introduction to this chapter and to the book at large, which argues that in current marital economies, business-based calculations structure the terms of marital pursuit and the measurement of its success. As I will argue, the wannabe wife must build her brand, be a self-starter, and expect a high level of competition for what is increasingly understood to be a scarce resource: marriageable men.

To analyze these mind-sets, in this chapter I focus most centrally on online dating, a practice that requires a set of strategies steeped in brand culture. "Branding entails marketing and selling immaterial things—feelings and affects, personalities and values, rather than actual goods," confirms Sarah Banet-Weiser, a sentiment that effectively expresses why branding logics are so applicable to the process of finding a husband.[9] One of the central premises of this study as a whole is that the lived realities of contemporary wifedom are newly disconnected from the sort of domestic, privatized identities previously connoted by the moniker "wife." By engaging with current vocabularies of selfhood and aspirationalism, the figure of the wannabe wife renders these shifts visible and highlights how success in the dating market requires professionalization. These realities in turn cohere with the demographic sociological reality that marriage occupies an increasingly exclusionary space in American contexts. Whereas college-educated, upwardly mobile Americans (such as those attending a college like Princeton) continue to marry in legion, their contemporaries without high school or college degrees do not. Perilously in line with the sorts of polarizing income stratifications that now characterize American economies, these organizations clarify how marriage is increasingly a province of the wealthy rather than a lifetime commitment enjoyed by Americans who exist on varied social strata.[10]

With an eye toward the various labors demanded of the wannabe wife in online realms, and a concluding section on marriage panic, this chapter theorizes that discussions of dating and marriage increasingly reflect and concretize disparities. It asks: How are larger conceptualizations of marriage affected when hyper-rationalization of the terms and expectations for dating become de rigueur? How have the systems of online dating created the markets that they profess to be in the business of responding to? What forms of affect and personal identity display are encouraged by popular culture forms, particularly online dating advice? As I will assert, the current zeitgeist encourages women to self-assess, self-report, and self-advertise. These now-regularized aspects of the pursuit of matrimony locate marriage as a commodity most readily available to those who possess significant resources, including time, money, and emotional acumen.

Maximizing Exchange Value in Online Dating Markets

By 2009, online dating surpassed all forms of matchmaking in the United States other than meeting through friends.[11] This rise in the use of online dating—and a corresponding diminishment of the stigma associated with it—reflects changing marriage trends and the shifting contours of personal life in the United States.[12] As Dan Slater writes in his 2013 volume *Love in the Time of Algorithms*, a historical and journalistic overview of the online dating industry, "The ascension of women at work and their rising financial status, the lagging prospects of men, the ebb of the marriage rate, and the ever-rising marriage age—these are societal trends that have dovetailed with, and been a boon to, online dating in recent years." As a model that turns dating into a business of efficiency and uses the latest trends in social and digital media to do so, online dating has much to recommend it to Americans already comfortable outsourcing their lives to digital applications. One of Slater's interview subjects reveals, "Everyone in San Francisco is too busy to date. But everyone owns an iPhone. So dating becomes one more thing you access through an app. I have an app to get my music, another to suggest movies, another for news, another for friends, one to show me where a good bar is, and another app to help me find a date to go to that bar with."[13]

It should be acknowledged that many people use online dating not to find a long-term partner or a marriage but for myriad other reasons, including the chance to partake of sexual encounters that do not involve expectations of commitment. That said, many people use these services for the purpose of finding a spouse. Though eHarmony is the only popular site to explicitly reference marriage in its promotional materials (claiming that eHarmony's services account for "5% of new US marriages"), other sites use similarly weighty verbiage to convey their success at creating sustainable couples ("Each week, hundreds of JDaters meet their soul mates"). A 2013 ad for Match.com similarly proclaims, "Match is number one in relationships, in dating, and in marriages." Though online daters employ services for all sorts of reasons, dating sites undeniably exist in the cultural imaginary (and in practice) as places where couples can make connections that lead to long-term, perhaps even lifetime relationships. Even the supposed hookup app Tinder has, on occasion, interloped in marital economies and facilitated long-term unions.[14] Because I am most interested in marriage-minded users, I have chosen to focus this study primarily on conventional dating sites like Match.com, OkCupid, and eHarmony, which tend to cultivate belief in the attainability of long-term coupling.

The claim that online dating has shifted the marital landscape into an explicit commodity marketplace whereby users sort, judge, and quantify romantic value also deserves qualification. Admittedly, marriage's operation as a rationalized market of exchange rather than, say, a fortuitous outcome where soul mates experience love at first sight, long preexisted the proliferation of digital technologies. In his seminal 1973 article "A Theory of Marriage: Part One," economist Gary Becker coined the term "marriage market" in order to explain how "men and women compete as they seek mates . . . each person tries to find the best mate, subject to the restrictions imposed by market conditions." Becker unabashedly affirms the value of economic theory as it pertains to supposedly non-market realities; as he predicts, "economic theory may well be on its way to providing a unified framework for *all* behavior involving scarce resources." Becker's suggestion that suitable marriage partners were scarce resources seems prescient in light of the belief that, thanks to the shrinking of the middle class, the ranks of eligible and financially secure men have dramatically thinned, a formulation I address in the final section of this chapter. However, a number of Becker's other insights now appear as fairly commonplace, particularly the idea that marriage-minded adults seek to make the best matches possible and seek what he calls "compatibility or complementarity" in factors like physical capital, education, intelligence, height, and race.[15] (The only difference now, perhaps, is that these are search terms.)

That individuals date and marry people of similar backgrounds, classes, and educational levels is likewise hardly a contemporary phenomenon. Sociologists employ the terms "homophily" (love of the same) as well as "assortative mating" to describe this operation, explaining how marriage between similar types results in social reproduction, which shores up categories of racial, class, sexual, and cultural privilege. Admittedly, of course, most people do not regard their spousal selections in this way, preferring instead to couple romantic ideologies of love with notions of free choice that, if articulated, might sound like the following. "I simply chose to marry the person I fell in love with." There is evidence to believe, however, that the more rationalized the process, the more participants are aware of themselves as participating in a market where certain traits are sought and others devalued. In a study published in 1993, economists Aaron Ahuvia and Mara Adelman interviewed a group of singles involved in an "introductory service" (industries that were clear precursors to today's online dating companies) and found market metaphors were particularly prevalent among this group. Ahuvia and Adelman categorized their interviewees' understanding of the process as consumption (dating as shopping and people as products), production (one produces benefits to be consumed by a dating partner, or sells oneself), and macroeconomic metaphors about the dating world in general. As Ahuvia and Adelman conclude, "Seeing the dating process as a job search is perhaps the most fitting of the metaphors discussed in this paper. In the job market, as in the marriage market, the prospective applicants/partners are trying to promote themselves, while simultaneously assessing the desirability of the 'company.'"[16]

The mainstreaming of market metaphors is likewise evidenced in self-help literature and dating advice geared specifically toward women. In a 2009 article where she surveys dating advice in the UK version of *Glamour* magazine, Rosalind Gill usefully coins the phrase "intimate entrepreneurship" to describe a process whereby "relationships are cast as work, using analogies from finance, management, science, marketing and military campaigns." In one of the many examples of intimate entrepreneurship that Gill locates, the author of an article about online dating urges the reader to "think of yourself as a product that needs to be marketed. You have to write your profile as you would a CV, shortlist the responses, and systematically work through men you like the sound of."[17] As this quotation makes explicit, online dating shares a number of affinities with job seeking. Online profiles are often compared with cover letters, and readers are encouraged to treat dating like a job, recognizing the need to distinguish oneself from other competitors, as well as seek and find a match that is a good fit.

Despite this notion's prevalence and persistence, market metaphors can offend, insofar as they profane what many people consider the more sacred act of finding love in a less calculated way. Many would rather perceive romantic connection as a meeting of soul mates, not a rationalized pairing based on similar or complementary factors such as age, income, or education level. However, perceived difference between un-calculated versus rationalized choice in terms of whom one marries has been usefully blurred by sociologist Pierre Bourdieu. As he explains in his 1975 article "Marriage Strategies as Strategies of Social Reproduction," which was based on a study of marriage patterns in Algeria, marital calculations are at once subject to finely regulated social and familial rules but lived and experienced as far less regimented processes. "Unequal" matches (particularly those on the basis of income) tended to be outlawed, yet these rules are rarely explicitly codified as regulatory or disciplinary. Instead, they are lived as if a part of the person's "habitus," a term Bourdieu uses to indicate socialized norms or tendencies that guide individual behavior and thinking. He writes:

> Hence, since these patterns emerge "spontaneously," it is unnecessary to make them explicit or to invoke or impose any rules. Habitus is thus the product of the very structures it tends to reproduce. Predicated upon a "spontaneous" compliance with the established order and with the will of the guardians of that order, namely, the elders, habitus is the principle that will generate the different solutions . . . Marriage strategies as such must therefore not be seen in the abstract, unrelated to inheritance strategies, fertility strategies, and even pedagogical strategies. In other words, they must be seen as one element in the entire system of biological, cultural, and social reproduction by which every group endeavors to pass on to the next generation the full measure of power and privilege it has itself inherited.[18]

Societal norms structure propensities to think, feel, and act in determinant ways, inclinations that are often not recognized as the result of explicitly coercive or disciplinary regimes. Marriage decisions are implicitly a product of these operations; as Bourdieu usefully delineates, marital patterns serve to reproduce social hierarchies even when they are not perceived as such.

Online dating exposes and presupposes precisely the sort of machinations typically mystified in dating arrangements premised on the spontaneous meeting of a soul mate. Thanks to sophisticated site functionality, for example, users can search for dates according to specific terms.

The ideological underpinnings of this process are aptly summed up by economist Catherine Hakim, who refers to dating as "self-service mating."[19] Online daters, moreover, make selections on the basis of finding someone like themselves. According to a 2005 study of sixty-five thousand heterosexual users of an online dating system in the United States, "users' preferences were most strongly same-seeking for attributes related to the life course, like marital history and whether one wants children, but they also demonstrated significant homophily in self-reported physical build, physical attractiveness, and smoking habits."[20]

Despite this emphasis on sameness, the trade-off model where, for example, an attractive young woman might be willing to marry a less attractive older man if he has money, still holds sway in the cultural imaginary. Patton mentions that her Princeton-educated son married a classmate of his but "he could have married anyone." She continues, "Men regularly marry women who are younger, less intelligent, less educated. It's amazing how forgiving men can be about a woman's lack of erudition, if she is exceptionally pretty."[21] The wide cultural cognizance of these trade-offs informs Patton's logic and lends legitimacy to her claim that Princeton men exist as a highly desirable commodity. Coverage of her piece in the mainstream media, for instance, cited an irreverently titled 2012 study by the *Journal of Political Economy*, "Fatter Attraction: Anthropometric and Socioeconomic Matching on the Marriage Market," that quantified such trades. As the article reported, "Women can compensate for two additional units of body mass index with one additional year of education." Conversely, "men may compensate 1.3 additional units of B.M.I. with a 1 percent increase in wages."[22] Put even more crassly, women can be fatter if they are better educated, and money helps men to offset perceived physical detriments. A 2012 CNBC special report on online dating further clarified how these calculations would likely play out in real life. According to one researcher, a man who is 5'9"would need to add another $40,000 a year to his annual income to hold the same attraction as another who stands 5'10".[23]

Though the level of specificity in these accounts is perhaps startling, the basic principles of operation are nevertheless commonplace. Evidencing the American public's willingness to think of marriage as a set of quantifiable exchanges, in 2007 a woman posted to Craigslist New York stating that she was twenty-five, pretty, stylish, and wanted to know how to attract and marry a guy with a $500,000 annual salary or above. A response from a man purporting to be a "Wall Street banker" scathingly assessed her market value. As the banker declared, "Your looks will fade and my money will likely continue into perpetuity . . . in fact, it is very likely that my income increases but it is an absolute certainty that you won't be getting any more beautiful! . . . So, in economic terms you are a depreciating asset and I am an earning asset. It doesn't make good business sense to 'buy you' (which is what you're asking) so I'd rather lease."[24] It turns out the banker was apocryphal, which Reuters reported at the time. However, the same story continued to circulate for years as true and current, suggesting the longevity and attraction of the belief that marital agreements function on a principle of exchange (e.g., her beauty for his money). Yet, unlike money, beauty is a perishable commodity; as one snarky poster noted in 2013, "Girl better hurry up" since she only has "2.5–5 more years of marketability."[25]

Online dating blatantly encourages these calculations thanks to its parameters of age, race, and professional specificity; many sites even include an option where posters can divulge their income range. Daters can likewise sort for specific factors in their searches, and research supports the idea that they tend to narrow their range of choices precisely because they can be so selective. A study of a major dating site between February 2009 and February 2010, for example, reported that users display a strong preference for dating within their racial and ethnic groups. According to the study's primary author, Jerry Mendelsohn, more than 80 percent of the contacts initiated by white members were to other white members and only 3 percent were to black members. Black members, on the other hand, were ten times more likely to contact whites than whites were to contact blacks. (This emphasis on the first contact has been an important heuristic for researchers, and race appears to be a particularly predominant sorter in this regard.) Mendelsohn's study serves as yet another example of how entrenched patterns of social reproduction become concretized online. As Mendelsohn says, "Segregation, it seems, is sort of built into the social scene for the time being."[26]

Whereas Mendelsohn's study clearly focused on a site where users scroll through profiles, trolling for potential paramours (examples include OkCupid, JDate, and Match.com), similar selection criteria appear to inform the logic of operations based more overtly on pairing people on the basis of their stated preferences. These latter types of sites use algorithms to suggest partnerships based on what behemoth eHarmony calls the key "dimensions of compatibility," a process that is patented to protect its insights. This version also typically limits users' ability to see or communicate with those who fail to meet the algorithm's standards, which provides another example of how dating sites seamlessly incorporate the principles of selectivity in their sites' operations, normalizing finely tuned calibrations which in turn read as simply a commonsensical approach to informed selection. (Despite their cosmetic differences, all dating sites should perhaps be understood as blending user preferences with site recommendations. Even sites where users seem to have complete control use algorithms to determine a user's online patterns and suggest matches based on them.) These systems also point out the ubiquity of what Ted Striphas calls "algorithmic culture," whereby "the sorting, classifying and hierarchizing of people, places, objects and ideas" are determined by computational processes.[27] Online daters hence partake in hierarchical practices where algorithms sort and quantify potential dates, a process that likely will further entrench intolerance of difference as these algorithms "learn" user preferences.

Thanks to site design and/or predetermined personality questions, online dating sites also instruct users on what criteria count as acceptable points of similarity or desirability (age, location, education, previous marital status, income, religion, lifestyle, etc.) and may even mandate those synergies. These organizations suggest that complementarity or agreement serves as an important foundation for establishing successful unions. Though this understanding seems sound, it undeniably plays into the sort of wealth-consolidation patterns I discussed in the introduction to this book. Likewise, the prevalence of niche dating sites that cater to very specific lifestyles and interests encourages the perception that shared affinities, interests, or identity category markets will translate into more optimal pairings. According to Slater, the list includes "goth dating; pet-lovers dating; sites for military widows; nerd dating; plus-size dating; a large subset of dating sites for rich guys and the women who love them; sites for prisoners; a site for people who look alike; a site for Star Trek fans; sites for cowboys; a site for sea captains; sites for the fitness obsessed."[28]

Efficiency and selectivity exist as hallmark attributes of online dating as a service, since users roundly consider the ability to quickly sort through large inventories in short order as one of online dating's greatest virtues. Online dating dramatically expands the dating pool and then compensates for these expansions by offering users a way to pare down what could be an overwhelming number of potential matches. As Heino, Ellison, and Gibbs report in their 2010 study of online dating users, "One woman used an assessment tool on the site and discovered that only 6% of the male members had qualities she was seeking. Because her search was so specific, she appreciated that online dating allowed her to quickly identify those particular users." Sites cater to selective consumers who know exactly what they seek, allowing users to participate in what the authors of the study call "relationshopping." Further, as the researchers argue, many users consider themselves to be engaged in consumerist acts. Without prompting, more than half of the respondents in their study used economic metaphors to describe the experience of online dating, referring to online sites as a supermarket or a catalog. Many compared their profile to a resume that was meant to showcase their best self, and some even appreciated the opportunity to ascertain their relative worth/merit. As one female respondent put it, "I'm much more attractive than I thought, you know, so that was good."[29] Though the article does not frame the respondent's sentiment in this way, this woman's expression suggests her satisfaction with having procured an accurate sense of her brand value, a concept I explore in the next section. Online dating increases the likelihood of accurately determining one's market worth, an estimation based on the quality and character of responses to one's profile.

Online Dating and the Branded Self

This lack of discomfort with online dating is consistent with the modes of selfhood promoted by online existences in general, particularly the pleasures that come from having created a branded best self, notions that juggernauts like Facebook, Twitter, Tumblr, and Instagram have instantiated as commonplace. Here, it is worth making the distinction between commodification and branding: as Sarah Banet-Weiser distinguishes, commodification is an explicit economic strategy, whereas branding can be understood as a cultural phenomenon. As she explains, "In a moment of advanced global capitalism, the making—and selling and using—of things is often impossible to separate from the way we make our own lives. Brand strategies and logics are not only the backdrop but become the 'tools' for living in culture . . . brand logics and strategies become normative contexts for the forming of individual and social relations of affect and emotion."[30] Online dating is a clear example of a process whereby brand logics dictate the tools, prescribe the behaviors, and circumscribe the effects of mate seeking.

These logics are nowhere made more explicit than in Rachel Greenwald's 2003 volume *Find a Husband after 35 (Using What I Learned at Harvard Business School)*, which includes chapters on how women must build their brand, market that brand, increase their brand exposure, and even market test that brand, a suggestion that involves (gulp) having a friend call a failed date to find out why he felt it did not succeed. According to Greenwald, wannabe wives should construct a brand that meets the following criteria: "the brand rings true to who you are, both as you see yourself and as others see you; the brand will appeal to a wide range of men; the brand is memorable and unique; the brand positions you as 'marriage material.'" As she advises, women should begin by settling on three key words about themselves; one successful participant in her program used the brand "red hair, adventurous, great chef." This advice clearly premises itself on the understanding that entrepreneurial logics characterize every stage of the premarital process. "Now that you've developed your brand," Greenwald writes, "you will learn to advertise your brand, make your brand consistent with all details of your packaging, and reinforce your brand with online dating and other dating activities."[31] As this statement suggests, Greenwald's intervention is based on a thoroughly immersive experience: she recommends that her readers open a bank account from which funds can be channeled exclusively into the ancillary costs of finding a husband (buying new clothes, joining dating services, etc.), advice that points out how implicit assumptions of wealth and disposable income organize her program. This advice is nevertheless quite practical, insofar as marriage-minded sites tend to charge for use, with monthly subscription rates ranging from about twenty dollars per month to fifty dollars per month, fees that require users to possess at least a modicum of disposable income.

Online dating sites, indeed, play good host to branding labors. Consider, for example, the title of Damona Hoffman's dating guide, *Spin Your Web: How to Brand Yourself for Successful Online Dating*, in which Hoffman tells the reader, "From this point forward, I want you to think of yourself as a product: The Product 'You.'" Hoffman employs this terminology throughout her book, and includes a document template appropriately titled "The 'Product Me' Marketing Worksheet," which features questions such as "What would you liken your 'Product YOU' to?" and "What kind of person do you think would be attracted to this product?"[32] Rachel Greenwald additionally refers to online dating as "online marketing" and asserts that it is "the single best thing you can do to maximize your odds of finding a husband."[33]

Tech expert Amy Webb's part how-to guide, part memoir *Data, a Love Story: How I Gamed Online Dating to Meet My Match* offers a first-person account that inadvertently employs the theories that Hoffman and Greenwald advocate, a coherence that points out the mainstreaming of ideas that once seemed extreme.[34] Webb later filmed a successful TED talk based on her book, titled "How I Hacked Online Dating."[35] In order to perform "market research," Webb not only looked at other women's profiles, as Greenwald advises, but also posed as a variety of men to see how other women responded to them and then concocted a "superprofile" based on what she learned. To keep the most effective records of her progress, Webb formulated a weighted list of the qualities she sought in a husband (assigning more point values to those she was most desirous of), filled spreadsheets with details on the men who contacted her to see what point values they scored, and ultimately refused to communicate with anyone who failed to score highly enough. She writes, "Remember, you game a system by understanding it on a fundamental level so you can exploit its structure and gain a personal advantage."[36] Webb's language's insistence on gaining "a personal advantage" underscores her instrumental approach to the process of coupling. Like any participant in a stressed economy, Webb surveyed her competition, assessed which types of female profiles garnered the most attention, and mimicked the interaction protocols exhibited by the women who contacted one of her ten phony male profiles. (Webb largely discounts the ethical implications of this pretense, asserting that she never prolonged a conversation with an unknowing woman who believed the profile to be from a real man.)

Figure 1.2. Amy Webb's TED talk "How I Hacked Online Dating" has garnered more than six million views.

Webb's experiments underline what Alison Hearn calls "digital reputation" insofar as they illustrate that "the general public feeling or sentiment about a product, person, or service" can be both quantified and altered. As Hearn explains, "The number of times a name comes up in a Google search, an eBay rating as a buyer or seller, the number of friends on Facebook, or the number of followers on Twitter can all be seen as representations of digital reputation."[37] Importantly, the premise that reputations can be manipulated organizes what I would consider the first online dating reality show, TLC's *Love at First Swipe* (2015–16). In it, veteran *What Not to Wear* (2003–10) style expert Clinton Kelly along with online dating expert Devyn Simone face a series of misguided and ill-attired women hoping to find love online, who have already made missteps in putting together a profile. The sole focus on women goes unremarked on, though it does inadvertently confirm this chapter's contention that women bear the brunt of laboring for love. Prospective daters' first attempts at creating profiles feature prominently as negative examples, for they are too outlandish, too zany, too sex-obsessed, too obtuse, et cetera. Part makeover show, part dating instructional, *Love at First Swipe* has a two-pronged approach to the rehabilitation of its daters and their profiles. Kelly scrutinizes the candidates' looks, selects new outfits, and organizes a mini-makeover, whereas Simone tweaks their online profile, providing new photos, taglines, and advice on how to manage interactions. The show is deadly serious in what it considers the stakes of its mission: "A disastrous dating profile can kill your chances of finding love," says Kelly, as a picture of a woman with a cat on her head flashes on the screen. As well, the show thoroughly invests in the belief that a revised profile and a more sophisticated handling of one's online presentation writ large is a surefire vehicle for success. To illustrate the veracity of this claim, each episode begins by showcasing a contestant's pre-makeover profile and asking one hundred men if they could see themselves in a relationship with this person. Predictably, the number of takers is woefully low. The same question is asked again of the makeover profile, to dramatically improved results. This before-and-after assessment confirms the implicit wisdom of the show's experts and suggests that with some work even the most hopeless of dating candidates can be dramatically rehabilitated.

The sort of advice disseminated by Kelly and Simone is consistent with Webb's finding that successful profiles showcase women who seem upbeat and carefree. Webb recommends that users upload photos where they appear in nominally revealing clothes and where it appears that the camera caught them seconds after laughing; photos with these attributes feature prominently in *Love at First Swipe*. The show's hosts also keenly attend to the task of modulating any perception of excess. Women must be happy but not crazy; sexy but not slutty; individualized but not garish or odd. As these observations suggest, emotional and visual regimes organize online dating sites. Like any work milieu, online profiles demand certain outward manifestations of approachability, enthusiasm, and normalcy.

In fact, an emphasis on positivity is the single most repeated mantra in online dating advice. Laurie Davis, author of *Love @ First Click: The Ultimate Guide to Online Dating*, exhorts, "The most important thing to keep in mind when writing your profile is to be optimistic."[38] Greenwald writes, "Be brief, positive, and unique."[39] In *Love at First Site: Tales and Tips for Online Dating Success from a Modern-Day Matchmaker*, Erika Ettin counsels that prospective daters "stay away from talking about bad times in your life" and instead that they "be optimistic and happy."[40] This advice not only reflects the narrow range of affects afforded to online daters but also confirms the extent to which neoliberal affective regimes demand optimism. In *Meeting Your Half Orange: An Entirely Upbeat Guide to Using Dating Optimism to Finding Your Perfect Match*, author Amy Spencer elevates cheerful hopefulness to both a creed and an identity. Dating optimists (her term) simply believe that their "love life is going to work out for the best." To ensure this eventuality, wannabe daters must "start being the happiest person you can be now."[41] As cultural theorist Barbara Ehrenreich observes in *Bright-Sided*, "Positive affect seems to signal internal happiness," which also implies its obverse since it has become mostly unacceptable in American contexts not to demonstrate such wide-eyed sentiments.[42] Importantly, corporate logics regularly underpin emotional paradigms. As Melissa Gregg discovered in her study of professional culture, "the appropriate regulation of affect" is a key determiner of job success.[43] Online dating in this respect mirrors or replicates the affective conditions of the working world.

Displaying positive affect is, in turn, a good indication that one has successfully mastered the task of branding the self. If, as Hearn contends, "a smiley face and positive attitude are the hallmarks of a successfully branded person,"[44] the online dater's affect signals her relative brand savvy. One wrinkle in this format, however, is the need for one's brand to be both personalized and also rather indiscriminately inviting. To use Greenwald's formulation, brands must be "unique" and yet "appeal to a wide range of men."[45] The way to negotiate this difficulty is adaptability. Both Webb and Davis urge users to proclaim that they are as comfortable doing "this" as doing "that" even when those two attributes or interests are opposed. Webb's superprofile, for instance, included the following statement: "My friends would describe me as an outgoing and social world traveler, who's equally comfortable in blue jeans and little black dresses."[46] Pronouncements of versatility represent another fixture of the online profile. Davis rewrites a client's statement to read, "I'm as happy about finding a great pair of Diesel jeans as I am about tailgating."[47] As these lines suggest, sartorial choices are often stand-ins for personality traits. Yet, more than mere style, these sentiments mandate normalcy as a visibly middle-of-the-road ethos. Being comfortable whether fancy or casual (as both of these examples proclaim) signals a person who lacks rigidity or stubbornness. In short, it identifies the writer as someone whose goals and desires will not overshadow their partner's and whose adaptability assures their attractiveness.

Dating advice that encourages users to identify themselves as having an easygoing everyday persona nevertheless contains an additionally gendered subtext. To return to Webb's initial insights, in addition to being optimistic, profiles must adhere to rather narrow and conservative gender lines. Dateable women are sexy, easy to get along with, and not compromised by attending too closely to their own desires.[48] These postures culminate in the figure of the "girl," a self-identification that indicates one who is not taking herself too seriously. In order to "be a fun girl!" (one of her mantras) Webb changes her user name to "Tokyogirl" to reflect having lived for an extended period in Japan, though she does not mention the prestigious career that brought her there.[49] Webb obeys the long-held tenet that single women need to downplay their talents and ambitions and at the same time positions themselves in line with the sort of girlie rhetoric that Diane Negra identifies as a postfeminist hallmark.[50] These performances are "consummately and reassuringly feminine," to quote Angela McRobbie, and highlight that ambitious women continue to face pressure to dissemble not only their accomplishments but also their aspirations.[51] It is difficult to believe that the most interesting things Webb has to say about herself involve her girlishness, her casual nature, or her deft sartorial choices. (One of the book's repeated chords, in fact, involves her donning of a worn-out hooded black sweatshirt.) Yet, in order to attract an educated, upwardly mobile man, Webb downplayed precisely these factors in an effort to seem more normal and everyday.

While the tactic of minimizing female accomplishments has long been a fixture of dating advice, the market logics of this advice are in some ways as startling as their retrograde sexual politics. Marketing of oneself as "average," "easygoing," and "girl next door" paradoxically serves as distinguishing because it does not risk alienating or intimidating prospective dates. Despite all their pretenses of flexibility, online dating sites encourage a performance of personality that is actually quite rigidly defined. Online dating in this way perfectly encapsulates what I am characterizing in this book as a new marital zeitgeist, insofar as the project involves selling oneself to a potential buyer/mate and explicitly using new media technologies to do so. As Banet-Weiser details, "For the contemporary virtuous self, individual entrepreneurship is the conduit for self-realization, and online spaces are a perfect site for realizing this entrepreneurship."[52]

To effectively market oneself, in turn, entails formulating a profile that conveys one's ideal self, a terminology concomitant with an aspirational regime wherein the realization of one's best qualities becomes the subject's sole raison d'être. *Love at First Swipe* promises, for instance, to "help you present your best online self." Similarly, to quote Webb again, "I didn't want to try to hide who I was or to pretend to be someone else—I just needed to learn from the masters and present the best possible version of myself online."[53] Promotions of one's best possible self are also markedly in line with neoliberalist formulations designating only those who have fortified the self as entitled to achieve desired outcomes. As an example of the sometimes-backhanded logic of these strategic maneuvers, Webb's occupation as a digital strategy consultant is intrinsic to the sort of person she claims to be, yet she deliberately omits this detail from her online profile. As she comes to recognize, being a "fun girl" represents a more saleable identity than being a "serious professional." In this way, her book narrates a bildungsroman concerned less with the quest of finding a husband and more with her evolution as an entrepreneur of the self whereby she learns promotional and branding practices that deign her dateable and in turn marriageable. The ideological implications of these hard-won lessons are nicely summed up by Alison Hearn, who reminds us that "the branded self sits at the nexus of discourses of neoliberalism, flexible accumulation, radical individualism, and spectacular promotionalism."[54] These conceptualizations echo what Imre Szeman calls the "logic of entrepreneurship," which "not only offers possibilities of order and control but also makes claims on human flourishing and self-fashioning."[55]

The corrosive and myopic nature of the enduring myth that aggressive self-fashioning can solve all dating difficulties is nevertheless largely mystified in accounts like Webb's, since she does eventually find a husband and professes contentment in the union. More interesting perhaps is the way that rhetorics of self-improvement are employed to lay blame at the feet of those who do not accomplish their marital goals even when those obstacles are largely structural. Consider the operation of an Atlanta organization directed primarily at single African American women, The Single Wives Club. According to founder Koereyelle Du-Bose, the group, which features speakers, classes, online tutorials, and coaching, was created in 2011 out a of personal need to "figure out how we could better navigate the dating scene so that we could find quality men and prepare for healthy relationships . . . Our mission is to educate and to empower single ladies to become better women before becoming wives." DuBose's perception that unhappily single African American women simply have not worked hard enough on themselves and on preparing to be wives inserts neoliberal fantasies of deservingness into a conversation about marital prospects, substituting them for what might otherwise need to be stark admissions that for this demographic the odds of finding male partners are not especially good. When faced with a reminder that 42 percent of black women will never wed, DuBose demonstrates an almost quixotic commitment to the belief that nuptial success is in the hands of the individual: "We have to decide what we are willing to do about it, so instead of saying, 'woes me' . . . what are you going to do about it, what are you going to do to empower yourself, what are you going to do to prepare yourself, so that you don't become a statistic? . . . I'm going to have to put in some work . . . If I want something different, I'm going to have to *do* something different. That is what the single wife understands."[56] I read DuBose's verbiage as a valiant effort to mystify actual demographic realities confirming that marriageable African American men are in regrettably short supply, statistics hardly amenable to being altered by sheer force of will. In this way, DuBose's sentiments serve as a distressing reminder of the pervasiveness of what Lauren Berlant terms "cruel optimism," which Berlant defines as "a relation of attachment to compromised conditions of possibility whose realization is discovered either to be *im*possible, sheer fantasy, or *too* possible, and toxic." DuBose exhibits what Berlant might call a "compromised endurance" wherein "technologies of patience" enable "a concept of the *later* to suspend questions about the cruelty of the *now*."[57] Aspirational notions of goal setting, self-analysis, and maximization of assets allow "single wives" a perception of control, wherein biding time working on the self postpones a confrontation with the crippling social contexts that have hobbled economic assurance, disadvantages that serve as a primary stumbling block for American marital futures.

Another surprise in the lexicon of online dating is how well conceptions of the branded self gel with the quest for a soul mate. We might wonder: if one accepts that the branded self is in part a marketing device, can it sufficiently manage the burden of attracting a real soul mate?

Figure 1.3. Single Wives Club founder Koereyelle DuBose cultivates proper mind-sets on the path to marriage.

This dissonance is not as great as one might suspect in part because the best self rhetoric is oftentimes consistent with what people consider to be the "real me." The wannabe daters on *Love at First Swipe* confirm this perception. Though often attired and adorned in ways inconsistent with their everyday life, participants appraise their makeovers as uncovering their true selves and say they feel empowered as a result. Moreover, thanks to digital regimes like Facebook and Instagram, which emphasize and reward curated self-presentation, online forms of communication founded on the sharing of photos and tidbits of personal narrative, reflection, or observation seem as organic as any other. If anything, in fact, online dating has revitalized the predominance of soul mate rhetoric. Finkel and colleagues report that "destiny/soulmate beliefs have long been encouraged by the media," but "the pervasiveness of online dating sites' soulmate-related claims may well be exacerbating this general trend." A Marist poll taken in January 2011, for instance, found that 73 percent of Americans believe in soul mates, a number that was up from 66 percent just six months prior.[58] Another explanation for the pervasiveness of soul mate rhetoric is that online dating makes available scores of options that could not have been accessed in other eras. In turn, this leads to the perception that one has the opportunity to be selective and make the best choice possible.

If, as Banet-Weiser usefully posits, in the realm of the digital "to be authentic to oneself, one must first be authentic to others,"[59] then selfhood is constituted through acts of recognition. Finding a soul mate online is therefore perhaps even more natural than finding one through other means. Another way of framing this process is offered by Stig Hjarvard, who postulates, "As the media project sociability as the dominant mode of interaction in many institutional contexts . . . the media come to influence how recognition is exercised as love, respect, and esteem."[60] This observation points out how recognition and sociability become the bedrock on which romantic connection is made, an observation that again underscores how well-suited the practice of online dating is for the social and romantic requirements of the current era.

Gatekeeping and Exclusivity in the Online Realm

Thanks to site design and functionality, patterns of self-presentation and intra-user dialogue are well established in online dating realms. This section argues that by setting parameters for acceptable behavior in online dating, the process participates in setting hierarchies of value that contribute to marriage's increasingly exclusionary status in American contexts. In addition to demanding that one foreground a branded best self, online dating privileges what economist Catherine Hakim terms "erotic capital," the combination of "beauty, sex appeal, skills of self-presentation and social skills" that make people attractive in everyday contexts. Erotic capital entails what Hakim calls "a combination of aesthetic, visual, physical, social and sexual attractiveness to other members of your society."[61] Most dating advice marketed to women obliquely instructs them to maximize erotic capital, emphasizing the importance of looking good, seeming social, and using visual technologies to enhance their appeal. With its emphasis on photographs and pithy catchphrases, online dating is a perfect vehicle to operationalize optics; this description also explains why *Love at First Swipe* works so well in the televisual register. Specifically, it is a makeover show that allows viewers to revel in the pleasures of the reveal.

Visual appeal and the ability to communicate in savvy ways represent a structuring logic of the online dating sphere. Resultantly these topics also command vast attention in online dating advice. Erika Ettin offers a granular account of how many photos should appear in a profile (ideally three), cautions against including pictures of other people, and advises daters to include "one photo where you are doing something interesting."[62] Likewise, Laurie Davis spends the better part of a chapter telling people how to prepare and pose for profile photographs ("cropping makes you clickable"; "red is the best color you can wear in your main photo").[63] She similarly spends an exhaustive amount of time counseling readers on how to make a first contact, offering painstaking advice on how to formulate everything from greetings to subject lines to signatures.

On a more abstract level, online dating demands what Eva Illouz calls a "value rationalization of personality" insofar as users are asked to clarify their "values and beliefs . . . What do I want? What are my preferences and personality? Am I adventurous or in need of security?"[64] To communicate in this way involves not only an understanding of one's strengths and skills but also cognizance of how to express them in particularized, even atomized ways. Daters do this, according to Ettin, by "setting yourself apart by digging into the details" and avoiding what she calls "the curse of the empty adjective."[65] The experience of setting up an online profile privileges self-knowledge, demanding that it be channeled into a vocabulary that confirms self-actualization. Participants are meant to possess a keen and quite sophisticated level of emotional literacy whereby they know their authentic selves and translate that awareness into recognizable, iterative concepts. As Illouz explains, online dating encourages "the control of emotions, the clarification of one's values and goals, the use of the technique of calculation, and the decontextualization of emotions." Illouz additionally contends that emotions are instrumentalized so that they serve as the centerpiece of "selfhood and sociability."[66] To test her thesis, consider what was once my own online dating profile, which appeared under the tagline "Film Professor Seeks Leading Man":

> Is it wrong to say that my personality really is my best feature?
>
> I like long dinners and medium-length runs (outside, though, not in a gym!). I'm almost as good at facilitating a discussion with a class of forty as I am sharing a glass of wine with a friend, and I think I'm a good listener, which is probably why I love being around people so much. I have one of those faces that shows everything I'm feeling, and though I don't think this is necessarily a bad thing, I probably am the worst poker player ever!
>
> I have an admitted soft spot for good writers, though I'm more likely to be described as friendly, optimistic, and good-natured than pretentious. And when it comes to movies, I promise, I will watch almost anything.
>
> In the last year, I have sampled a Scottish breakfast in Edinburgh, gone horse-back riding in Bryce Canyon, white-water rafted in Maine, snorkeled in St. Thomas, and shopped in Miami (that last one actually felt like a sport, believe me).
>
> My ideal guy is all the things you'd expect (smart, funny, adventurous, kind) and some you wouldn't (someone willing to go dancing in a 1970s disco outfit at least once—I'll explain later).

I see in this profile a presentation eerily consistent with the diagnosis that the control of emotions, the clarification of one's values, and the regimented specifications of what one is—and what one seeks—rest at the very heart of an online presentation of self. To emphasize my emotional fitness, I make dramatic points of my ability to listen, my fondness for people, and my openness. To clarify my interests, I stress athleticism and travel. I frame what I am looking for as both commonplace (smart, funny, adventurous) and rarified (disco outfit). Yet, at the same time that I strive for transparency, I also earnestly attempt to control what the audience will see. To modulate a perception that, as an academic, I might be a snob, I promise "I will watch almost anything." This admission likewise serves to create an opening for a partner to outpace me in an arena in which I have considerable experience—I am, in fact, a film professor promising not to critique films, hence my own "girling" moment.[67] Along these lines, I also use the colloquial "guy" in place of "man." In all, this profile illustrates the requirement that one present a self who is confident, well-rounded, and emotionally transparent.

Online daters likely feel compelled to present such selves, as I did, because they symbolically entitle coupledom. Much like reality television's makeover participants who, as Brenda Weber argues, warrant full citizenry rights only if they exhibit traits like power, confidence, and happiness, so, too, are affective performances the lingua franca of online dating sites.[68] Likewise, as Beverley Skeggs discusses, if emotional competence signifies mastery of one's inner self, "feelings and emotions become *value statements about one's capacity*."[69] In this respect, it bears noting that I unwittingly followed Webb's advice to "keep language aspirational, positive, and optimistic"[70] to a tee. I, too, wrote a profile circumscribed by cheerful attitudes, even using the words "optimism" and "good-natured" in the text. Rosalind Gill has pointed out that when extraordinary emphasis is placed on positive affect, it leaves very little room for any other types of emotions: "Excised from this repertoire is any sense of the loneliness, anxiety, or hurt that might accompany being single while wanting a partner."[71]

My profile likewise emphasizes versatility—my jeans / little black dress formulation takes the shape of describing myself as comfortable with a large group of people ("class of forty") or in small intimate gatherings ("sharing a glass of wine with a friend"). Even more crucially, as I now see, I say nothing of my work as a scholar or writer, confining professional references to my tagline and my experience as a teacher. As my profile illustrates, one becomes legible and legitimated as a dating subject through such displays, rhetoric that I approximated in the suggestion that I, too, exhibited these emotional as well as (frankly) gendered and classed competencies. Or, as Illouz writes, "there are now hierarchies of emotional well-being, understood as the capacity to achieve socially and historically situated forms of happiness and well-being."[72] Dating sites act in accordance with a cultural zeitgeist where emotional performances determine "dateability." Dating profiles like mine therefore demand to be read in terms of their exclusionary understandings; as Skeggs reminds us, "The therapeutic injunction to communicate is then not just a privatized form of labor but a form of class and gender reproduction, promoting a bourgeois model of how intimate relationships should be performed."[73]

My reference to travel, and the rather performative list of the places I had been in the last year, also underlines the persistence of affective and economic hierarchies, a point buttressed by Adam Arvidsson's finding that Match.com users espoused what he terms an "experiential ethic" of "self-discovery, an orientation towards touching, revealing or sharing one's true self through open-hearted and intimate communication with others, or through an active or experientially rich life conduct." The fact that successful forms of emotional well-being must be testified to in language, reinforced via consumer culture, and necessitate a type of life experiences that it takes resources to procure (e.g., the type of travel I mention) collectively highlight the classed dimensions of online dating. Arvidsson tentatively hints at these distinctions when he notes that online daters seek partners with whom to share "a life conceived as an ongoing quest for enriching experiences," and speculates that "this could be a matter of class habitus. Perhaps such quests for self-expansion through continuous experiences make up the ideal of the particular class of 'culturally mobile,' urban, college-educated symbol workers that make up the main target for Match.com."[74] My own experiences certainly corroborate this sentiment.

Online dating norms likewise operationalize the notion that some users are fitter than others are for the process. Much like any job description featuring a list of competencies that applicants must possess in order to be considered for employment, users of online dating sites are tacitly encouraged to highlight the sorts of skills and aptitudes (and even life histories) that characterize successful behavior on new media platforms. eHarmony codifies this hierarchy outright, rejecting candidates for "being married too many times, for responding to items in a way that suggests that they may have emotional problems such as depression, and for being identified by the algorithm as providing misleading or inaccurate information on the survey."[75] Quality control may also occur in more subtle ways. In *Love @ First Click*, Davis advises her readers not to overshare about past relationships, complain about their lives, or discuss sex, politics, or religion. *Love at First Site* similarly recommends that prospective daters refrain from talking about sex—"sex and your online dating profile should not mix."[76] Such counsel contributes to the perception that online daters need to self-censure in order to enhance their wider appeal.

Users are likewise directed to identify themselves in terms that translate not only from person to person, but also across markets and platforms. Dissuaded from identifying oneself through potentially incendiary or controversial attitudes, daters utilize tastes, hobbics, and interests as a way to perform individuality.[77] Instead of any discussion of politics, Davis urges the atomization of product tastes: "Think 'spicy tuna rolls' over 'sushi' and 'racquetball' over 'working out.'" This advice nods to how social media forms encourage users to list their likes and dislikes, incessantly categorizing what they are listening to, buying, watching, or reading as a way of establishing their personality. To further compel daters to reveal similar information, Davis refers to research findings culled by OkCupid and clarifies that "every niche word or phrase the site has data on has a positive effect on messaging, such as 'vegetarian,' 'band,' and 'grad school.'"[78] This advice underscores the importance of commodity culture to the experience of online dating and to its presentation in female popular culture. This point was made saliently in an Amazon.com reviewer's critique of Love @ First Click. Derisively labeling it "chick lit," the reviewer complained that "there are too many references to stilettos and specific gadgets. The easy, breezy, cool girl about the city voice didn't resonate with me, and product placement mentions are off putting. I realize that this is part of trying to convey a certain vibe, but I just found it irritating."[79] Postfeminist cultures inculcate femininity according to formulistic and narrowly defined parameters, expectations that many women perceive as exclusionary. These observations remind us how, even in a postrecession context, female popular culture is dominated by tones of whimsical confidence, steeped in references to consumer culture, and peppered with references to the markers of easy luxury, all of which assume an audience with similar degrees of privilege. Postfeminism sees "capitalism as a vehicle for self-fashioning," a point that author Stephanie Harzewski makes, not incidentally, in a scholarly investigation of chick lit.[80] As it is presented in female forms like advice manuals, online dating is a practice bound in a larger nexus that encourages women to think of—and present themselves as—nested firmly within consumer cultures. As in chick lit, female online daters are called on to identify themselves via their consumptive practices and to communicate within taste cultures.

Targeted acts of self-disclosure are also quite useful to advertisers. While perhaps an obvious point, online dating sites gain valuable income through advertising revenue. The more users disclose their product tastes and preferences in their online profiles, the more information advertisers can cull. Surveying the advice Match.com gives its customers about how to construct a profile, Arvidsson notes that it is designed to create the impression that Match has "quality singles," a necessary perception for users *and* for advertisers.[81] In this way, the requirements of the capitalistic market set the rules not only in terms of who qualifies as datable but also by circumscribing the parameters of what constitutes acceptable (read: useable) content for corporate interests.

These content norms also begin to suggest the highly classed aspects of the online dating experience, since being able to write with some degree of flourish about one's likes, hobbies, or interests also attests to a user's social and cultural capital. This observation has nevertheless garnered scant research attention. Indeed, one of the most provocative takes I have seen on the subject of class and online dating comes from a 2012 study written by a graduate student who sought to determine how "people's performances online construct subjective, *classed*, identities." As Kate Aurigemma asserts, "Through providing information both about class-constitutive demographic indicators and *habitus*-dependent social tastes, dating site users are simultaneously constructing their own class identities along with their personal profiles." Aurigemma conducted a linguistic analysis of thirty-six online dating profiles of women on OkCupid, segmented according to educational levels. Her analysis suggested several key themes that may serve as class markers: how people talk about their goals, how satisfied people are in their jobs or careers, the role of family in people's lives, and the importance of intellect. Significantly, Aurigemma concluded that those with college or graduate degrees used a tone that communicates more certainty and confidence, whereas those without degrees were less convinced of their eventual success. When talking about their careers, those with high school degrees "use verbs like 'trying' and 'working' . . . the others use more certain verbs like 'will' or . . . 'continue to upgrade' (as opposed to *trying* to upgrade)." Analyzing the way that class is codified via linguistic cues, she speculates that "those with greater education have practice in maintaining middle-class norms," and hypothesizes that "their confidence and certainty is born from a sense of self-esteem fostered through successful compliance with these norms." Aurigemma's data suggests an interesting distinction based on the fault line of education and class, one consistent with the sort of new marital economies that constitute the impetus for this book. Class divides in the nation increasingly correlate with marital status, an outcome assured by the reality that well-educated Americans with cultural and economic capital tend to select others in the same bracket. As she concludes, "The major cultural implications of these findings are that such classed performances and vocabulary reinforce notions of meritocracy and an ideology of upward mobility; create often-hidden class injuries; obscure institutionally based inequalities; and perpetuate the ideology of self-esteem that rewards people who maintain their privilege."[82]

Online dating's emphasis on appearance, sociability, and confidence underscore how thoroughly postfeminist attitudes have melded with entrepreneurial logics, and confirm that effecting a presentation of assuredness, openness, and versatility qualifies one for dating markets. Likewise, while postfeminist attitudes have long been understood to stress a culture of competition, advice about online dating builds on this foundation in order to emphasize the need to constantly jockey for position, with the understanding that like many markets, the dating market is a glutted one. To maximize their exposure, online daters should be on at least two dating sites simultaneously (though preferably three) and dating multiple people at the same time, experts urge. As Rachel Greenwald articulates, "You always want to increase the chances of selling your product by expanding your market—by targeting as many relevant consumer segments as possible."[83] Advice literature likewise assumes dating success exists in direct proportion to the amount of effort one puts in. *Spin Your Web*'s author guides readers to "date like it's your job," and "send at least five messages a week for the first month."[84] Other common advice includes the suggestion that daters should upload new pictures or tweak their profile descriptions on a regular basis in order to ensure that their profiles continue to turn up in other people's searches.

These markets again cater to those who have the time and money to procure the sort of access and experience they desire, and the process can even be outsourced. For a price tag of $147 per date, or for a monthly rate of $1,200, the company Virtual Dating Assistants helps clients select prospective matches and plan dates, right down to the minutiae of wardrobe selection.[85] As these new realities remind us, online dating seems most suited to those who inhabit elevated class structures, appealing to people with busy work lives who are also under career and time pressure. As Arvidsson concludes, "It seems that internet dating users in general, and Match.com members in particular, belong disproportionately to the urban, college-educated symbol analysts that make up the upper echelons of the new working class of the information economy."[86] Relatedly, online dating seems to be directed toward and constructive of a certain type of urban femininity most prized by advertisers, one that imposes a strict set of guidelines for affective performances, calls for social media savvy, and rewards users familiar with effective self-presentation in online settings. Romantic norms exist in compliance with these rationalized realities, and represent yet another way that coupledom has become a business.

Coda: Marriage Panic and the New Scarcity

In a 2006 issue of *The Atlantic*, author Lori Gottlieb attempted to investigate the promises and realities of online dating, at the time a burgeoning but not wholly mainstream practice. In the article, she narrates a meeting she had with Dr. Neil Clark Warren, the head of eHarmony, where she asks why, despite having taken the site's exhaustive 436-question personality test and expanding her search to the world, she elicits zero matches. Dr. Warren tells her that she is too good: "You are too bright. You are too thoughtful. The biggest thing you've got to do when you're gifted like you is to be patient."[87] Flash-forward exactly two years and Gottlieb pens an article in the same magazine titled "Marry Him!" which she later expanded into a book, *Marry Him: The Case for Settling for Mr. Good Enough.*[88] In both pieces, Gottlieb bluntly counsels women in their twenties and early thirties to couple early, writing, "Settle! That's right. Don't worry about passion or intense connection."[89] As she rationalized, although their impulse might be to hold out for Mr. Right, that decision too actively risks singlehood in one's forties. Describing how she dumped perfectly adequate but nonetheless uninspiring boyfriends, had a child on her own, and then faced even more difficulties as a single mother trying to find a husband, Gottlieb's trajectory provides a fascinating through line for this chapter, insofar as it narrates a transition from dating in a market economy to, as she argues, the necessity of lowering one's expectations when the market refuses to accommodate those demands.

Gottlieb's advice was simultaneously of the time and highly antici-patory. Her exhortation coheres in obvious ways with female popular culture's incessant admonition to single women that they marry in time, before it is *too late*. As Anthea Taylor diagnoses, "The most visible single woman in postfeminist media culture is she who proves her profound wish to be otherwise,"[90] a desire both encouraged and cultivated by media outlets that stress the centrality and urgency of marital impera-tives. The belief that time is a quantity that cannot be squandered has been most usefully delineated by Diane Negra, who suggests that "one of the signature attributes of postfeminist culture is its ability to define var-ious life stages within the parameters of 'time panic.'" As Negra argues, for women "time is conceived of as a threat," in no small part because of reproductive requirements that delimit female options in ways that are not so acutely visited on men.[91] These insecurities (loosely defined as "How will I find a man in time, before I am too old?") have been in-flected and amplified by related pressures brought on by the worldwide economic recession. Introducing a notion of scarcity into a rhetoric al-ready infused with high amounts of insecurity, the recession highlighted the imperiled status of the men once meant to be mates for marriage-inclined women. An attendant preoccupation for wannabe wives, ac-cording to female popular culture, is the requirement that they find men of substance and means because the supplies grow ever scarcer.

As I have argued elsewhere, one of the resounding drumbeats of the recession was the observation that this period of widespread financial insecurity hit men harder than it did women; reports postulated that inequities were bound to continue since women were outpacing men in terms of college degrees earned and jobs procured.[92] Though there is considerable evidence that women's newfound economic dominance is a convenient yet specious narrative, these conversations have contin-ued to dominate popular culture.[93] Moreover, men's supposed finan-cial downfall has been narrated through the lens of the heterosexual imperative. Put simply, widespread male un- or underemployment has spurred media consideration of what these developments will mean for women in search of suitable husbands. These discussions twin the working sphere with the domestic one, aligning their understandings of marriage with shifts in professional economies. These slippages and overlaps between professional and marital economies represent an in-

augurating premise of this book, recalculations that confirm their inter-
dependency despite the fact that they are so often kept separate in the
cultural imaginary.

The worry that women's newfound economic dominance will in turn
imperil their marital prospects reflects entrenched gender patterns. Specifically, it rehearses the long-standing assumption that men's birthright
ensures their status as higher earners than women and assumes that ambitious or successful women are bound to have a harder time coupling
or staying coupled. A 2013 *New York Times* article, "Breadwinning Wives
and Nervous Husbands," for example, reports on a study which found
that women's gains in the economic sphere tend to lead to disadvantages
in the personal realm. The study's authors speculate that "the trend in
the percentage of women making more than men explains almost one-
fourth of the marriage rate's decline." Though the causes for these findings are unclear, the article speculates that men's discomfort with having
to occupy a secondary economic role may be having a dampening effect
on marital futures.[94] Women are charged with the responsibility of miti-
gating and managing this supposedly new state of affairs, a reality that
reveals precisely the sort of logics of supply and demand I have been
tracing in this chapter.

To return to the beleaguered Lori Gottlieb, it bears noting that she was
ahead of the curve insofar as she divined a realistic solution for women
faced with this widespread scarcity. Gottlieb's rejoinder that women settle
instead of continuing a search for perfection anticipates a conversation
about marrying down that emerged forcefully during the global recession. As this advice goes, women should consider accepting men who are
in some way their inferiors, be that designation tied to income, ambition,
or job prestige. These solutions are not, of course, unique to the current
moment. Similar advice has long had its roots in strapped marital economies and has been particularly prevalent in communities of color. Attesting to the long-standing reality of scarcity, in the provocatively titled *Is
Marriage for White People?* Ralph Richard Banks confirms not only black
women's inability to find black men who equal their level of education or
financial security (regardless of their own position vis-à-vis these demographics) but also that settling is a popular response. As he asserts, "Black
women more frequently marry less-educated and lower-earning men than
any other group of women in our nation."[95] Such accommodations are

also routinely accounted for in women's popular media. In a comparison study of relationship advice found in *Marie Claire* (a publication with a predominantly white readership) and *Essence* (a publication with a predominately black readership), Sanja Jagesic found that "the reality of the marriage market is accounted for in relationship advice, and since several of the articles in *Essence* advocate for embracing relationships with men less economically successful, it seems that black women are asked to respond to their marriage market by embracing non-traditional structures of male-female romantic relationships."[96]

In a prescient move, in 2011 Banks predicted that "if the fortunes of white men and women diverge as they have among blacks . . . professional white women may confront the same challenges that professional black women do today."[97] The marriage panic I identify here has much to do with the perception that, thanks to all men's declining statures, the marital calculations demanded of women of color have become the lot of all women. These changes in marital economies have of course been pervasive everywhere except affluent communities for quite some time, but it is only as they make their way into the upper echelon that popular culture begins to recognize this dearth.

Notions of panic, scarcity, and the need to account for these shifting economies tend to consume reports that concentrate on female marital futures, and these extend from personal accounts to more widely accepted demographic studies. Kate Bolick's November 2011 *Atlantic* cover story "All the Single Ladies" was exemplary in terms of offering a memorable autobiographical account. On a cover emblazoned with the words "What, Me Marry?" stood an image of a well-dressed, thirty-something white woman visibly perturbed by the sentiments superimposed on her image: "In today's economy, men are falling apart." (The image is actually Bolick herself.) As Bolick writes, "American women as a whole have never been confronted with such a radically shrinking pool of what are traditionally considered to be 'marriageable' men—those who are better educated and earn more than they do. So women are now contending with what we might call the new scarcity."[98] Bolick's observation rehearsed conversations which predicted that disparate levels of education and aspiration between the sexes take a toll on marital futures, predictions that appear to have come to fruition. According to a 2014 Pew Center report titled "Record Share of Americans Have Never

Married," "Changing gender patterns in the link between education and marital status have contributed to an educational mismatch between never-married men and women. Today, never-married women ages 25 and older are more educated overall than never-married men: one-third of these women have either a bachelor's or advanced degree, compared with one-quarter of never-married men ages 25 and older."[99] As this study implies, this mismatch presents a problematic state of affairs because the ranks of well-educated men have thinned, and consequently heterosexual women will lack suitable, equal partners. It is nevertheless notable that only when women are more educated than men is this considered troublesome. Consistent across much of this rhetoric is the idea that it is bad for women to outpace or outearn men, yet the reverse has never generated comparable hand-wringing.

These disparities continue to register as problems that women must account for and plan around. As if to reinforce their own culpability for remaining single, Bolick and Gottlieb both at some point highlight that they could have married perfectly nice men, options they now somewhat wistfully recall. Displaying a tendency to personalize the scarcity, these authors blame their current lack of a husband on having been too choosy, and on having held out for an unattainable ideal. Interestingly, they also echo the sentiments espoused by Single Wives Club founder Koereyelle DuBose, insofar as they individualize their lack of a spouse and suggest that they simply did not work hard enough to understand and accommodate the marital marketplace. Neoliberal notions of personal responsibility, in turn, bring us back full circle to Susan Patton's advice: as these authors insinuate, women who wait to marry face thinner marriage markets. In the face of these realities, female popular culture urges women to bootstrap their way into marriage.

While postfeminist regimes have always been intent to illustrate to women the importance of finding suitable mates, and doing so before it is too late, this exhortation has become all the more complicated in an era characterized by a supposed shortage of eligible men. This situation reaffirms the need for a famine mentality where one must marshal all available resources to pair off. This chapter has surveyed how the need to poise oneself for wifedom must be met with urgent deliberation. Marriage scarcity rhetoric, bar none, reminds women of the increasingly more austere conditions under which the wannabe wife now toils.

2

Almost Wives

Emotional Regulation, Marriage Television, and the
Plight of the Modern Bride

In November 2010, the E! network premiered the reality competition come bridal showcase *Bridalplasty* (2010–11), a show that touted the questionable slogan "The only competition where the winner gets cut." As the tagline suggested, in each episode eager brides-to-be compete for a minor plastic surgery from their wish list, facing off over tasks such as decorating wedding cakes, creating a bridal bouquet, writing vows, and planning honeymoons. Once determined, the overall winner received a full-scale surgical makeover as well as an all-expenses-paid wedding of her dreams, an event that provided the show with its culminating episode. To add to the intrigue, the groom had not seen his wife-to-be since her transformation. In the terms now typical of a synergistically focused reality television industry, the surgeries were performed by celebrity plastic surgeon Dr. Terry Dubrow, himself a familiar face to audiences thanks to his having led the surgical team on Fox's controversial *The Swan* (2004). In 2012, Dubrow also began appearing in *The Real Housewives of Orange County* (2006–) alongside his wife, aspiring actress Heather Dubrow. He garnered his own show in 2014, *Botched*, where he and fellow *Real Housewives* veteran Paul Nassif repair plastic surgeries gone wrong.

Due to its conflation of makeover, weight loss, and wedding tropes coalescing to convince women of the necessity of changing and perfecting the self, and of taking invasive and dramatic measures to do so, *Bridalplasty* prompted much predictable hand-wringing.[1] The show nevertheless represented a natural outgrowth—and perhaps even a logical endpoint—of the sort of wedding-themed reality television that has long peppered female culture. While the show made many uncomfortable and did not return for a second season, it unfailingly called on the logics of discipline and punishment that have become staples of the genre.

As the previous chapter documented, processes of efficiency, quality control, and maximization of marketable assets circumscribe twenty-first-century marriage markets. Wedding-themed reality television similarly announces itself as a rationalized form of labor, and this chapter examines the way this programming encourages women to work physically and emotionally in order to declare their fitness as wedding (and eventual) marital subjects. Though rarely as punishing as the body modifications featured on *Bridalplasty*, the types of labors demanded by wedding-themed reality television are explicitly linked to the bride's establishment of credibility, legitimacy, and desirability. Moreover, as I will document, the sorts of attitudes and dispositions bridal culture compels women to cultivate in many ways mimic the skills and aptitudes demanded by contemporary workplaces. Learning the requirements and figuring out the optimal mind-sets for being a perfect bride exist as fitting precursors to the eventual task of becoming a wife.

My analysis is grounded in and influenced by seminal work on the relationship between reality television and neoliberalism. As Laurie Ouellette and James Hay argue in *Better Living through Reality TV*, the genre cultivates good citizens, subjects who learn to self-govern so that they might more effectively and efficiently manage their homes, families, appearances, health, and finances. As Ouellette and Hay write, "At a time when privatization, personal responsibility, and consumer choice are promoted as the best way to govern liberal capitalist democracies, reality TV shows us how to conduct and 'empower' ourselves as enterprising citizens."[2] Reality television is likewise undergirded by market logics that stress principles of competition, hard work, and personal responsibility, and at the same time disregard factors that may disadvantage certain groups such as age, race, or socioeconomic status. As it pertains to wannabe wives, I argue that an unending series of rejoinders to work on the self organizes bridal television, labor conceptualized as both affective and corporeal. Only when the bride has proven herself a responsible citizen able to regulate her emotions, manage her body, and discipline her whims does she confirm her suitability for wifedom. Inculcating a corporate mentality that demands that brides accommodate to specific and demanding conditions, the bridal realm asks for optimism and a willingness to get along with others. Similarly, it requires a driven determination to work hard and prove that one that not only desires but also deserves a husband.

To analyze the process by which a dater turns into a proper bride, this chapter begins by analyzing reality dating shows, particularly *The Bachelor* (2002–) and *Millionaire Matchmaker* (2008–15), offerings that provide a bridge from the previous chapter in that they translate online dating's focus on efficiency, selectivity, and instrumentality into a public display. I argue that *The Bachelor* is anchored by an affective regime whereby bachelorettes must prove their sincerity, willingness to believe in the promise of true love, and ability to reproduce discourses of authenticity in a milieu nevertheless permeated by artificial constructs, staged scenarios, and falsified rhetoric. *Millionaire Matchmaker* similarly disciplines its participants in order to ensure their fitness for romance, demanding from them submission to the withering gaze of guru Patti Stanger. An ability to withstand scrutiny and even to thrive in the face of surveillance in turn legitimizes prospective daters as serious and commitment-ready.

Turning to "bad bride" television, the chapter documents how female popular culture embarrasses brides who do not adequately self-regulate. In particular, the long-running *Bridezilla* (2004–13) reminds viewers that its featured women are not worthy of the weddings or marriages they have, particularly by pointing out their extreme affects, inappropriate behaviors, and mistreatments of friends and relatives, transgressions that confirm the bride's status as a bad boss. These offerings also tend to reinforce exclusionary cultural hierarchies, shedding negative light on brides disadvantaged by class or race. The chapter contrasts these unflattering representations with those offered by series such as *Bridal Bootcamp* (2010) and *Shedding for the Wedding* (2011), shows that document the lengths—both physical and emotional—that brides can be expected to go to in order to declare their marital fitness. In total, the chapter surveys offerings that underline and applaud the work that goes into preparing oneself to be a proper bride and censure those activities that do not. Ultimately, it argues that postfeminist neoliberal entrepreneurialism inflects the bridal industry, turning the process of becoming a bride into a labor for respectability and deservingness. The chapter concludes with a brief meditation on mediatized weddings, arguing that the wedding serves to inaugurate a woman's brand identity as a wife.

Reality Dating Shows and the Husband as Prize

In the female popular imaginary, reality dating shows (and the celebrities they inaugurate) have supplanted the romantic comedy as the optimal site for generating interest and excitement about the process of coupling. While the American romantic comedy surged in popularity during the 1990s, the genre began to seem creaky and formulaic by the 2000s, when it was also somewhat hijacked by the bromance.[3] By the early 2010s the romantic comedy was roundly considered a tired genre. Referencing 1989's *When Harry Met Sally* in an article titled "R.I.P. Romantic Comedies: Why Harry Wouldn't Meet Sally in 2013," the *Hollywood Reporter* argued that increasingly globalized film markets favoring action and serialization over dialogue, a dearth of marketable young stars, and fatigue with rom com's "meet cute" predictability sounded the genre's death knell.[4] Relatedly, the romantic comedy has not kept pace with the sort of data-driven formulas that now structure romantic conceptualization, technological parameters that circumscribe the experience many daters actually have.

In a 2014 *Atlantic* article that again references *When Harry Met Sally*, Megan Garber's "When Harry Met eHarmony" observes that "the axis romance has revolved around—the guiding sense of mystery, of uncertainty, of *otherness*—is giving way, under the influence of digital capabilities, to more pragmatic orientations. . . . The promises of big data—insights! wisdom! relevance!—are insinuating themselves onto relationships. Love, actually, is now more data-driven than it has ever been before."[5] Garber links these new realities to the decline of the romantic comedy, though it should be said that online dating does figure prominently in a number of romance films, including traditional romantic comedies such as *You've Got Mail* (1998), *Must Love Dogs* (2005), *In Search of a Midnight Kiss* (2007), *Because I Said So* (2007), and *The Ugly Truth* (2009). It likewise structures teen capers like *Eurotrip* (2004) and *Sex Drive* (2008), and references to the practice appear in myriad television shows.[6] Garber's assertion that big data and algorithmic functionality organize modern dating climates also coheres with the investigations presented in my previous chapter.

Reality dating shows, I argue, are more attuned to data-driven realities and inject tension, intrigue, and uncertainty back into the coupling process. Specifically, reality dating shows reinvigorate the concept of choice, stressing the many-options principle that is both the seduction and (for some) the danger of online dating, perpetually dangling the prospect that someone better will be on the next screen, in the bus, or about to get out of the limo. Reality dating shows also allow for the same "will they, or won't they" deferral that structures the pleasures of romantic comedy, though they up the ante considerably since it is rarely clear which prospective dater will win or whether the couple that forms on a show will retain a connection. As compared to romantic comedies, dating shows may appear significantly less invested in marriage outcomes. I nevertheless wish to retain this focus on dating shows as a training ground for marriage because the language of lasting commitment focalizes competitions and remains central to how contestants frame their intentions. In keeping with the competitive logics on which this book focuses, it should also not be forgotten that many reality dating offerings situate a marriage proposal as, quite explicitly, a prize to be won.

The dating show format is not unique, of course, to the latest iteration of reality television, what we might think of as the *Real World* / *Survivor* / *Big Brother* era that began in the mid-1990s. Dating shows like *The Dating Game* (1965–73), *Love Connection* (1983–95), *Studs* (1991–93), and *Blind Date* (1999–2006) featured contestants choosing someone to date, rehashing the details of a date, or literally on a date. In the most popular twenty-first-century versions, dating shows explicitly broadcast an efficiency model meant to lead to a lasting relationship. Typically, the star chooses between eighteen and twenty-five options and decides on a final winner. These shows have taken many forms, from the sensationalized *Who Wants to Marry a Multi-Millionaire?* (2000), *Flavor of Love* (2006–8), *Rock of Love* (2007–9), and *A Shot at Love with Tila Tequila* (2008–9); to the controversial *Joe Millionaire* (2003) and *More to Love* (2009); to the gimmicky *ElimiDate* (2001–6), *Mr. Personality* (2003), *Who Wants to Marry My Dad?* (2003–4), *Boy Meets Boy* (2003), *Average Joe* (2003–5), *Date My Mom* (2004–6), *Dating Naked* (2014), and *Love at First Kiss* (2016); to the long-lasting *The Bachelor* (2002–) and its spinoff *The Bachelorette* (2003–), which are, as of this writing, gearing up for seasons twenty-two and fourteen, respectively.[7]

Despite dating shows' outward performance of encouraging marriage-mindedness in their contestants, critics have been divided on how to read their ideological impact. Debates turn on the question of whether they are mandating heteronormative sexuality in service of a marital imperative or making fun of these codes, presenting a more carnivalesque parody that points out their absurdity.[8] Though I have myself previously staked a claim in this conversation, identifying *The Bachelor* as contributing to a cultural sensibility that identifies marriage, particularly for women, as a scarce but highly desirable commodity, my interest here lies less in the series' portrayal of marriage as a site of fantasy and more with the recognition that the show's format complies with current marital logics of competition and calculation.[9] By hybridizing a contest structure with the voyeuristic pleasures offered by the docusoap, dating shows allow viewers to witness people on dates, learn the reasons for the star's choosing some contestants over others, and watch the winners and losers interact before their respective positions have been determined. *The Bachelor* franchise (and in this category I include both *The Bachelor* and *The Bachelorette*) has a paradigmatic role in this conversation because it places marriage, however unlikely an outcome, as the impetus for the series writ large.

Thanks to the sheer number of contestants, *The Bachelor/Bachelorette* insists on the necessity of evaluating dating candidates against one another. Choice is, in this way, instantiated into the series' narrative structure, since the process of whittling down the star's top choices from a pool of candidates provides these shows' most fundamental organizing principle. This ethos coheres with sociologist Beck-Gernsheim's notion of the "elective relationship," a term she uses to describe how an individuated society relies on personal choice as an explanatory framework for familial relations.[10] Dating shows like *The Bachelor* affirm choice as the only appropriate framework through which to understand romantic partnership, albeit promoting the notion that the selection process is a regulated and disciplined undertaking at every turn. Much like filters on online sites encourage users to search according to certain criteria and make estimations of a candidate's desirability on this basis, the show's producers assiduously select the show's contestants, women between the ages of twenty-one and thirty-five who are described by longtime host Chris Harrison as "adventurous, ready for marriage. She should be intelligent. She should be ambitious. And of course, attractive."[11] Though perhaps an obvious point, Harrison's list affirms the necessity of possess-

Figure 2.1. Season 13 bachelor Jason Mesnick charms his gaggle of aspiring wives. Also pictured is Molly Malaney, whom he eventually married. Photograph courtesy of Photofest.

ing the sort of erotic capital I detailed in the previous chapter, making these aptitudes and attitudes determinant of a woman's placement in the marital hierarchy. (The odds of making the cut are nevertheless minuscule: seasons 2 and 3 of *The Bachelor* reportedly saw eleven thousand applicants vying for twenty-five spots.)[12] Moreover, it is not a stretch to suggest that the contestants who appear on the show well understand the need to sell themselves as viable wife material. Observing Molly Malaney, a *Bachelor* season 13 contestant who makes a fervent statement of her worth after being cut from the competition in the season finale, the authors of a study titled "Arrested Emotions in Reality Television" note that her plea resembles a "sales pitch" whereby she seeks audience support to remain on the show.[13] Perhaps not incidentally, Malaney actually ended up married to bachelor Jason Mesnick after he realized he made a mistake in selecting her competitor.

The need to sort through a glutted economy of potential daters exists as a structuring premise of shows like *The Bachelor*, a genre Misha Kavka calls "real love TV." Kavka names the show's investment in selection and selectivity a "process of progressive discrimination" and posits that real love TV reflects "the fundamental means by which the polyvalent world of desired objects is turned into the monogamy of romance. Romantic choice thus functions as both the premise and the promise of real love programmes . . . the promise of 'choices made' suggests that one has been discriminating and thus has mobilized the core values of agency and feeling in the search for 'real love.'" She continues, "How do you know you're really in love? Not because someone took your breath away, but because you've been choosy."[14] The people on real love television, it should be said, are entitled to be choosy—they are typically white, attractive, and conventionally abled. Making a choice for choice's sake nevertheless assures viewers that the marriage seeker has labored to sort through available choices and earned his or her right to the spoils. Pierced by the logics of productivity, shows like *The Bachelor* illustrate that contestants merit the romantic experiences to which they inevitably gain access thanks to their willingness to do this work. The difficulty—and emotionality—of making romantic selections is likewise well underscored by the visual and auditory cues of the series, which tend to call on the tropes of classic film melodrama. Shots favor close-ups of the star's anguished face, and music is manipulated to lend emotionality and tension to this decision point.[15]

The language of "making difficult choices" and the fact that the mise-en-scène of the series cooperates to underscore the decider's dilemma points to the peculiar emotional register of *The Bachelor* franchise, where one must believe in "real love" and even a soul mate, while actively dating scores of people who could fit that bill. In her book-length study of the franchise, Rachel Dubrofsky locates the language of emotional openness and "risk taking" as fundamental to this process, and points out that these logics apply to the bachelor/bachelorette as well as to those vying for the coveted rose (a signal that one has been chosen to move on to the next round). "Participants regularly invoke their ability to take the risk of being emotionally vulnerable as evidence of their commitment to finding love," Dubrofsky observes. Much like online daters who must engage in proper emotional performances, so, too, does the series prescribe a limited affective range, one that falls in between what Dubrofsky calls "two dangerous extremes in this economy of emotion (not showing enough emotion or showing too much)."[16] The ideology that typically informs the presentation and typecasting of women on *The Bachelor*, argues Susan Ostrov Weisser, can be characterized as Victorian since it pits women who throw themselves at the bachelor sexually and emotionally against those who are cold and "withholding of sex and emotion."[17] Weisser's categorizations add a useful historical dimension to Dubrofsky's argument about the necessity of emotional modulation.

The show's emphasis on affective regulation, according to Dubrofsky, demands that a contestant "confess her feelings and emotions, but not too much or too soon"; "see the process as a therapeutic experience but not change herself"; "reveal herself increasingly on the series, but never reveal anything new or startling"; and "be empowered through her choices, but give up power to her emotions and to a man who will make important choices for her."[18] Looking at this list, it is worth thinking about how the milieu of *The Bachelor* mimics a workplace where the improper display of emotion can negatively affect how one is evaluated. On the one hand, it is perhaps an obvious point that dating involves emotional labor, a term that sociologist Arlie Hochschild famously coined to describe the process by which workers are expected to manage their feelings in accordance with employer-defined rules and guidelines.[19] Though it might seem like a stretch to think of the bachelor/ bachelorette as boss, the show inculcates rigid strictures for the proper performance of emotion and suggests that like any professional space, the premarital dating world mandates affective regulation. Structured parameters for emotional expression may indeed borrow explicitly from corporate cultures where "the appropriate regulation of affect" is a key determiner of professional success.[20]

Given the group nature of the series, contestants likewise obey a process of "emotional socialization," whereby they must mimic one another's behaviors, reactions, and understandings of events.[21] Contestants that cannot get along with their fellow housemates routinely get typecast as villains. On the other hand, those who keep calm and mobilize audiences in their favor reap multiple rewards, particularly since the producers have begun to select future bachelors/bachelorettes from the crop of previous contestants, typically tapping a fan favorite whose heart was broken in a previous season. This sort of internal spin-off builds brand awareness in audiences, encourages serial viewing, and rewards losers for having played nice with their direct competitors.

The Bachelor's formulation for proper emotional displays involves a register characterized by the following affective states: the aspiring bride must be "hopeful," "excited," and "ready." Relatedly, she must "believe in love" and be prepared to "share her heart." These future-directed sentiments clarify the aspirational temporality of the series, since contestants wait for their true love, remaining eternally optimistic about finding that person. In this way, they performatively confirm the sagacity of mainstream dating advice that exhorts women to remain persistently merry. Indeed, the author of the determinedly sanguine dating manual *Meeting Your Half-Orange: An Utterly Upbeat Guide to Using Dating Optimism to Find Your Perfect Match* explicitly hails contestants on *The Bachelor* for their no-holds-barred aspirationalism. She writes, "The women who end up on air have something positively special going for them: All of them are saying—not just to themselves but to the bachelor they want and to millions of viewers—'I want a relationship. I want to find true love.' To that I say, good for them!"[22] In *The Bachelor*, optimism is likewise overlaid with an earnest sense of possibility. Prospective brides say things like "I could definitely fall in love with him" and "I want it so badly." Yearning to find love and professing oneself open to this experience serve as qualifying statements.

The show also scrutinizes the veracity of declarations of readiness for love, instantiating a finely calibrated emotional spectrum whereby contestants self-monitor and surveil one another for confirmation that their "feelings are keeping up with the experience," a favored phrase. Contestants must submit to breakneck emotional pacing whereby they move from strangers to prospective spouses in six weeks, which is an unforgiving timetable, to be sure. Again, this situation is not unlike being on deadline in a workspace; it is perhaps not surprising that bachelors/bachelorettes often exhibit conflicted feelings, voicing apprehension over how well they are gauging their own emotions and verbalizing their struggles to make the right choices. Contestants labor to figure out if they can fall in love with a person they have just met, sensibilities that contribute to the show's work-like ethos. This labor was evident in season 9 of *The Bachelorette* (2013), which featured a somewhat unprecedented last-minute twist. Frontrunner Brooks Forester left bachelorette Desiree Hartsock during the show's concluding trip, though she was likely to choose him as the show's winner. Sitting down with host Chris

Harrison to discuss why he had extracted himself from the competition, Forester confides that he asked himself, "Am I really ready to say this is the love of my life, that I really want to be with this person?" Forester's rhetoric revolves around a growing sense of his lack of readiness and the shrinking possibility that he could love Hartsock. Harrison asks, "You are sure this isn't the girl for you?" and "Could you be in love with this person?" As these questions posit, only a sense of certainty that one *couldn't* be in love merits disqualification. If participants remain hopeful and open to the possibility, on the other hand, their candidacy remains viable. Notably, the show encourages the sort of adaptive, flexible ethos valued in nimble corporate cultures where it is important to stay agile and open. At the same time, it foregrounds emotional excavation as a contestant's most pressing obligation. In this realm, the true measure of one's fitness for couplehood relies on whether one wants it badly enough to will his or her emotional state in the direction of romance.

Faced with the pressure to explain what would it feel like to be in love, contestants sometimes struggle. At base, however, participants on *The Bachelor* are not asked for a unique definition of love, merely that they remain hopeful, ready, and excited. Doubt, on the other hand, has no place in the marital industry. This requisite emotional openness dovetails with the idea that contestants must talk about marriage in appropriately reverent terms, and one concern in the later years of the franchise has been whether a contestant is "serious about being here," a phraseology used repeatedly on the show.[23] As reality television has increasingly served as a vehicle for ordinary Americans to pursue fame, contestants are scrutinized for whether they are appearing on *The Bachelor* for sincere reasons or instead to (crassly and unacceptably) increase personal exposure. Contestants are frowned on for participating on the show to gain celebrity rather than love, and for attempting to fake who they really are. This obsession with authenticity reverberates with the mores and operations of reality television more generally, and Brenda Weber offers the appraisal that "popular television narratives are stringent in their punishment of falsity and vociferous in the approval they offer the pursuit of the real and stable self."[24]

Despite the enforcement of these mores, some contestants on *The Bachelor* have shamelessly transitioned from appearing on the show to promoting personal brands and acting as spokespeople for others. To cite one example from Instagram, noted by Yanyi Luo and Kate Brennen in their website devoted to the franchise, "Becca Tilley from Seasons 19 and 20 of *The Bachelor* promotes her friendship with JoJo from Season 20 in an ad for Bumble, a dating app marketing a new feature for finding friends on the service."[25] Clearly, both women received payment for the campaign. Branding efforts on the part of bachelorettes are nevertheless typically papered over in the cultural discourse surrounding the show, and bachelorettes do not tend to have the reputation that Bravo's *Real Housewives* do, of using their reality television stints in service of personal brands. (This reality may, however, be shifting as more and more reality television appearances become a springboard for personal publicity, and as social media endorsement deals provide former contestants with vehicles to extend their exposure. A pipeline exists, for instance, between *The Bachelor* franchise and ABC's *Dancing with the Stars*.)[26] While on the show, however, bachelorettes are expected to convince audiences that their sole motivation for appearing on camera is to find true love.

The Bachelor reassures audiences that bachelorettes enjoy a secure class status. This is to say, it affirms that thanks to their already middle-class posture, these women do not (or *should not*) need the show for any reason besides having been formerly unlucky in love. This exclusionary and privileged ethos was in turn thrown into relief by a number of copy-cat offerings, among them VH1's *Flavor of Love* and *Rock of Love*, and MTV's *A Shot at Love with Tila Tequila*, all of which had more racially diverse casts, and featured contestants who tended to be coded as lower class. Many cast members on these shows were in the business of attempting to profit from their exposure, in turn laying bare the financial incentives for appearing on reality television. The most famous of these was *Flavor of Love*, which mimicked *The Bachelor*'s format but cast former Public Enemy rapper Flavor Flav as the lead. The show is mainly considered a "ghetto" version of *The Bachelor*, with ghetto explicitly meant to signal blackness, argue Rachel Dubrofsky and Antoine Hardy, though the featured women in fact came from a variety of ethnic and racial backgrounds.[27] By contrast, all of ABC's bachelors and bachelorettes were white, until the casting of bachelorette Rachel Lindsay in 2017.

In many ways a satirical send-up of *The Bachelor*'s faux authenticity, *Flavor of Love* gleefully traded in the outlandish and grotesque. Rather than awarding winners roses, Flavor Flav gifted them gold grills. During its two-season run, female contestants were filmed vomiting, describing masturbation, and (in the case of one contestant) defecating on the floor. Behind the swagger of shamelessness, however, many of the women vying for Flavor Flav's affection were themselves quite disadvantaged. "The competition itself is not only a chance to win Flavor Flav's heart, but it's a chance to improve their class status," Jon Kraszewski elucidates. The women's tight financial circumstances positioned them as competitors in a contest where the rewards of winning were as much economic as they were affective. Much like *The Bachelor*'s "right reasons" rhetoric, contestants policed one another to see if Flavor Flav's wealth, and the platform the show could grant, was the real reason the women were there. "Repeated casting of women with minimal talent and training trying to start or further their careers in entertainment contributed to the overall neoliberal logic of working-class and poor women managing their own economic problems," argues Kraszewski.[28] The economic peril that *Flavor of Love*'s contestants negotiated departs in important ways from the easy luxury that *The Bachelor*'s participants enjoy, and also points out the exclusionary and often hidden relationship between entitlement to love, whiteness, and an elevated class status.

Access to affective experiences like love and affection, white privilege, and materialistic luxury are indeed virtually axiomatic of *The Bachelor*. From the high-end exotic locations to the borrowed ball gowns to the dramatic rose ceremony that apes a prime-time awards show, the show is steeped in both style and substance—in markers of wealth and advantage. These defining features also confirm Eva Illouz's contention that romantic love is increasingly embedded in the experience of consumer capitalism.[29] Doubling as an orgy of consumption, *The Bachelor* features contestants adorned in designer clothes while partaking of adventurous and expensive outings (helicopter rides, excursions on private yachts, solitary walks through otherwise off-limits foreign locations) in exotic and breathtaking locales (Thailand, Fiji, Bali, Hawaii). Again, the staying power and, frankly, the whiteness of the franchise speaks to this book's investigation of the exclusivity of marital imperatives. A 2013 report in the *New York Times* about the lasting dominance of *The Bachelor* franchise noted not only that the show's viewership was thriving, but also that the series was proving increasingly capable of captivating affluent viewers: "ABC emphasizes that the show, far from having the economically downscale profile of some reality shows, is especially strong with women of financial means. In homes with more than $100,000 in income, it scores 34 percent above the television average."[30] One might speculate, as does Susan Ostrov Weisser, that viewers take pleasure in learning how to succeed at the dating game: comparing the show to the experience of reading novels by Jane Austen, Ostrov notes that *The Bachelor* offers a road map for wealth and luxury: "Just as the Austen heroine marries only for love but somehow manages to love and be loved by the man who has a comfortable income or better, *The Bachelor* fuses 'finding' the Right One with a picture of a lifestyle that is as close to the American Dream as the viewer imagines."[31] In keeping with Ostrov Weisser's notion of the American Dream, it bears noting that the show traffics in the most upscale and exclusive of experiences. Though couples may profess to aspire to the suburbs and multiple children, their road map to achieving middle-of-the-road visions is paved with jewels. In this way, *The Bachelor* normalizes the trappings of affluence and functions much like other lifestyle shows that draw a privileged viewership such as *The Real Housewives*, a franchise I discuss at length in chapters 3 and 4.

Detecting Defective Daters on *Millionaire Matchmaker*

Dating-themed reality television centralizes the idea that wannabe spouses must work in a variety of registers to illustrate their worthiness as marital subjects. Media offerings provide a tangible plan for these objectives, and for this chapter's second focal point I turn to Patti Stanger's "Millionaire Matchmaker" franchise, and the show that bore its name. Stanger is an outspoken and opinionated marital guru, and her exclusive Millionaire's Club has a premium entrance fee, ranging from $25,000 to $150,000 a year, with a minimum commitment of one year. Beginning in 2008, Stanger began starring in her own show on the Bravo network, an offering that fit snugly in the network's brand of upscale lifestyle programming, and complied with its proclivity for featuring female entrepreneurs with formidable economic clout.[32] After leaving Bravo and ending *Millionaire Matchmaker* in 2015, Stanger moved to WE tv, helming a similar series called *Million Dollar Matchmaker* (2016–).

Stanger's status as a marriage mogul is multipronged: "In addition to the Millionaire's Club, Stanger has a presence on Facebook and Twitter, a self-help dating book, a weekly call in show on XM Radio, a weekly Yahoo! blog, and her own dating website for non-millionaires (a subsidiary of JDate, subtly reinforcing Stanger's heritage as a third generation Jewish matchmaker)," Lindsay Giggey notes.[33] Stanger's self-help book *Become Your Own Matchmaker* (2009), and her video *Married in a Year* (2011), similarly affirm her status as a businesswomen publicly in the business of making marriages.[34]

In keeping with the logics of affluence and cross promotion that characterize Stanger's empire, *Millionaire Matchmatcher* filmed in Los Angeles (save season 4, where Stanger transplanted her business to the East Coast for a season titled "Helping New York Find Love") and routinely featured other "Bravolebrities" (as they are often termed) as consultants and clients. Stanger and her clients thread through exclusive homes, clubs, cars, and restaurants, prioritizing the visible accoutrements of wealth, creating a visual spectacle that complies with Bravo's emphasis on conspicuous consumption. In each episode, Stanger counsels two single men (and the occasional single woman) on how to find love, sequencing them through self-scrutiny, the selection process, early dating, and follow-up appointments.

Calling quite overtly on the tradition of the outspoken Jewish matchmaker, Stanger's dating advice unabashedly reinforces traditional gender norms. She tells women that they should have long hair, and has two rules she repeats constantly on the show: "no sex before monogamy" and "two drink maximum." (Monogamy is a definitive time stamp on Stanger's relationship trajectory: she frequently uses the phrase "after monogamy" to indicate that clients must purposefully progress to this phase, and name it as such.) Stanger's breed of marital disciplining nevertheless coheres with the neoliberal self-improvement ethos I have been describing in this chapter, thanks to what have been described as her "Darwinian" attitudes and her "abrasive to the point of abusive style."[35] Featuring services that are both expensive and exclusionary, the premise of her business is that millionaires are not only interesting and worthwhile dating candidates but also those most deserving of her breed of tough love. Though they often act in ways that infuriate her, Stanger's clients' net worth in essence ensures they are serviced. Relatedly, they benefit immediately from her expertise, quickly learning from her their value on the romantic market. Stanger introduces her show with the following voice-over: "Love. Everyone wants it, but not everybody gets it. That's my job. . . . Meet my millionaires!" The juxtaposition of the "it's a jungle out there" attitude with the introduction of her millionaires again plays into an American cultural climate hospitable to the idea that the rich deserve boutique services ("everyone wants it, but not everybody gets it"). The premise that the rich can—and perhaps should—outsource their dating lives likewise organizes the hour-long show's narrative trajectory. Episodes feature Stanger meeting her clients, screening potential dates for them, and staging a mixer where millionaires meet multiple options, a competitive fixture that calls to mind similar events on *The Bachelor*. The show then films the dates that ensue, and finally Stanger's follow-up with the millionaires and their dates.

Particularly indicative of the hierarchical logics that underpin the series is the screening process, where Stanger and her associates seek women for their eligible millionaires. Holding resumes and head shots, Stanger and company witheringly judge the women who stand before them. Faced with a woman who claims to be thirty, Stanger asks, "What is your real age?" Scrupulous about atomizing a mixer candidate's aesthetic defects, Stanger pays meticulous attention to clothes, hair, and body type: "What's with the hair?" "I don't like what you are wearing." She frequently encourages women to maximize their feminine assets and to wear clothing that reveals their physique with exhortations like "Flaunt the ta-ta's" or "You need to sexify yourself." For someone who frowns on casual sex, Stanger nevertheless expects a high level of sexual appeal from the women she selects as potential dates for her male clients. Explaining the thought process of her clients to a woman Stanger feels needs to dress in a more provocative manner, she charges, "I don't want to fuck you because I think there are granny panties under that dress." Many a woman's admittance to a mixer is likewise contingent on promising to wear a sexier outfit to the event or to change her appearance in some way (hair, shoes, etc.). In another savvy cross-promotional brushstroke, in a season 3 episode Stanger gifts all the women a premixer makeover, using her own makeup line, "PS the One." Stanger's appearance advice likewise seeks to erase visible markers of ethnicity that may signal class disadvantage. A news profile of her begins with her

Figure 2.2. Matchmaker Patti Stanger and her associates sort through piles of single women's head shots, making determinations about their suitability for her millionaires. Photograph courtesy of Photofest.

demanding that a hippie-seeming client straighten her hair to tame a mass of wild curls, a suggestion that seems to favor a gentrified and sleek look indicative of an elevated class status.[36]

The selection and improvement techniques that define Stanger's screening sequence tellingly rehearse the sort of scrutiny of the female body that routinely occurs in makeover shows: the camera often does a vertical tilt, beginning with the shoes of a candidate, and then slowly travels up her body. Exacting gazes are in turn coupled with literal commentary on the flaws they reveal. As Brenda Weber observes in a book devoted to the ideological subtleties of makeover reality programming, and in a section specifically on the show *What Not to Wear*, "Turning the body into a ledger sheet is in some ways a practical strategy premised on the desire to claim an objective viewing position outside the body, but it also evokes a chattel economy where racialized bodies under the gaze are assessed for market value."[37] Stanger makes a similar evaluation, basing her market evaluation on how her aspirants stand, dress, and respond to questions about their careers and interests. Candidates receive instant feedback as they are told they are too old, are too tall, or, more specifically, have the wrong set of interests or ambitions for the bachelor at hand. With quick assurance, Stanger renders her judgments, a process that recalls the sorts of expedited behavior encouraged by online dating formats where users are encouraged to assess the market value of potential dates, make a fast decision, and move on to another likely candidate.

Stanger is particularly incensed by women who should be eligible for her mixers but act in a manner that purposely disqualifies them. When a woman in her thirties who appears to be a good fit for one of Stanger's clients nevertheless rejects the idea of dating a fifty-year-old, Stanger yells at her, "This is why you will always be single in this town!" Stanger's vitriol hints at the cutthroat and profusely utilitarian understanding that she has of the selection process, since creating the perfect blend of eligible women for her mixers relies on these women's amenability. Women not willing to play by her rigid rule systems particularly rile Stanger, who seems genuinely baffled by their refusal to adapt to a flexible ethos. In these instances, she dresses down her recruiter for not bringing in the right sort of candidates. These sequences highlight cheerful adaptability as a nonnegotiable qualification for potential daters, a sensibility that represents an optimal mind-set not only for dating (as described in chapter 1) but also for success in the twenty-first-century workplace. Variation among the women thus arrives in the form of more cosmetic attributes such as hair color or height, and Stanger overtly acknowledges the need to fulfill certain quotas: "I need more blondes, there are only brunettes." The carefully calibrated microcosms of female identity that Stanger sends to her mixers hence rely on sameness of disposition but variation in presentation.

The professional success (or lack thereof) of mixer candidates also provides a telling indicator of the skills and aptitudes that a stratified dating market rewards. Stanger routinely asks the women whether they are employed full-time and critiques any perceived ambition gaps: "You're a makeup artist—do you have the aspiration to do anything else?" While these questions may seem to privilege a certain brand of occupation, what is actually at issue in these queries is whether the woman is willing to do what it takes to achieve a goal. Though Stanger may insult those not employed full-time, when faced with a recent college graduate who waitresses at Olive Garden because, as the woman admits, it represents the only work she can find, Stanger offers a sympathetic direct-to-the-camera address acknowledging the economic pressure many Americans face. (The waitress is later chosen to go on a date with the millionaire who rather uncouthly insults her job, and the two decidedly do not make a love connection.) In perhaps perfect neoliberal terms, Stanger seeks the capacity for hard work in the dating realm, an attribute for which professional success may serve as a harbinger. This sort of resolve is Stanger's holy grail, particularly since she believes without exception that women must be willing to put the same effort into their dating life as they do into their professional life. Explaining why she has chosen to invite a girl to a mixer who is much younger than her millionaire client, Stanger explains, "Jennifer has the drive and the chutzpah to get the job done, and I just know Justin is going to fall all over her." The suggestion that Stanger selects women with the particular aim of "getting the job done" perfectly bespeaks the workhorse ethos on which the show, and Stanger's brand identity, rely. It also provides a stunningly clear explanatory rationale for the sort of hierarchical understandings that underpin exclusionary marital mind-sets, since not working hard enough again serves as justification for blaming those who fail.

Neoliberal mentalities reflect the marital zeitgeist around which this study is focused and are also in strong evidence in Stanger's printed dating materials. In her book *Become Your Own Matchmaker*, Stanger divulges that she has adapted her "Ten Commandments for Dating" from her Millionaire's Club, reworking it for the general female public. Tellingly, many of these commandments rely on reminding readers of the necessity of devoting oneself wholly to the process of finding a mate, including "Thou shalt return calls promptly," "Thou shalt honor thy dating commitments," "Thou shalt be engaging," and "Thou shalt express sincere interest and appreciation." To be sure, all these mantras simply represent good manners. Stanger nevertheless consistently asserts that wanting a commitment and being willing to work hard at securing it are *the* most important qualities to demonstrate in competitive markets. Not surprisingly, perhaps, the book's epigraph reads as follows: "I dedicate this book to single women everywhere. If you take one thing away from my book, know this: If you want him, he's out there."[38] Rhetorics of self-sufficiency and hard work call on an American meritocracy that relies on bootstrapping, yet Stanger's is at every turn an empire based on a plutocracy. This sleight of hand is nevertheless disguised with a neoliberal emphasis on confidence, deservedness, and drive.

In keeping with the observation that uneven social organizations are implicitly just and justified, finding good women for Stanger's millionaires (or refitting them to conform to a classed beauty ideal) is a task rather cleverly positioned in her oeuvre as a way to teach the men something. In this, her advice exhibits a fascinating form of pseudo-feminism whereby scrutinizing and insulting women—and only selecting what she deems to be the best representatives of their gender—contributes to a larger effort to modulate chauvinistic tendencies on the part of her male clients. Predictably, a number of Stanger's clients are men whose money has enabled a fairly superficial engagement with women; as a result, Stanger attempts to fix her clients psychologically in order to get them ready to date. Most of her male clients need a wake-up call of some sort: they are too materialistic, after the wrong sort of woman, formerly unfaithful, too expressive, overly controlling, or commitment-phobic. Describing her willingness to work with Kevin, a movie producer with little respect for women except as sex objects, she says, "The reason I take difficult clients like Kevin is to help my sisters. To help the world and the female race. They're good-looking and they've got money and they're just messed up inside; someone needs to tweak them." The notion that women deserve a better Kevin fits squarely in a culture where the rich are entitled to betterment whereas others lacking resources merit dismissal.

To stage an intervention on behalf of her clients (or was it on behalf of all women?) Stanger routinely relies on hypnotists, psychotherapists, and life coaches. A watered-down therapeutic imperative organizes dating preparation for the wealthy, and clients are rarely pathologized as unredeemable. Instead, Stanger's recommended treatments are designed to loosen men up, transforming them to ensure they are open to the possibility of love. A typical diagnosis from Stanger, for example, sounds like the following: "He's so obsessed with the physical that he can't get to know women emotionally"; or "Bradley is cheap, he's borderline narcissistic, and it's all about him." Being ready to date entails a willingness to rectify mistakes, start a healing process, or get to the root of commitment-phobia. Similarly, Stanger exhibits a tough love sort of ethos—she figures out the client, and determinedly announces what she or he needs. Stanger's matter of fact sensibility, her confidence, and the reliability of her judgment go unquestioned, as does the presumption that these men deserve fixing.

Though Stanger's is ostensibly a dating show and not a marriage show, the slippage between them is telling. In fact, many of Stanger's clients profess themselves ready for marriage and reproduction. In keeping with the aforementioned Darwinian attitudes, it might be said that Stanger's larger goal is to produce not only fitter dating subjects but also fitter spouses and parents. The show's tendency to traffic in heteronormative paradigms was perhaps most obviously on display in the one and only episode where Stanger counsels a lesbian, wherein she treats the client with great fanfare ("I get to fix up my first lesbian ever!"). In addition to repeating the phrase that the butch-seeming lesbian has "a softer side," Stanger makes hay with the notion that her client, Chef K, wants children. Chef K and the other millionaire featured on the episode (a white man) are repeatedly said to be in search of the "white picket fence," a desire that ostensibly informs a key question for the screening sequences: are the prospective dates (all women) ready to have children right away? Stanger seems to have no other frame of reference, or set of standards, by which to match women with women, except to graft male heterosexual leanings onto a prospective lesbian couple. This is to say, the desire to begin a family immediately was the stated desire of the male millionaire, not Chef K. Bereft of insights into other characteristics that might attract a woman to another woman, Stanger defaults to a limiting pattern of reproductive futurity, insofar as it shoehorns lesbian desire into a one-size-fits-all heteronormative matrix. Stanger's exuberance over the "white picket fence" ideal also suggests her brand's almost eugenically inspired notion of what types of people qualify as fit for marriage and reproduction.

In total, *Millionaire Matchmaker* demands daters who are resilient and responsible. To meet Stanger's standards, they must demonstrate a willingness to be flexible, fix their appearance, and do the necessary psychological work of getting themselves ready to embark on long-term relationships. Choice, individual empowerment, and personal responsibility underpin Stanger's presentation of the marital market, and she witheringly holds men and women alike accountable when they refuse to get themselves ready for love (to borrow a phrase from *The Bachelor*) or fail at making a connection with a date she has deemed suitable. Key to this process, again, is Stanger's insistence that her clients must be willing to labor for the affection they seek and to follow her rigid advice for how they can shape up their looks and personality so that they are poised to find it. (An autocrat whose tone is frequently derisive and impatient, Stanger is ironically the antithesis of the flexible laborer she demands.) Stanger's dictatorial and unyielding posture is nevertheless meant to be commensurate with a high-stakes dating market. Above all, she imparts that dating is cutthroat matter demanding utmost seriousness.

Bad Bridal Subjects: The Origin and Execution of the Bridezilla Phenomena

Stanger's advice and mantras are scalable to much wider populations; as this section will explore, failing at being adaptable, cheerful, and selfless in turn subjects one to the disciplinary mechanisms of the media machine. Particularly evident in what might be termed the "bridezilla cottage industry," these discourses shame wannabe wives who do not appropriately manage their emotions and behaviors. The term "bridezilla" rose to prominence in the mid-1990s, a trenchant combination of the words "bride" and "Godzilla," the monster first featured in Japanese horror films in the 1950s. Capacious in definition, a bridezilla may exhibit a number of unseemly traits including, but certainly not limited to, micromanaging wedding details; mistreating service professionals; exploiting family and friends; getting angry and screaming, shouting, or crying; acting ungrateful; wanting and insisting on perfection; exhibiting overly materialistic tendencies (particularly by going overboard with the cost of a wedding); testing the groom's devotion and loyalty; and overreacting to perceived slights. Taken as whole, this list of misbehaviors has at its center the bride's lack of self-regulation and failure to appropriately temper her desires and emotions. It also demonstrates an investment in the belief that brides should be serene, graceful, and above all feminine, and suggests that becoming overly invested in the self at the expense of others merits censure. (One example of the sorts of popular sentiments mobilized against bridezillas arrives in the form of a mystery novel title—Laura Levin's *Killing Bridezilla* [2012] summarily dispatches with the problem bride, and the assignment of solving her murder falls to Jaine Austen, the novel's likeable protagonist.)

The bridezilla made her first appearance on American television in 2003, thanks to an eight-part cable documentary called *Manhattan Brides*. Edited down to a one-hour special, *Bridezillas* appeared on the Fox network, to the delight of audiences and the chagrin of the unaware bridezillas. Later picked up by WE tv, a network specializing in programming for women, *Bridezillas* proved to be one of the network's most reliable and popular offerings for almost ten years. Though the first season featured mostly affluent brides, the show was retooled in its later years to focus on less rarified celebrations. Seasons 2 through 10 showcased more socioeconomically and ethnically diverse casts, and the later years of the series focused increasingly on brides of limited financial means and cultural capital. Though the series continues to cast women of all ethnic backgrounds, its attraction to downscale circumstances also seems linked to its racialized imaginary. Put simply, as the show got more diverse it also became more sensationalized. Uniting the series throughout its tenure were the bridezillas' emotional and physical outbursts, exhibitions of laziness and anger, spoiled and materialistic behaviors, displays of entitlement, and attempts to over control all wedding-related situations.

The bridezilla's status as an object of scorn rather than admiration is of course the series' most basic premise, one underscored by *Bridezillas'* derisively ironic female narrator. The narrator's persistent voice-over cattily points out the bridezilla's personality defects ("Let's check back in with the coddled and commanding bridezilla"), highlights the inappropriate nature of her behaviors ("She is a teen terror with the social skills of a serial killer"), and ultimately deems the bride undeserving of the attentions being lavished on her. This removed, judgmental tone educates viewers on the importance of treating the bridezilla with a sense of amused and ironic detachment, a sensibility that (as I have argued elsewhere) characterizes postfeminist female popular culture.[39] This oration assures viewers of the show's awareness of the bridezilla's atrocious behavior and flirts with the possibility that the bridezilla might receive a much-deserved comeuppance ("When she pushes too hard, will it be game over?") as well as questions the long-term stability of her coupling

("Who will be left in the dust?"). The wedding almost always happens, of course, a fact credited again to the bride's bullying tendencies. Part of the narrative sequence of *Bridezillas* involves showcasing the wedding itself, and in many cases the bridezilla continues her rampage even while dressed in her bridal gown. As Erika Engstrom notes, "Complaints just minutes before or after the wedding ceremony mark these episodes, illustrating just how demanding a bridezilla can be."[40] These sequences confirm that despite frequent protestations to the contrary, the bride's outbursts are less the result of singular wedding stresses and more a function of her defective personality type.

It perhaps bears noting that like the aforementioned *Flavor of Love*, *Bridezilla* could easily be read as camp. I want to acknowledge this possibility and link it to the hyperbolic nature of dating and wedding reality programming, which has tended to resort to ever more preposterous contrivances for prospective daters and brides. Read in this light, *Bridezillas* could be said to have circumscribed a set of patterned behaviors the bridezilla (once designated as such) is encouraged to follow. This reading mitigates the portrayal's purely disciplinary effects and suggests that bridezillas must on some level be aware that their behaviors are being actively monitored to highlight deficiencies. To read the series as a thoroughly ironic text where bridezillas are playing up to the camera and completely in on the joke nevertheless fails to account for its larger sociocultural implications, and the fact that viewers are actively encouraged to regard bridezillas with class-inflected distain.

Importantly, the class and racial politics of *Bridezillas* turned increasingly troubling over the series' ten-year run. As the show moved to more middle- or even lower-class milieus, female behavior became increasingly over-the-top and involved tantrums, screaming, and even physical violence. This tendency to push the envelope in terms of the bridezilla's more overtly abusive behaviors corresponded with its showcasing of brides for whom the financial stresses of a wedding involve visible strain. Evidencing the limited economic means of many bridezillas, Tifani, a black woman, converses with her mother about how much it will cost to make dirty rice for the guests. After running through a variety of cost-saving measures (encouraging her mother to buy a bag of rice rather than boxes, nixing the idea of a salad, deciding to use food stamps for the purchase, and eliminating meat from the recipe), Tifani entertains the idea of not feeding her guests at all ("When you're on a budget you don't have many options, so I had to eliminate their options"). One compelling reading of these difficulties has been offered by Katherine Morrissey, who speculates that "bridezillas play out the tension between the mediated images of feminine beauty women are expected to reproduce on their wedding days and the limitations that real bodies and finances present to this quest." Morrissey reads the bridezilla's outbursts against vendors, particularly, as expressing frustration over the disappointments of consumer culture, and reiterates that financial realities "block many women's abilities to afford feminine ideals."[41] This is a compelling and sympathetic reading of how the series articulates economic obstacles since, as Morrissey argues, many a bridezilla's sense of outrage stems from her inability to produce her own "wedding imaginary."

We might contrast *Bridezillas*, for instance, with the women featured on *My Big Redneck Wedding* (2008–11), where couples embrace and even flaunt their low-class status. Episodes feature receptions held in mud pits, wedding meals that double as hotdog-eating contests, cakes made entirely out of cheese, brides and grooms attired in camouflage, and decorations comprising nothing but beer cans. If redneck brides embrace their campiness—fully in on the joke, so to speak—bridezillas appear unable to dispense with the wish to partake in the markers of a high-class wedding or abandon their associated feminized ideals. Far from the redneck brides who resist such trappings, bridezillas desire but are excluded from the sort of high-end experiences that characterize other wedding programming such as *Say Yes to the Dress* (2007–), where brides shop for gowns at Kleinfeld's, an exclusive bridal boutique; or *Whose Wedding Is It Anyway?* (2003–10), about wedding planners. If the redneck bride fully embraces the mockery of wedding culture, in a sense letting go of the myth and evacuating it of symbolic strength, the bridezilla invests too heavily in it, losing control of her own image in the process.

Reading the bridezilla as a scapegoat also reveals the show's larger interest in emphasizing that limited financial means leads to emotional mismanagement. Privileging instead what can best be termed upper-class decorum, the show suggests that bridezillas violate good manners. It is striking, for instance, how often the bride's lateness for events occurring in her honor (including the wedding itself) constitutes *Bridezillas'* narrative content. The bridezilla's willingness to inconvenience others because of her self-involvement dovetails with the increasingly classed nature of these portrayals, which is to say that upper-class regimes support the appearance—though not necessarily the actuality—of thinking about others instead of oneself. Hence the bridezilla's refusal or inability to affect such a pretense seems to disqualify her from this celebrated position. If weddings are, as Gwendolyn Audrey Foster claims, "the class-passing event of your life," *Bridezillas* suggests that its featured brides are not necessarily up to the challenge, even if those obstacles are the result of limited financial or personal means.[42]

Though the bridezilla's lack of education regarding what it means to get along with others or consider their viewpoints presents itself in myriad ways, one consistent theme in *Bridezilla* is that the bride is a bad boss, inattentive to the needs and desires of her husband-to-be and of those friends and professionals working on her behalf. The show typically includes sequences, for instance, where bridezillas express the opinion that professionals hired to execute her special day are sabotaging the event. Sequences typically center on the brides' trials, as brides profess that they have not eaten, or slept, and that the products or services requested do not meet their wishes or specifications. The most frequent complaints have to do with the aesthetic details of the wedding—gowns, hair, flowers, and cakes—and bridezillas often fail to acknowledge their accountability for having changed their minds at the last minute or misjudging how long a service takes to execute. As one petulant bride repeats, "I want my chocolate cake!" despite having ordered a different type. In this respect, the wedding represents the source/cause of the bridezilla's breakdown, her stress exacerbated by the failures of others to do what she thinks they should. Predictably, the camera work in these sequences sympathizes with the beleaguered professionals, featuring close-ups where they are forced to be polite to the out-of-control bridezilla.

The show typically includes a section where the bride and groom talk about the origins of their coupling and features vignettes where the two make mutual decisions on weddings plans. Here, brides often demand an object or service more expensive than the groom believes prudent. In their communications, bridezillas readily and eagerly fault grooms for missing appointments, not being supportive, neglecting to pull their weight, and failing to understand the stress the bride is under. Bridezillas also frequently test grooms, making them prove their loyalty and devotion by agreeing to unreasonable demands, such as changing their appearance, dressing in specific or uncharacteristic ways, or ceasing to socialize with friends she has deemed unsuitable. Bridezillas retaliate against incompliant grooms by threatening to call off the wedding, refusing to speak to them, or staging colossal fights.

Friends and family members fare no better, particularly the unlucky women who compose the bridezilla's wedding party. It is against these women whom the bridezilla seems to vent a significant portion of her rage. I suspect this focus speaks to the fact that WE's primary audience is women, meaning that spectators are most likely to cast themselves in the role of the bridezilla's friends. Scripting the series in this way offers viewers a point of entry, and a chance to either imagine how they might react to an unruly bride or revisit the times when they endured one already. Bridezillas often overtly attempt to coerce their bridal party into acting like servants: as one bridezilla says of her bridesmaid, "She should have more of 'whatever you would like ma'am' attitude." It is not exactly an exaggeration to say that the bridezilla expects bridesmaids to deny their selfhood to meet the requirements of her wedding—one bride, Gloria, angrily berates a bridesmaid who missed a dress fitting because the bridesmaid was in the hospital. Similarly, Mai-Lee explains how she plans to crack the whip at her wedding party on her big day: "Saturday morning, the girls, at 10:00 a.m., you belong to me." As the aforementioned Tifani says, "Unless they die, they need to be there." Tyrannical brides manage their attendants as if commanding a batch of underlings in a hierarchical order that has no place for dissent: "Everyone's hair is going up, everyone is getting the same makeup, too. If they don't like it, they are just going to have to suck it up," Mai-Lee proclaims. These rejoinders confirm the bridezilla's inflexibility, and indict her for violating the populist pretenses that tend to enshroud successful players in the neoliberal order. To be a successful manager in the twenty-first century involves a willingness to disavow absolute power. One of the bridezilla's major violations is therefore her abuse of her position and lack of self-awareness. Proving herself to be a bad boss—an infraction that is perhaps more egregious than being a bad friend—the bridezilla transgresses by failing to even pretend to value reciprocity.

Bridezillas refocus onto their bridesmaids the sort of surveillance cultures that have long scrutinized women's bodies and appearances. A typical story line involves a bride trying to put her bridesmaids on a diet: "I'd rather have no bridesmaids than big ones . . . I bought a scale to weigh all the girls," one bridezilla asserts. A striking feature about this request is that losing weight for a wedding is a frequent requirement for *the bride*, one that, as I will highlight in the subsequent section, serves to establish her willingness to labor appropriately on behalf of her incipient wifedom. The bridezilla's deflection of scrutiny away from herself in favor of turning a misogynistic and often sadistic gaze on her bridesmaids instead suggests a rejection of the responsibilities that rightfully attend her. It also exhibits a shockingly cavalier propensity to throw other women under the bus, so to speak, in her place. One of the more incongruous features of the series is that unlike the paid weight loss and image experts that populate reality television and are generally revered in their narrative contexts (though not always by audiences), the bridezilla possesses a specious authority, insofar as she dispenses dangerous and self-serving advice. Angela's bridesmaid collapses, for example, after not having eaten, in an effort to accommodate the bride's request that she don a too-tight gown for a wedding that is a mere two days away. Part of the show's mobilization of bad will toward the bridezilla results from her misguided understanding of her role visà-vis reality television's stratified order, and the show itself could be seen as her comeuppance. This punishment is at times meted out through a bridesmaid's lack of devotion to the bridezilla since, in addition to questioning whether grooms will actually marry these shrews, the show queries whether the bridezilla's tension with her bridesmaids will result in an attendant's purposeful absence from the wedding.

The symbolic significance of the bridezilla's fractured friendships with other women can be traced to the wedding's position as a stand-in for cultural ties more generally. As Elizabeth Freeman argues, "The wedding seems to work as an emblem for the condition of belonging to constituencies *beyond* (if also sometimes constitutively connected to) the male-female couple: to proper gender, extended family, ethnic or religious constituencies, the nation, or a particular niche market."[43] In larger terms, the bridezilla evidences her ostracism from systems of belonging, violating the community of the wedding and acting as a bad citizen. This violation of citizenship not only casts doubt on the bridezilla's fitness for marriage but also seems to provide a larger referendum on her personhood.

Not incidentally, the dictum to question the bride's worth and, more specifically, the longevity of her marriage now serves as the future of the franchise. Retiring its decadelong juggernaut in 2013, WE quickly introduced a spin-off series, *Marriage Boot Camp* (2013–), featuring former bridezillas with imploding relationships. The couples underwent a two-week therapy session, at the end of which they decided if they wanted to stay married. While husband and wife often share equally in the blame for a couple's marital woes, the bridezilla's designation as such provided a structuring framework.

Weight Loss as Marital Labor

As this chapter has argued, dating- and wedding-themed shows eagerly display their knowingness that brides need to behave in a manner befitting the term, and forcefully shame brides who do not. Offerings like as *Buff Brides* (2003), *Bulging Brides* (2008–10), *Bridal Bootcamp* (2010), *Bridalplasty* (2010), and *Shedding for the Wedding* (2011) illustrate how this ethos is manifested in corporeal terms, linking fitness for marriage to body shape, size, and appearance. Much like *The Bachelor* associates finding love with emotional fortitude, these shows adopt a neoliberal model of perseverance that rests on the notion that only when one is "in shape" does one qualify as worthy of marriage. Putting this observation in conversation with the idea that marriage exists as a site on which to reify citizenship claims, Tiara Sukhan asserts that *Bulging Brides* "stands out for the way that it explicitly and unapologetically reinforces ideas of heteronormative femininity while linking a slim female body with social health and marital longevity."[44]

In many ways, bridal weight loss shows cohere with reality makeover and weight loss tenets more generally. Typically featuring a panoply of improper bridal bodies, the shows foreground a competition to see which bride (or, sometimes, altar-bound couple) can lose the most weight before a culminating reveal. On *Shedding for the Wedding*, *Bridal Bootcamp*, and *Bridalplasty*, brides overtly compete for their dream wedding—*Bridalplasty*'s withering dismissal line is "Your wedding may

Figure 2.3. *Bulging Brides'* experts advise women on how to alter their eating and exercise habits in time for the big day.

go ahead, but it won't be perfect." The bridal industry's typical accoutrements provide the rationale for body modification (*Bulging Brides* uses the wedding dress as a motivator) as well as lend a structuring theme to the challenges that contestants face, such as running with a life-size groom doll or wrestling in a fifteen-foot cake. The wedding imaginary is also typically grafted onto the objectives of weight loss. *Bridal Boot-*

camp's contestants, for example, receive invitations embossed with cal-ligraphy, asking them to participate in "marital missions," compete for prizes such as their dream flower arrangements and vacation packages, and participate in weigh-ins that take place in what is the termed the "fitting room."[45] To be sure, turning the often-mythologized aspects of wedding culture into props suggests a certain irreverence for the perfect wedding as a concept. As evidence of this cheekiness, *Bridal Bootcamp*'s first episode begins with brides in dresses and combat boots: the women run through an outdoor obstacle course, rendering their gowns muddy, blackened, and ruined. Despite this mockery of bridal iconography, brides tend to speak with solemnity and earnestness about their quest to fit into their dresses, listen intently to nutritionists who decry their previous eating habits, and often push their physical limits, sometimes to the point of exhaustion and illness.

Brides-to-be turn themselves over to the structures of governmental-ity that inform reality television's disciplinary imperatives, as they strive for bodily perfection (and the dangled reward of an all-expenses-paid wedding). As well, the specter of not being able to fit into their wedding dress, or not looking as one would wish on their wedding day, legiti-mates the humiliation that many brides voluntarily undergo. On *Bulging Brides*, for instance, brides walk down an "aisle of shame," which literal-izes their eating habits based on a recorded food diary. In one episode, a bride is faced with a heaping table of fried food, meant to represent one month of her takeout meals, while the nutritionist recounts their extreme caloric and fat counts. Another bride watches as the nutritionist makes a monster batch of cookies, purportedly representing the bride's monthly intake. By scaling up daily food choices to abject representa-tions of monthly or even yearly quantities, en masse food depictions prompt visual recoil, turning the desirable into the repugnant. These tac-tics nevertheless read as reasonable and helpful responses to unchecked eating. Audiences' general tolerance for such displays has been con-firmed by Katherine Sender, whose comprehensive survey of makeover television concludes that viewers tend to find shame "socially useful" if the process of "looking at oneself through the eyes of another and see-ing one's shortcomings" leads to "transformative self-reflexivity."[46] These findings suggest that the tactics present on *Bulging Brides*, where nutri-tionists and trainers work with participants to achieve their stated weight loss goals, read as legitimate strategies that help the bride and serve her desired end of being a more fit wife, both literally and figuratively.

With few exceptions, bridal weight loss shows illustrate the physical toll that weight loss regimes take on bridal bodies as both worth it and necessary. Replicating the ethos that informs almost all weight loss shows, fat indicates a moral failing. Repurposing the heavy-handed tone found in offerings like *The Biggest Loser* (2004–16), where fat and the fat body represent an enemy in need of eradication by virtuous efforts, bridal weight loss television operates by assuring brides and viewers alike that working hard at achieving weight loss proves a woman's fitness and/or rightness as a bride. The notion that some aspirants are more deserving than others also makes ready appearance in the competitive nature of a number of bridal offerings. Nearing the finale of *Shedding for the Wedding*, ultimate third-place finisher Allison asks her fiancé, David, "Do you know how much stress this would take off us, like, if we won this?" Allison's comments betray the sort of financial literacy/ economic instability I described earlier in the *Bridezilla* section, insofar as the dangled promise of an all-expenses-paid wedding seems to be as much a motivator as is the prospect of a fitter body. Allison also proclaims that she and her partner are more worthy than the couple she perceives as their primary rival. Assessing the male in that duo, Allison says, "I don't really know if he's genuine or not, and that's why I don't like him." Again, the neoliberal imperative to be "authentic," as Sarah Banet-Weiser reminds us in her eponymous study, bespeaks virtue.[47] The show's primary basis for this judgment is how hard its respective contestants have worked, a metric tied (whether justly or not) to the amount of weight they have lost.

Sentiments that legitimate effort as righteous and principled are in turn peppered throughout wedding weight loss offerings. Statements like "I will do whatever it takes" become structuring mantras, alongside proclamations of the bride's unwavering commitment to the task of weight loss. As one *Bridal Bootcamp* contestant proclaims, "I no longer want it; I *need* the wedding of my dreams . . . Every workout is 180%. I'm never giving up." Trainers are also afforded reverence as the emissaries who will deliver prospective brides to the promised land of achieved weight loss if they follow the trainer's stated brand of tough love. As one trainer says, "If either of them wants the wedding of their dreams, they'll have to give me more than they've ever given me." These demands exist in comfortable juxtaposition with the contestant's proven desire to work hard to achieve weight loss, a sentiment that, as Sender suggests, invites audience approbation. Audiences tend to support and root for candidates who appear to be expressing their "true inner selves," concludes Sender, "the evidence of which is their expression of feeling."[48] Brides seem to genuinely want to perfect themselves both inside and out, and candidates are wont to say they learned about "being strong" and "tough" and oftentimes proclaim themselves a "totally changed person." This transformation often hinges explicitly on this notion of bridal labor, since the subtext of many a bridal show is that the bride must learn to work, instruction that correlates with the larger interest that bridal television has in positioning the hard worker as worthy of her wifedom.

This conjoining of bridal and weight loss culture serves to fortify a narrative of constant labor and to identify wedding preparation as a type of work that takes place in public. As Erika Engstrom explains, "In FitTV's *Buff Brides* the women take on additional 'shifts' in addition to their regular jobs and personal lives. The first shift involves their job, another shift is devoted to working out and going to the gym, and a third shift is spent planning their weddings. The notion of increased labor and work is mentioned at the beginning of every *Buff Brides* episode by the narrator, who reminds viewers that not only are these brides trying to get buff, they also have big weddings to plan." Relatedly, the narrator describes wedding plans as "chores" that brides must fit into their already busy lives.[49] This terminology again reminds us of the overarching premise of this study since it relocates a seemingly domestic task (the "household chore") into the public space, translating it into an act of public labor.

That the bride's efforts are a matter of public knowledge—and are destined to take place in a discursive context of surveillance—is a posture likewise instantiated in the final round of *Bridal Bootcamp* where the top two contestants' final challenge is to go home for a month and continue to lose weight. This structure inculcates an understanding of bridal (and by extension wifely) behavior that hinges on a model of continual self-betterment. These expectations mimic those found in any professional setting, where one is expected to outdo one's previous efforts and accomplish more, in line with standardized performance reviews. Similarly underscoring the premise that brides must demonstrate practices and behaviors that ensure continual achievement, *Bulging Brides* includes a segment where brides face digital representations of themselves if they were to gain ten to fifteen pounds a year. These visual high jinks serve as tangible reminders of the need for brides to keep to fitness regimes even after they marry. Faced with the contestants' revulsion at the sight of these extrapolated photos, Tiara Sukhan speculates that these women are motivated by "an anxiety that becoming fat would constitute a breach of their social contract."[50] Sukhan's comments importantly remind us of the multifaceted pressure that women face to be marriageable and then to stay worthy of those marriages. In this context, losing weight and being able to keep it off illustrates a readiness to meet the psychological challenges of marriage and suggests how popular culture links bodily discipline with emotional control.

Conclusion: The Wedding Special as Cultural Event

On the finale of *Bridal Bootcamp*, the winner tearfully proclaims, "The dress is a symbol of the journey that I have made through *Bridal Bootcamp*. I could never have worn that dress forty-four pounds ago." These comments usefully situate the wedding as a space in which women showcase their best selves, celebrating their soon-to-be-achieved identity as a wife. Taken in the context of this chapter, the wedding serves as the crowning achievement (sometimes quite literally) of the emotional, physical, and psychological labor that the wannabe wife has undergone in service of her goal.

In addition to serving as a site where networks can feature lucrative advertising that showcases bridal products, reality weddings unabashedly call on idealized and mythologized tropes. Brides weep, proclaiming this the happiest day of their life, and gauzy pictorials relish aesthetic details including flowers, cakes, and table settings. Reality weddings also invariably luxuriate in consumptive excess. Though a running subtext of this chapter has been the financial struggles (or lack thereof) of wannabe wives, reality wedding specials tend to obscure the price tag of these events since, in many cases, the wedding is being funded by the show and its multitude of sponsors. In this way, the wedding serves quite literally as the prize, one awarded to the woman who most willingly aligns her personal habits and desires with the sanctioned edicts of the show on which she appears. The interplay between the bride's individualism and her submission to the dictates of the reality genre exists as a culmination of her branding as a wife, insofar as she makes choices within a prescribed set of models. The bride may select her color palette—and often is rewarded with the services of celebrity stylists, designers, hair and makeup artists, caterers, and wedding planners—yet the general parameters of every reality show wedding remain the same. Reality weddings linked to dating shows obey a pantheon of visual cues dictated by the televisual genre itself: weddings must be lavish and colorful, grand affairs that appeal to highly feminized aesthetics.

There is nevertheless one glaring exception to this formula—the bridezilla wedding, an event that tends to read as garish. In large part because of the bridezilla's continued misbehavior, bridezilla weddings lack the solemnity and sense of earned accomplishment that characterize other wedding programming. To understand this dichotomy, we might be reminded of Beverley Skeggs and Helen Wood's observation that transformations on reality television are structured through class relations and that one group's standards versus another's generate the featured conflict. Respectable or aspirational women are typically pitted against those considered rough or excessive, and working-class participants are principally the ones in need of alteration. Moreover, "domestic and emotional labour becomes the mechanisms by which bad subjects are subject to transformation."[51] Even at their weddings, bridezillas continue to register as subjects in need of alteration.

The weddings featured on offerings like *The Bachelor* or *Bridal Bootcamp*, on the other hand, serve as a reward for a goal achieved, celebrating women who have earned the right to become wives. As this chapter has detailed, these women have obeyed the affective parameters that dictate hopefulness, readiness, and a willingness to work hard as the foundational aspects of wifely preparation. Wedding media invites brides to undergo a "brand management process of transformation"; the authors of the study "Here Comes the Brand" eloquently sum up this process, arguing that "wedding media are shaped by a brand management culture that emphasizes a need to transform the self, as well as encouraging active competition in doing this. This discourse of transformation is associated with the aspiration to become more distinctly visible, and to realize a new perfect self."[52] Untethered from the achievement of romance per se, reality weddings afford the bride the chance to singularly enjoy the attention and elegance that rightfully rewards her efforts. Being physically and emotionally well managed are achievements that culminate in the wedding celebration, where the highly visible display of her body and her selfhood legitimate the bride's status as worthy of grand celebration.

According to Skeggs, "Through its focus on transformation, reality television offers a new model of mating based on fault and failure, generating expectations of 'proper' heterosexual, gendered, and classed relationships, enabling audiences to recognize similar affectual situations through their own experiences."[53] As this chapter has surveyed, dating and bridal shows not only inculcate a specific idea of how brides must behave, but also confirm the risks and rewards of adhering to established protocols. Those who work hard enough to accomplish prescribed goals announce themselves as better people and confirm their legitimate access to lavish luxury. In the next chapter, I begin my investigation of how married women begin to lay claim to their identity as wives, and specifically investigate how and why the housewife has become an ironically aspirational figure in twenty-first-century America.

3

Return of the Housewife

Putting an Icon Back to Work

The housewife, relatively absent from prime-time programming since the departure of *Roseanne* in 1997, has returned
with a vengeance.
—Sharon Sharp

In July 2012, *Forbes* online published "Are Housewives to Blame for the
Plight of Working Women?"[1] Its glib title notwithstanding, the article glossed a serious and sobering study. According to a report titled
"Marriage Structure and Resistance to the Gender Revolution in the
Workplace," powerful men with stay-at-home wives have a negative
view of female employees and female leaders, and also "deny, more
frequently, qualified female employees opportunities for promotions."
In addition to bringing necessary attention to what can only be called
rampant workplace sexism, the *Forbes* article participates in what has
become a commonplace heuristic, pitting the housewife against the
working woman. In customarily inflammatory terms, the title of the
piece not only intertwines the housewife and the working woman but
also suggests that one can be blamed for the trials of the other, rather
than, say, the men in power who exhibit these troubling views. Though
one of the authors of the featured study explicitly expressed her reluc-
tance to participate in the "mommy wars," the author of the *Forbes* piece
apparently felt no such compunction. Repeatedly, the article refers to
stay-at-home women as "yoga-mat-toting housewives," and a still from
the ABC drama *Desperate Housewives* cheekily flanks the story.[2]

I begin with the *Forbes* article because it serves as an apt metonym
for a cultural tendency to reduce complicated power dynamics to catfights between women. Relatedly, and as importantly, it reminds us
what a convenient straw figure the housewife has become in twenty-

first-century American media. As this chapter will explore, the housewife has a storied history in the popular consciousness, a visibility that began in earnest during the 1950s. This chapter is nevertheless anchored by the recognition that the housewife has reemerged in the popular consciousness in a different form than she inhabited in the 1950s, one where she is now a stand-in for all that is considered feminine in the twenty-first century. In keeping with this book's focus on wifedom as a public labor, this chapter identifies the housewife, paradoxically, as the most high-profile form of wifedom in contemporary America. This reintroduction of the housewife as public laborer is especially odd, given the housewife's historical definition as one who lacks paid work outside the home and whose meanings would seem to be anchored in and by the domestic sphere. This chapter will trouble that idea, suggesting, for one, that the housewife has always been as much a mediatized (and hence public) figure as a private one. Moreover, questions of for whom (and on behalf of whom) housewives labored have long circumscribed her iconicity. I begin by revisiting some classic texts and conversations about the 1950s housewife in order to illustrate how her image has always accounted for and dialogued with issues of work, labor, and professionalism.

Central to my analysis and argument about the current era is ABC's much-debated *Desperate Housewives* (2004–12). The series birthed a new conceptualization of the term "housewife" whereby she is no longer a woman who lacks paid employment outside the home. In this new order, housewife serves as a placeholder for a set of popular culture preoccupations surrounding the strictures of modern femininity. Specifically, she exists as a metonym for *all* women and provides popular culture a vehicle through which to minimize and miniaturize complicated gender dynamics. By limiting women's matters to marital and reproductive imperatives, devoting unflagging attention to the supposed tension between "work" and "life," and obsessing over the aforementioned supposed tensions between working women and stay-at-home mothers (housewives), women's media culture suggests that these issues constitute the whole of contemporary femininity. The housewife in the twenty-first century is therefore less an identity than a convenient opportunity, presenting a way to remind women about the facets of femininity the American media considers most salient.

Wife, Inc. chronicles the rise of the wife as an occupation, and this chapter argues that the wife's professionalization hinges on the figure of the housewife. I make this point most decisively in this chapter's concluding section on Bravo's *Real Housewives* franchise, insisting that the term focalizes logics of productivity and branding, turning this identity quite literally into a job. While *The Real Housewives of Orange County* (2006–) began humbly in 2006, promising to take a behind-the-scenes look at the privileged existences of the real-life women that the fictional offering *Desperate Housewives* gently lampooned, it has spawned a reality television explosion wherein women become wives precisely in order to be paid for their fame work. Women monetize so-called feminine experiences, affects, and activities such as shopping, dining out with friends, negotiating romance, attending parties, and engaging in rituals of leisure and self-care. Exploring the forms of labor that these televised offerings foreground, and recognizing that self-identifying as a housewife remains a burgeoning business opportunity, this chapter contends that the housewife nomenclature was oxymoronically instrumental in turning wifedom into paid work.

The Housewife: Histories and Contexts

Because this is a study of wives in media representation, it is perhaps worth a reminder that the housewife is as much a theoretical construction as she is a real-life figure. She has been supremely instrumentalized, meant to serve as a mythologized paragon of femininity, one whose selfless devotion to housework, husbands, and children justifies her beatification. The housewife is, however, a supremely relational figure: defined by her familial connections, she encourages comparison with other women. Because popular culture encourages women to measure their worth against that of the idealized housewife, her perfection stands as a rebuke to those who fail to live up to her impossible standards of homemaking.

Central to the image of the housewife is her apocryphal nature; as a construction, she has tended to exist as an amalgamation of media images of smiling, apron-clad women. She is also tied quite strongly to the 1950s, and particularly to the televised representations in which she appeared. As Stephanie Coontz writes in her aptly titled historical treatise *The Way We Never Were*, "Our most powerful visions of traditional families derive from images that are still delivered to our homes in countless reruns of 1950s television sit-coms." The housewife as image did have roots in real-world sociological shifts, specifically the reorganization of family life in the 1950s. Coontz recalls, "Nineteenth-century middle-class women had cheerfully left housework to servants, yet 1950s women of all classes created makework in their homes and felt guilty when they did not do everything for themselves." In reality, the amount of time women spent doing housework in the 1950s increased from previous eras, despite the advent of convenience foods and laborsaving devices. Tethered to homes, and encouraged to believe that their primary purpose was to nurture husbands and children, real-life housewives expressed their frustrations in sometimes self-destructive ways. The use of alcohol and drugs (oftentimes tranquilizers) rose to combat the sense of boredom, loneliness, and despair that characterized the lot of many. Referencing discussions of this phenomena in *Ladies' Home Journal*, *McCall's*, and *Redbook*, Coontz recalls, "By 1960 almost every major news journal was using the word *trapped* to describe the feelings of the American housewife."[3]

It is this version of the housewife—restless, unfulfilled—that many early feminist tracts sought to release from her symbolic imprisonment. The most famous of these was of course Betty Friedan's *The Feminine Mystique*, which brought needed attention to "the problem that has no name," and arose from a series of interviews Friedan did in 1957 with former Smith College classmates who for the most part became stay-at-home wives. There have rightfully been a number of critiques of Friedan for her exclusionary understandings and predominant focus on white, middle-class women. This limited focus undeniably informed Friedan's adamant and somewhat myopic assertion that women's problems stemmed solely from their domestic positions and could be solved by entry into the professional sphere: "It is urgent to understand how the very condition of being a housewife can create a sense of emptiness, non-existence, nothingness in women," she proclaimed.[4] Friedan's excoriation of women's magazines and the advertising industry more generally—which she lambastes for exploiting women's anxieties and selling them false images—nevertheless speaks directly to my point that the housewife has always been a media construction as much or more so than an accurate representation of actual women's lives.

Friedan's engagement with the housewife, notably, took place on the level of the literal *and the mediatized*. In addition to interviewing real-life housewives, Friedan interrogated the housewife as a media icon whose prominence resulted in material damage to real women, though Friedan admits that "there may be no psychological terms for the harm it is doing." Friedan wondered, "What happens when women try to live according to an image that makes them deny their minds?"[5] Friedan's wariness of images and their power serves as a potent reminder that housewives as a category must be identified and understood in mediatized terms. Combating the potency of the "happy housewife heroine," as Friedan called her, meant interrogating and dismantling the myths surrounding her.[6]

The twinning of the housewife as real-life woman and as a media construction is central to the argument of this chapter, for I will suggest in the next section that *Desperate Housewives'* winking humor rests on understanding and making deliberate use of this slippage. The way the image of the perfect housewife affects *real* women has long preoccupied feminist media scholars, as has the housewife's symbolic power. The housewife's existence as both mediatized figure and target audience importantly dovetails with the history of American television: one of the first figures to appear as a stock character, the housewife was also early television's most well-defined and easily segmented audience. The industry arose conterminously with increasing numbers of real-life housewives; between 1948 and 1955, television was installed in nearly two-thirds of American homes, a time period that corresponded to what Lynn Spigel calls a "new suburban family ideal." The national mood emphasized the reconstruction of family life in the wake of World War II and evinced "a renewed faith in the splendors of consumer capitalism."[7] The housewife sat at the nexus of this vision, for in many ways the promise of reconstitution rested with her ability to serve as a paragon of domesticity.

This position was simultaneously fraught with pressure, as women strove to approximate the sort of effortless perfection of home and appearance that was thought to indicate fulfilling marriages and successful motherhood. "The pleasures of domesticity as a site of psychic and social success for women became something posited as an ideal to be labored towards," explain Helen Wood, Beverley Skeggs, and Nancy

Thumim, "placing emphasis on the detailing of female (often maternal) failure, thereby repositioning domesticity as a set of practices and performances through which one constantly needs to try harder, get advice, and potentially transform for the future, as a form of necessary labor."[8] This description rightly emphasizes labor as a central organizational category for the housewife, a point this chapter also seeks to underscore. Constantly striving, and constantly failing, the housewife served as both aspirational and cautionary.

This double bind is usefully categorized in Nina C. Leibman's study of 1950s television and film, wherein she addresses the question of the housewife's professionalism. Leibman finds evidence that media representations elevate homemaking and motherhood to "career-like" status, and identifies "a two-tiered strategy of minimization and punishment for careerist desires or an explicit celebration of domestic activities, both of which function to render careerism as anathema for women and domesticity their salvation." In a backhanded twist that nevertheless speaks to the convoluted logic of these attitudes, magazine articles geared toward women in the 1950s and 1960s offered advice *from* television wives and mothers on how to excel as homemakers. Leibman cites "Barbara Billingsley's Advice to Homemakers: Dress Up to Your Role," which appeared in *TV Guide* in 1961, a piece that saw the *Leave It to Beaver* star (herself a real-life working woman, it should be noted) advising housewives to dress up, no matter how hectic things get.[9] This example perfectly encapsulates the slippage I document in this chapter, wherein a television celebrity speaking as a sitcom icon advises real women on how to comport themselves.

The housewife exists as a paragon of potent impotence. Symbolically, the role had significant value to the national mythos whereas the behaviors of actual women were often scrutinized and denigrated. What little power she did have typically arose vis-à-vis consumer culture. As the family's primary purchaser of domestic goods and services, the housewife maintained a responsibility for dispensing money, and manufacturers and advertisers recognized the importance of appealing to her consumer tastes. Yet, the housewife had little if any income of her own, rendering her power discretionary at best. "In her value to the economy, the homemaker was at once central and marginal. She was marginal in that she was positioned within the home, constituting the value of her labor outside of the means of production. Yet she was also central to the economy in that her function as homemaker was the subject of consumer product design and marketing, the basis of industry," Mary Beth Haralovich reiterates.[10] Historian Elaine Tyler May casts this ability to spend on behalf of the family in a more sanguine light, writing that "the economic importance of women's role as consumer cannot be overstated, for it kept American industry rolling and sustained jobs for the nation's male providers."[11]

Consumption *as* an occupation—another notion that carries through to the contemporary era—also reflects discourse that positioned women as "experts," "managers," and "executives," attributions that frame the home as a business or factory. "Since at least the mid-1800s, domestic advisors have advocated a model of domesticity rooted in rational housekeeping and efficiency," Elizabeth Nathanson recalls.[12] Likewise, as Stacy Gillis and Joanne Hollows document in their introduction to the volume *Feminism, Domesticity and Popular Culture*, 1920s culture increasingly positioned middle-class women as responsible for making and managing the home. The lure of professionalism accompanied these roles, since rationalized systems and technologies apparently improved domestic outcomes. "The housewife was imagined as a woman who used knowledge from business, science, and medicine to run her home in an efficient and rational manner, one who made intelligent use of new consumer products that promised scientific and technological solutions to household problems," Gillis and Hollows remark.[13] Again, it warrants notice that society hailed the housewife as a consumer responsible for greasing the wheels of the national economy, in sync with popular ideals of time saving and rationality. Encouraged to take responsibility for reimagining the home and modernizing it, housewives served as the architects of domestic space.

As American society interpellated women as laborers *and* consumers, television bore increased responsibility for teaching women how to consume in a manner befitting their roles as domestic managers. Examining the question of the housewife's work, or the work of wifedom as this study proposes, necessitates identifying consumption as a cornerstone of the housewife's duties and considers the historical role that television played in conveying these lessons. Marsha Cassidy locates audience-participation shows as serving a pedagogical function, offerings such as *Queen for a Day* (1956–64), *Strike It Rich* (1951–58), or *Truth and Consequences* (1952; 1956–65). Hailing home workers as "active participants" who partook in attentive daytime viewing, Cassidy clarifies that, "like the turn-of-the-century department store, the television studio theater authorized women's public visibility in the pursuit of commercialized goals, while the daily transmission of a vibrant community of women into domestic space, paired with the possibility for homebound interaction and sorority, justified paying close attention to commercials, a mandatory preface to shopping."[14] Amber Watts likewise identifies audience-participation shows as training grounds for proper consumerism. Surveying the popular *Queen for a Day*, Watts believes that it forged an ineluctable link between having a stable life and the goods that populated suburban homes. The shows positioned household products as necessary for staving off a bad situation or, at the least, ameliorating it: "They seemed to assert that owning the right merchandise could help one avoid both crisis and the labor of recovery and that every woman deserved to own the right merchandise . . . all women could feel that they deserved the same consumer goods, whether to solve problems or ensure their families' future security."[15] These shows hence promoted a fantasy of consumption by equating the benefits of a middle-class lifestyle with having a stable of goods and services; as I discuss at the end of this chapter, today's reality show housewives ably take up that charge.

The housewife's status as a consumer should also not be disarticulated from her racial and class status. Whereas early sitcoms featuring housewives such as *I Remember Mama* (1949–57), *The Goldbergs* (1949–56), and *The Honeymooners* (intermittently between 1952 and 1967) included representations of racial and class diversity, subsequently, the white, middle-class model "came to be identified—against much of the sociological evidence—with the majority collective American identity in the 1950s," Andrea Press asserts.[16] This exclusionary ethos dogs the figure to this day. In her study of 1950s television, Mary Beth Haralovich finds that "the working class is marginalized in and minorities are absent from these discourses and the social economy of consumption."[17] The racial, ethnic, and class exclusions promoted by the figure of the white, middle-class housewife haunts her media presence, a fact that nevertheless made her ripe for rehabilitation during the postfeminist era, wherein similarly exclusionary practices predominate.[18] The housewife's relationship to discourses of normalcy becomes all the more troubling when seen in this light. If the housewife's iconicity is tied to her standing as a common woman, her whiteness serves as a salient and unsettling aspect of this attribution.

The prototypical white housewife adheres to proper tenets of femininity and exists as an other to the feminist and/or working woman. Though feminist scholars sought unity with the housewife, they also disarticulated themselves from her, locating her as their abandoned or fictionalized other, argues Charlotte Brunsdon.[19] This disjuncture should perhaps be traced to Friedan, who urged a stark separation between housewives and career women, and who believed that working outside the home would solve the housewife's dilemma. "In early second wave writing paid work represented much more than a pathway to economic independence for women. It was often constructed as freeing women from the tyranny and monotony of domestic life and expanding the horizons of what it means to be fully human," explains Rosalind Gill.[20] Yet, as bell hooks importantly points out, the exhortation to work is itself racially inflected: "The racism and classism of white women's liberationists was most apparent whenever they discussed work as the liberating force for women. In such discussions it was always the middle-class 'housewife' who was depicted as the victim of sexist oppression and not the poor black and non-black women who are most exploited by American economics."[21] The image of the downtrodden white housewife relies on the symbolic erasure of the labor of women disadvantaged by class and/or race. Similarly, the feminist exhortation to work as a form of liberation often lacked a nuanced understanding of female labor outside the confines of the white middle class.

Despite these multiple advantages, feminist discourse tended to paint the housewife as one suffering from stunted development and confined to unfulfilling domesticity. Hence, the housewife appears as a figure who must be disavowed and rejected in the name of claiming a more self-realized existence, as evidenced by entry into the realm of paid labor. As I will go on to explore, this bifurcation between the housewife and the working woman misrepresents and oversimplifies their respective status, a misattribution that contemporary media texts complicate and trouble. These texts point out the multiple ways that housewives engage in work and reframe the term housewife so that it suggests public as well as private acts of labor.

Desperate Housewives Redux

Feminist media scholars commonly reference a *Cosmopolitan* article titled "Meet the New Housewife Wannabe's" published in 2000 as an exemplar of the sort of thinking that characterizes postfeminist doctrine.[22] In the piece, twentysomething women profess their desire to quit their jobs, relish domesticity, and embrace the role of being a stay-at-home mother, an attitude that could signal rejection of the professional gains for which feminists fought. More specifically, these women's views cohere with what some have termed "new traditionalism," a strain of postfeminism that valorizes old-fashioned feminine postures and roles, appealing to "a nostalgia for a prefeminist past as an ideal that feminism has supposedly destroyed."[23] As Elspeth Probyn explicates, "New traditionalism hawks the home as the 'natural choice'—which means, of course, no choice. If new traditionalism naturalizes the home into a fundamental and unchanging site of love and fulfillment, the discourse of post-feminism turns on a re-articulation of that choice."[24]

Postfeminist mindsets frequently position the housewife as a revitalized and newly attractive icon, understandings that fuel what Diane Negra calls "housewife chic." "This idealized category of femininity celebrates the affluent (usually white) stay-at-home mother for her retreatism, which is to say her opting out of paid work and largely out of the public sphere in favor of a reconnection with the essential femininity that is deemed to only be possible in domestic settings," Negra clarifies.[25] The return of the anachronistic housewife troubled feminists, who felt that the figure portended an embrace of essentialist ideals. If "the housewife is precisely constructed by feminism as what the feminist is not,"[26] her resurgence on the cultural scene in the early years of the twenty-first century was greeted by many progressive women with chagrin.[27] In this section, I argue that the housewife's revitalization represented a turning point in the cultural trajectory of wifedom.

The housewife's reinvigorated cultural presence was forcefully in evidence in 2004, when she blazed onto the popular consciousness in the form of the hit television series *Desperate Housewives*. Focusing on the lives of the women of Wisteria Lane, the show aimed to highlight the plight of women in the "suburban jungle," according to creator Marc Cherry.[28] From first blush, the show appraised its featured women with a complicated mix of empathy and disdain. On the one hand, the trials of five suburban women negotiating the travails of marriage and mother-hood as they concurrently tried to solve the mystery of a close friend's suicide invoked many of the same themes that Friedan highlighted forty-odd years prior. Dysfunctional marriages, disappointing sex lives, domestic boredom, female community and competition, and parenting challenges constituted the show's bread and butter. The following synop-sis represents a typical description of *Desperate Housewives*, and its lan-guage reveals affinities with the struggles Friedan wanted to elucidate: "Trapped behind the hedges of affluent suburban Wisteria Lane, the five female leads experience life and marriage through a haze of infidelity, loneliness, thwarted ambition, sexual dysfunction and drug addiction. Gabrielle cheats on her husband with the teenage gardener. Bree ter-rorizes her family with her perfectionism. Susan sets slutty Edie's house on fire in the course of their competition over a man, and Lynette, who opted out of her high-powered career but cannot seem to keep up the pace as a housewife, steals her children's ADD pills."[29] That the show sought to take a sympathetic approach to these dysfunctions and the women who suffer from them was roundly circulated as its origin story. Creator Marc Cherry proclaimed that he arrived at the conceit thanks to a conversation he had with his own mother after hearing the 2001 news story of Andrea Yates, a Texas mother who drowned her five children in the family bathtub. Following this tragedy, Cherry's mother admitted that faced with caring for three young children alone, she, too, suffered from feelings of helplessness and desperation. Reportedly stunned to hear this revelation, Cherry deduced, "If my mother has had feelings like that, then every woman has had those feelings. I thought, I need to write about this."[30] Many of those who admired the show praised it on the grounds that it centered on these feelings of quiet desperation: Jessica Seigel lauds the impulse to "skewer the myth of motherhood and subur-ban bliss with *Feminine Mystique*–inspired irony."[31] Ironically filmed in the same back lot as *Leave It to Beaver* (1957–63), *Desperate Housewives* was redolent with the impulse to illustrate the grimmer realities that lie behind perfect facades.[32]

To be sure, the women in *Desperate Housewives* suffer indignities that have historically been the lot of women, and the show participates in a rich tradition of televised offerings focusing on women who negoti-

Figure 3.1. Though flanked by a quintessential white picket fence, the bored affect displayed by *Desperate Housewives'* female cast challenges the "happy housewife" ideal. Photograph courtesy of Photofest.

ate love, marriage, and friendship in both comedic and dramatic terms. Cherry—who was the executive producer and writer on *The Golden Girls* (1985–92) before helming *Desperate Housewives*—"grew up admiring series starring Mary Tyler Moore, Lucille Ball, Marlo Thomas and Bea Arthur. In some ways . . . these 'desperate housewives' are their daughters."[33] Finding echoes in the tradition of the family sitcom, as well as the prime-time docusoap, critics have drawn comparisons between *Desperate Housewives* and *Bewitched* (1964–72), *I Dream of Jeannie* (1965–70), *Dallas* (1978–91), *Dynasty* (1981–89), *thirtysomething* (1987–91), *Married . . . with Children* (1987–97), and *Roseanne* (1988–97).[34] *Desperate Housewives* closest cousin is, however, *Sex and the City* (1998–2004). When that series ended in 2004, it left a void in programming for women that *Desperate Housewives* arrived to fill.[35] Thanks to its similar focus on friendship and sexuality, some touted *Desperate Housewives* as "*Sex and the City* grown up and moved to the suburbs."[36]

If we take seriously this genealogy, *Desperate Housewives* shares with its foremothers its sense of the labor of femininity. Though an admittedly exaggerated and hyperbolic portrayal, it reflects back on the stultifying 1950s (where homemaking was both the norm and the expectation for middle-class women) and attests to the way domestic ideals persist into the modern era. Cognizant of the need for women to perform contentment with familial identities, even at the expense of lying to themselves and others, *Desperate Housewives* understood the coercive expectations that fuel these performances. The pilot, for example, features a scene that mimics a touchstone sequence in *The Stepford Wives* (1975). In the film's closing, the camera pans across a grocery store, where placid women (all robots) in long dresses and hats float effortlessly through the aisles. In *Desperate Housewives*, the same shot begins the sequence and settles on Lynette (Felicity Huffman) flanked by rambunctious children, where she demands a return phone call from her absent husband. Running into a former colleague who tells her that her coworkers always say that if she had not left her job she would be running the place, the colleague asks, "How's domestic life? Don't you just love being a mom?" Lynette dissembles her frustration and anxiety, turns on a fake smile, and responds, "It's the best job I've ever had." (Meanwhile, her out-of-control boys wreak havoc on unsuspecting patrons.) A flashback likewise reveals that Lynette's decision to quit her job came at the behest of her husband during an ultrasound when she was pregnant with her first child, when he claims that "kids do better with stay-at-home moms. It would be so much less stressful."[37] Lynette's wild and poorly behaved children as well as her persistent sadness not only undercut that sentiment, but also illustrate how unthinking notions of essential feminine identities get discursively reproduced, often by those with no firsthand knowledge of the work it takes to inhabit these mythologized roles.

As they strive to make the domestic realm (which encompasses marriage, motherhood, and sexual relations) function according to imposed scripts, *Desperate Housewives*' protagonists undeniably engage in the labor of wifedom. Likewise, they view their labors more as chores than expressions of their unique subjecthood. Even Bree (Marcia Cross), the quintessential housewife, demonstrates exasperation after learning that her son has no appreciation for her osso buco or her basil puree, a dinner that has taken her three hours to prepare. When she looks to them for approval and affirmation, her children confess that they would be just as happy with a can of pork and beans. Bree often refers to "the actual

work, the drudgery and effort required behind the image of the perfect housewife rarely acknowledged in the earlier popular incarnations,"
Anna Marie Bautista comments.[38] Perhaps surprisingly attuned to the
thankless nature of housekeeping, Bree even excoriates the father of psy-
choanalysis when she laments that Freud's mother must have "felt so betrayed. He saw how hard she worked; he saw what she did for him. Did
he ever think to say thank you? I doubt it." (Friedan similarly charges
Freud with completely misunderstanding women's lives.) By making
visible the labor of wifedom, *Desperate Housewives* offers a rejoinder
to 1950s sitcoms where houses appear effortlessly clean, and children's
foibles signal charming weakness rather than threatening defiance.

The show takes on these televisual predecessors—paragons of perfection—in both serious and comedic terms. At the same time, it reveals
that unrealistic ideals persist in the twenty-first century. In the presence of her children, Lynette's emotional spectrum runs the not-so-wide
gamut from frustrated to weepy. Gabrielle (Eva Longoria), on the other
hand, thumbs her nose at domesticity, and her character's behaviors register as parodic—she mows the lawn only to hide from her husband the
fact that she has been distracting her gardener with sex, and jokes, "Do
you know how bored I am? I came within an inch of doing the housework." Importantly, Gabrielle reads as the only nonwhite cast member;
her retorts challenge the hegemony of idealized white femininity and
rebuff the strictures of an imposed traditional femininity. On the other
hand, the show codes her promiscuity and generally shallow demeanor
as problematic and self-centered, and some have accused the character of being painted in racist terms. Gabrielle softens in later years of
the series, especially after she becomes a mother. It is nevertheless true
that on the show "women are not generally presented as being naturally
disposed to the domestic sphere, challenging the assumptions within
the separate spheres ideology," remarks Bautista. She adds, "Domesticity
and motherhood are now largely depicted in terms of skills and abilities
to be acquired and cultivated; thus, while domesticity and motherhood
might still be idealized in many ways, the efforts required to achieve
these ideals are also exposed."[39]

By taking seriously *Desperate Housewives'* focus on the labor of femininity, I do not mean to discount the charge that thanks to its campy and
ironic tone the series makes light of many serious issues facing women.

Desperate Housewives' evocation of Friedan's housewives was under-cut by a number of factors, including its visual emphasis on eroticizing whiteness; its glamorous, thin, and conventionally attractive stars; and its sometimes-smug tone. The exaggerated nature of the show's plotlines, in turn, makes it difficult to take seriously the legitimate problems that it elliptically addresses. For instance, while the show narrates the lengths Bree goes to in order to project a domestic ideal, the show simultane-ously seems to ridicule her for being too concerned with cupcake baking and not attentive enough to the actual desires and problems of her fam-ily members. ("Everyone thought of Bree as the perfect wife and mother. Everyone, that is, except her own family," quips Mary Alice in her om-niscient voice-over narration.) As I have argued elsewhere, and in refer-ence to *Desperate Housewives* specifically, tones of ironic detachment characterize much postfeminist media culture, a sensibility that coheres with a strategy of showcasing female travails from a cold distance.[40] Postfeminist products sell women's insignificance and narcissism back to them under the mantle of irony, a charge that helps to explain the dis-comfort so many feminists had with *Desperate Housewives*, a show that was, at least cosmetically, supposed to be sympathetic to their plight.

This said, I argue that the show's contribution to the cultural milieu rests less with its feminist inclinations than with its revitalization and redefinition of the term "housewife." For some, the fact of organizing a series around the outdated premise of foregrounding a group of stay-at-home wives and mothers in an era where most women keenly felt the necessity of laboring outside the family confirms *Desperate House-wives'* conservative impulses. Its "worldview harks back to a time when two-parent, middle-class families could comfortably thrive on single in-comes, women's identities were primarily determined by the men they married and the children they raised, and husbands were not expected to trouble themselves with such pesky matters as child care and house-work," charges Jennifer Pozner.[41] The act of depicting gendered divisions was, for some, taken as an endorsement of this arrangement. As Sharon Sharp asserts, "*Desperate Housewives* puts forward the assumption that domesticity is a female-oriented sphere."[42]

The show nevertheless repeatedly troubles the notion that women bear primary responsibility for—and are best contained in—the home, which it accomplishes thanks to melodramatic plotlines and what Janet

McCabe calls the "sheer artificiality of these lush images."[43] As suggested previously, few of the characters on the show serve as traditional examples of housewives (with the exception of Bree, who is herself quite troubled) and none inhabits the role in a seamless manner. Gabrielle's disdain for all things domestic rivals the abjection written all over Lynette, whose disheveled hair, bedraggled appearance, and barely contained hostility toward her unruly children confirm her despair. Susan (Teri Hatcher), a divorced single mother, works from home as a children's book illustrator, agonizes over her love life, and fails to possess any domestic prowess or feminine grace. Though Bree oozes domestic efficiency, models impeccable manners, and exhibits aesthetic elegance, even the supposedly perfect housewife finds herself assaulted with the reminder that her family members find their domestic experiences joyless. When her husband, Rex, announces that he wants a divorce, he laments the cold, perfect thing she has become.[44] "I just can't live in this detergent commercial anymore," he says, a line that suggests his awareness of the way media icons have influenced his wife's personality and behavior. Similarly, the line betrays the show's wider cognizance that the housewife icon exists primarily as a media construction and troubling artifice. If enacted in life, the perfect housewife ideal reads like a grotesque caricature, and later years of the series witness Bree turning to alcohol to manage these pressures. *Desperate Housewives* exposed the false promises, hypocrisy, and unhappiness that undergird media images of domestic bliss.

While a recognition of the inaccuracy of the perfect housewife icon and her tendency to intimidate real-life women would seem to be a tired and unnecessary intervention in a post-Friedan era, the cultural discourse in the early 2000s tended to mythologize domesticity and in particular motherhood. *Desperate Housewives* emerged in a cultural context that exhorted women to craft the role of motherhood as an art—a là Martha Stewart (to whom Bree is often compared). According to Susan J. Douglas and Meredith W. Michaels's 2004 volume *The Mommy Myth: The Idealization of Motherhood and How It Has Undermined All Women*, thanks to a mind-set they call the new momism, women feel acute pressure to pursue perfect motherhood: "Because of this sheer increase in output and target marketing, mothers were bombarded as never before by media constructions of the good mother." Moreover, the new momism emerged at a time when women entered the workforce in record numbers, pulling women's psyches between what Douglas and Michaels call "powerful and contradictory cultural riptides" insofar as they must be doting and self-sacrificing at home, and achievement-oriented at work.[45] *Desperate Housewives* offered a rebuke to the widespread ideal of perfect motherhood, argues Niall Richardson, and was one of the first series to actively critique the cult of new momism.[46]

In addition to speaking back to these punishing cultural norms, *Desperate Housewives* recirculated and redefined the term housewife by bringing it into common parlance. I contend that the nomenclature allowed culture watchers to inaugurate discourse about *all* women, with an eye to the topic of female labor both inside and outside the home. "Until the advent of this show, the word housewife was almost a put-down," commented Australian journalist Rosemary Neill. With "its glamour, intrigue and women who stand up to their men, this dangerously dysfunctional neighborhood has reclaimed the word housewife for generations of women."[47] Though "housewife" formerly existed as a pejorative, Neill suggests that the show helped to modernize—and glamorize—the moniker. I offer a related observation, which is that *Desperate Housewives'* status on the cultural vanguard assured the widespread visibility of the slippage it indoctrinated, whereby housewife became a placeholder for a set of popular culture debates. The housewife's reappearance on the cultural stage reenergized long-standing media conversations, offering a convenient heuristic for the "mommy wars," since the distinction between women working outside the home and within it is a separation that popular culture has tended to frame as the most pressing concern of female lives.

That the show offered an opportunity and platform for these conversations was confirmed by the fact that much of the publicity surrounding *Desperate Housewives* centered on the idea of the housewife and, implicitly, her shadowboxing match with working women. In her piece about the show, *USA Today* contributor Ann Oldenburg argued that the problem with the word housewife was that it made women who work inside the home and those who work outside it equally uncomfortable. Women who do stay home "don't like the connotations of being 'just a housewife'—you're a housewife, organizer, mother," she writes. "But working women get the same anxious emotional attachment, because it means a choice they have not made. 'Housewife' evokes a lot more ambivalence today than it did in the '50s and '60s."[48] This pat division between housewives and working women nevertheless represents a reductive understanding of how gender functions in real-world contexts. Sketching out their objection to these categorizations, Douglas and Michaels state that it serves to place "mothers into two, mutually exclusive categories—working mother versus stay-at-home mother, and never the twain shall meet. It goes without saying that they allegedly hate each other's guts. In real life, millions of mothers move between these two categories, have been one and then the other at various different times, creating a mosaic of work and child-rearing practices that bears no resemblance to the supposed ironclad roles suggested by the 'mommy wars.'"[49] The housewife discourse is nevertheless ready-made to enter into this debate, and is one reason, I suspect, that the term garners such apprehension. Talking about housewives invokes these polarizing positions and confirms yet again that media portrayals mire women in binaristic logics.

Despite this seemingly easy distinction between working women and housewives, a closer look at *Desperate Housewives* illustrates a more nuanced vision, one that the show's title somewhat belies. Writing about housewives in a postfeminist context, Stephanie Genz urges a worldview that highlights "the challenges and paradoxes of a postfeminist femininity/domesticity that can no longer be conceptualized along a sharp split between feminism and housewifery, agency and victimization, work and family life." Likewise, she notes the need to resist the "analytical temptation" to retreat to "a safe, binary order that differentiates housewives from feminists, mothers from career women, domesticity from paid work."[50] *Desperate Housewives* enacts the sort of slippage that Genz encourages, insofar as it deploys "housewife" as a placeholder for all women, and fails to distinguish between them based on labors or reproductive identities. Importantly, not all of the show's primary characters have children, some are not married, and some do (or come to) work outside the home. The term does, however, place all women in relation *to* the domestic. Even though women may escape the housewife/working woman binary, they cannot so handily evade a conceptualization that puts their marital and reproductive identities at the forefront of understandings of their personhood. In turn, these identities circumscribe women's marketability in a branded economy, as I will discuss shortly.

In an excellent argument about *Desperate Housewives*, Janet Mc-Cabe credits the show with "assign[ing] representational form to the paradoxes and uncertainties defining contemporary femininity."[51] The housewife as a media figure embodies these paradoxes and uncertainties; she is, in short, less an icon than an empty signifier for all things feminine in the twenty-first century. *Desperate Housewives* invoked this figure to interrogate and ironize her—not to offer a definitive solution to women's desperation, but rather to reflect on her positioning as the sine qua non of feminine identity. By doing so, the series inaugurated its own zeitgeist, where housewife became synonymous with a certain type of upper-middle-class (typically white) femininity, the kind, indeed, that media outlets focus on to the virtual exclusion of all others. Confirming the housewife's representational dominance is the fact that she tends to be the figure who is invoked in discussions of women's lives. In this way, the housewife's return to the cultural forefront was both ironic, recalling her role as a media icon, as well as diagnostic, insofar as it acknowledged that traditionally feminine interests and preoccupations continue to frame American women's lives, regardless of their particular marital status, sexual identity, or profession. These same roles also soon became monetizable since performing wifedom and femininity, and doing so under the rubric of housewifery, became a shortcut to both fame and financial gain, as I will explore in the next section.

The Advent of the "Real" Housewives

A 2006 press release announcing *The Real Housewives of Orange County* included the following telling line: "Here is a series that depicts real-life 'desperate housewives' with an authentic look at their day-to-day drama."[52] A *People* magazine spread devoted to celebrating *Desperate Housewives'* concluding season in 2012 further outlined the link between the two shows, as Bravo producer Andy Cohen explained the debt the Bravo juggernaut owed to the ABC series: "We had this show in development, about this group of women in Coto de Caza, Calif. And it was originally called *Behind the Gate. Desperate Housewives* was heating up, and we realized, wow, well, what these women are is *real* housewives.

So it was a play—not only on *Desperate Housewives* but on the idea of what the modern housewife was. Certainly, with *The Real Housewives of Orange County* holding oranges in the credits, that was absolutely a wink to the original *Desperate Housewives* ad campaign of the ladies with the apples."[53] More than a happy coincidence, the development of *The Real Housewives of Orange County* attests to Bravo's willingness to capitalize on housewives' increased visibility in the popular consciousness. This recognition has paid dividends for the network which, as of this writing, has shepherded nine *Real Housewives* shows as well as multiple spin-offs into production.[54] While Cohen's words suggest the visual nods that the reality series makes to its fictionalized predecessor, more saliently, *The Real Housewives* revitalized and complicated the term housewife. Though Cohen references the idea of "what the modern housewife was," he actually means the modern *woman*: even in the first iteration of the series, *The Real Housewives of Orange County* featured an unmarried principal cast member (Jo De La Rosa).

According to the terms set by *The Real Housewives of Orange County*, housewives need not be married or mothers, but rather, wealthy and prone to performative femininities. The franchise's content flatly rejects traditional notions of housewifery. These housewives rarely labor in-side the home but rather revel in acts of pampered consumption and leisure, engaging in aesthetic rituals and regimes of self-care including shopping, dining out, and hiring others to assist them with their cloth-ing, hair, makeup, fashion, and jewelry. As Carina Chocano writes in an article titled "Housewives, Rebranded," "The 'real housewives' of Bravo fill their days with shopping, grooming, lunching, gossiping and feud-ing. What they don't do, naturally, is housework." The housewives do, however, self-disclose ad nauseam, both in group settings and in the talking heads sequences that pepper the programming, rendering their life events in dramatic and often inflammatory ways. This programming starkly departs from the "housewife as home laborer" ideal rehearsed earlier in this chapter. Instead, Bravo's housewives exhibit a relation to the domestic that is ancillary at best. Inside homes, housewives prepare for lunches or evenings out, direct household servants, or host group gatherings involving other housewives—they do not typically care for children or husbands, cook, or clean. Chocano calls this "confusing, con-tradictory, neo-housewife behavior," noting that they "proudly show off

Figures 3.2 and 3.3. *Desperate Housewives'* iconic use of apples informed and inspired the presentation of oranges, held here by the season 11 cast of *The Real Housewives of Orange County.*

their incompetence in the kitchen," "their lack of interest in sex," and "their limited patience for parenthood."[55]

Whereas one might expect the housewife's family to constitute her most central or prized affective bond, in fact, the relationships the housewives have with one another more often take precedence. Housewives routinely engage in catty interplay, a reality even more pronounced in the later years of the series, when housewives clearly doctored their relationships in an effort to create dramatic tension. The housewives' husbands, lovers, or partners, if they have them, tend occupy a sidelined or backseat role. So many marriages have dissolved during the franchise's now-twelve-year-long run that there is talk of a curse associated with appearing on it. As I will explore here, housewives commodify wifedom at the same time that they are commodified by it because their job is to be professional females, as defined by a network dedicated to upscale lifestyle programming. As I discuss in the next chapter, Bravo has staked its fortunes on cultivating an affluent consumer base.

Despite the docudrama ethos that first inspired the series—and here I refer to the promise that the show would reveal the reality of being a housewife—*The Real Housewives* programs quickly became known as career makers for their stars. The crashing of a White House state dinner in 2009 perpetrated by the status-seeking couple Michaele and Tareq Salahi, who were then cast on the short-lived *The Real Housewives of DC* (2010), stands as perhaps the most preposterous example of how the show has historically rewarded the drive for exposure with more exposure. Not incidentally, Michaele and Tareq eventually divorced and Michaele's marriage to classic rock band Journey's guitarist Neal Schon was broadcast in a pay-per-view event in 2013, an occurrence that speaks volumes about the way that wifedom operates as a commercializable happening. For numerous women, in fact, appearing on *The Real Housewives* is tantamount to the start of a new career. Their appearances in the franchise testify to an impulse to utilize an already wealthy lifestyle in service of both profit and exposure.

This trajectory nevertheless traffics in deep irony. In actuality, few of the women featured on the franchise ever resembled traditional housewives and, if anything, they become less like housewives by being cast *as* them. Ramona Singer, for example, ran a lucrative jewelry line with her husband when producers approached her about appearing on *The Real*

Housewives of New York (2008–). She initially demurred, until being told that "this would be a good platform for your businesses," according to the *Hollywood Reporter*. Similarly, reports credit Teresa Giudice's starring role on *The Real Housewives of New Jersey* (2009–) with bringing in enough money to keep her struggling family afloat. After years of irresponsible spending, a filing for bankruptcy, and an indictment on fraud for both her and her husband, Giudice became her family's main provider, relying for funds on her *Housewives* paychecks, royalties from her two cookbooks, and her appearances on the cover of gossip tabloids like *In Touch Weekly* (for which she reportedly earns $20,000 per shot).[56]

Further evidence in support of the oxymoronic notion that housewifery serves primarily as a public, professional career came from housewife Peggy Tanous, who explained in 2011 that she suffered from postpartum depression, an affliction she attributed in part to her position as a stay-at-home mother. She believed that appearing on *The Real Housewives of Orange County* would give her something else to do. Indeed, Bravo's housewives are in many cases women who seek paid professional work *outside* the home, and their casting as housewives makes the transition to waged labor possible. The participation of Beverly Hills housewife Camille Grammer also follows this logic. She began appearing in 2010, encouraged by her now ex-husband Kelsey, who advised that she do the show as a way to have something of her own. This advice soon looked like his own cynical calculation, a move designed to divert her attention while he pursued an extramarital affair and eventually a new wife.

In keeping with the idea that women become housewives to launch or relaunch careers, around 2015 the franchise began casting C- and D-list actors from sitcoms, soap operas, and nighttime serials looking to expand their performative registers, as manifested in the addition of 1980s stars Kim Fields and Lisa Rinna to *The Real Housewives of Atlanta* (2008–) and *The Real Housewives of Beverly Hills* (2010–), respectively, and by the casting of soap opera doyen Eileen Davidson on *The Real Housewives of Beverly Hills*. "The success of the franchise presents these former celebrities or wives of celebrities with another chance at fame, and draws new attention to their otherwise passé careers," comments Martina Baldwin.[57] These examples illustrate an organizing principle that has only intensified during the show's tenure: in essence, women become housewives in order to have a job, with the ancillary benefits of self-worth and independence that feminists touted as the perks of professionalization in ample supply.

My argument about the professionalization of housewifery also applies to women for whom the show paves the way for entirely new professional opportunities. Atlanta cast member NeNe Leakes, for example, parlayed her popularity into a full-fledged television career. In addition to appearing on *The Real Housewives of Atlanta* from its inception until 2015, Leakes headlined the spin-off *I Dream of NeNe: The Wedding* (2013). Continuing to serve Bravo parent company NBC, Leakes had stints on *Celebrity Apprentice* (2008–) and on *The New Normal* (2012–13) before branching out to recurring roles in Fox's *Glee* (2009–15) and ABC's *Dancing with the Stars* (2005–). Rounding out this profile, Leakes appeared on Broadway as an evil stepmother in a production of *Cinderella*, started her own production company, and launched a clothing line. All these roles in some ways reference Leakes's housewife persona; as Baldwin observes, "Her t-shirt line invokes her personality using her classic one-liners such as, 'Bloop,' 'Girl Bye!,' and 'Bye Wig!' Even in the scripted television series she appeared in (*The New Normal, Glee*), her characters have been very similar to her persona on *TRH* [*The Real Housewives*]—a sassy, blunt, no-nonsense force to be reckoned with."[58]

Appearing as a housewife is a gateway to potentially more lucrative and high-profile opportunities, an observation perhaps best illustrated by the most commercially successful housewife of all, Bethenny Frankel, former and current cast member on *The Real Housewives of New York*. As Diane Negra and I have argued elsewhere, Frankel made a career out of living out the stages of the postfeminist life cycle in the public eye, and her monetization of those phases speaks to the new logics of self-branding and entrepreneurialism that characterize twenty-first-century female media culture.[59] I want to reprise part of that argument here, with an eye toward Frankel's iconic status as a wife and with the larger goal of suggesting that Frankel serves as a quintessential example of the sort of upstart efforts that this book has traced throughout. As if plucked from the pages of a chick lit novel, Frankel began her public life as the witty, no-holds-barred, natural foods chef who appeared on but did not win the reality food competition *The Apprentice: Martha Stewart* (2005). She refers to her decision to participate in *The*

Real Housewives of New York, though she was unmarried at the time, as a professional calculation. At that juncture, Frankel was writing a cookbook titled *Naturally Thin*, and nearly a decade later she shared her thought process about joining the show: "It's not that easy to get on television, and I'm writing this book, and I can use it as a platform." She asserts, "I went on the show single-handedly and exclusively for business."[60] Admittedly, this could be revisionist history. Prior to the publication of this 2015 article, Frankel was never quite so outspoken or flip regarding her motivations for appearing on reality television. Regardless, since she first appeared in the public eye, Frankel has relentlessly used her personal life as grist for her professional mill.

Cast on *The Real Housewives of New York* as a singleton with a boyfriend she hoped to strong-arm into a more serious commitment, Frankel began crafting her signature brand, Skinnygirl Margarita, while on the show. Frankel's personal life and her quest to become a wife perfectly fit the parameters of her casting since she actively aspired to wifedom at the same time that she marketed a product that fit a lucrative demographic of which she was a part. As a single sophisticate herself, Frankel's flavor of product development—a low-calorie alcoholic beverage marketed to image-conscious women—aptly echoed her characterization. In short, Frankel both created and was the Skinnygirl, a feedback loop that masterfully linked her brand identity with the affective qualities and class positioning associated with her as a person. Frankel hence presented a seamless alignment of her product with her larger lifestyle. In 2011, Frankel sold the right to produce Skinnygirl cocktails to Beam Suntory (the parent company of Jim Beam) for a reported $100 million but retained access to the use and promotion of the name Skinnygirl. The feat landed her on the cover of *Forbes*, and today she helms a food and lifestyle empire, with the Skinnygirl name attached to low-calorie alcoholic drinks, a daily cleanse, nonalcoholic drink mixes, a dizzying array of foods (nutrition bars, chocolate, popcorn, chips, salad dressings), coffee, teas, sparking drink mixes, sweeteners, lotions, shapewear, online personal training, and workout gear. A *New Yorker* profile of Frankel noted that by 2015 the Skinnygirl label had been attached to over one hundred products, and in a 2016 article titled "Skinnygirl, Fat Wallet" *Forbes* again diagrammed how masterfully Frankel's licensing deals benefit her bottom line.[61]

Figure 3.4. Despite selling her low-calorie line of alcoholic drinks to behemoth beverage purveyor Beam Suntory in 2011, Frankel retained the rights to the Skinnygirl name. Since then, she has built a product empire on this brand.

Frankel's spin-off series *Bethenny Getting Married?* (2010) and *Bethenny Ever After* (2011–12) testified to her commodification of her wifedom. As they narrate, Frankel met a different man, Jason Hoppy; faced an unexpected pregnancy at the age of thirty-nine; and quickly married. The shows featured her wedding planning, baby preparation, negotiations with her new spouse, struggles with in-laws, attempts at homemaking, and the pressures of her professional aspirations as she built the Skinnygirl empire. Frankel's feverish juggling of marriage, career, and motherhood—in short, the vicissitudes of mediatized modern femininity—form the basis of the series. "What was perhaps most surprising about Bethenny's reality show," maintains Emma Lieber, "was the extent to which it perpetuated the long-established housewife formula and frame: the focus on domesticity, its conflicts, its demands."[62] Yet, despite the lip service she pays to the domestic realm, Frankel's efforts always double as professional endeavors for which she receives compensatory rewards. As Julie Wilson explains, "Within the context of the show, Skinnygirl-related plotlines, which are certainly promotional vehicles, feel authentic and completely in step with Frankel's star persona, as they are woven into her other, everyday struggles at womanhood. . . . With the lines between her public and private personas erased at the level of representation, the entirety of Frankel's 'real life' becomes a context for her own self-branding."[63] Even the sequences that seemed the most personal and private (and unconnected from her business)—as when Frankel allowed cameras into the hospital room while she was in labor—speak to her embrace of the professionalization of wifedom.

Frankel's success as a media icon relies in part on her compliance with the dictates of niche marketing in the early twenty-first century, as exemplified by the fact that her personal milestones worked in tandem with branding imperatives no matter what the phase. Frankel appeared on the covers of *Engagement 101* (before her wedding); *Parenting* and *People* (after the birth of her daughter); *Self* (while juggling marriage and motherhood); and *People* and *Redbook* (during her divorce proceedings). She even ostensibly found a way to monetize her marital failure, penning another self-help book, *I Suck at Relationships So You Don't Have To* (2015) after her divorce.[64] Frankel's marital aspirations and failures also comply with this book's contention that marriage remains of interest to and a boon for the affluent. Put simply, her story closely hews to the normative sequencing of life phases for affluent, white, professional women, a compliance for which she has been generously remunerated. Frankel's willingness to commodify her life undeniably augmented her fame, as did her metonymic function as a number of hallmark types such as "single girl in the city," "married working mother," and "divorced professional." As this book goes to press, Frankel is touring with self-help guru Tony Robbins in 2017, serving as a featured speaker in "The Ultimate Wealth and Success Summit." Frankel is the only woman on the roster, and it seems both summarily ironic and completely fitting that a seminar focused on wealth growth and self-realization would rely on the expertise of a "housewife."

Though Frankel is today clearly considered a consummate businesswoman, it bears remembering that the origins and the longevity of her fame can be attributed to her willingness to perform the attendant and relentless cycles of self-doubt and self-assurance that pepper feminized media culture, performances that have and continue to bolster her relatability. In an intriguing audience study, Kavita Ilona Nayar examined two online fan forums in which audiences of *Bethenny Getting Married?* and *Bethenny Ever After* commented on what Nayar calls Frankel's "transformation into a branded self," a change that Nayar ties to the Jim Beam deal.[65] While audiences varied in their responses to and perceptions of Frankel, those who tended to be her strongest supporters—labeled by Nayar as "brand ambassadors"—comment on how Frankel seems emotionally relatable because of her willingness to share her struggles with work and family. Nayar writes, "The vindication of Frankel's branded self is made even more enjoyable by her emotional labor on the reality television show, and audiences recognize this performance as a 'gift' she has given them."[66] According to Nayar, audiences see Frankel's brand as a work in progress and identify with her authenticity and willingness to admit her vulnerabilities.

Housewives like Frankel clearly traffic in emotional labor. Focalizing on what she calls "affective enterprising," Jacquelyn Arcy suggests that "by performing emotional excess, the Housewives construct compelling narratives as platforms to market their engineered personas and their branded merchandise." Arcy rightly locates Frankel's mastery of affective enterprising in the synergy between her branded enterprise and her emotional life, and calls attention to her willingness to emote on the show, even if that emotional realism involves performing degradation. Putting Arcy's observations in conversation with the arguments of this chapter helps to clarify that Frankel's laboring takes place in a feminized register, even as these labors frequently occur in public spheres and spaces, such as during promotional appearances for Skinnygirl. Frankel worries about her personal life, struggles with her friends, experiences bouts of self-doubt, and frets about child rearing, much like the 1950s housewife. Yet, these emotional investments pointedly earn Frankel economic rewards, specifically through the building of Frankel's branded image. Moreover, Frankel has proven capable of emoting in ways that make audiences trust her, which in turn leads them to support her business efforts. As Arcy discusses, in a season 2 reunion special for *The Real Housewives of New York*, audiences chastise the other housewives for attempting to shill their products in ways that feel crass and calculating. Frankel has never been subject to this critique, in part because her venture Skinnygirl so closely aligns with what seems to be her actual persona.[67]

After the demise of her marriage and a short-lived stint as a talk show host, in 2015 Frankel returned to the cast of *The Real Housewives of New York*, where she talked openly about the pressures of single motherhood. Frankel has also been quite forthcoming about how her appearances on reality television serve as examples of crafted labor. On a *Today* show interview in the summer of 2015, Frankel testified to the lack of reality in the Bravo show ("I think the show is a comedy, it's almost like a satire") and confirmed her efforts to appear compelling and interesting before the camera. She made similar comments in a *New Yorker* profile, calling herself a marketer: "I know how to communicate to people, and I think that's what marketing really is."[68] Frankel's self-identification as a housewife and return to the cast of *The Real Housewives of New York* clearly represents another sleight of hand since Frankel never appeared on the show when she was *actually* a wife and only returned to it after her divorce. Again, the term housewife reveals itself as an empty signifier, meant merely to signal Frankel's status as a heterosexual woman disposed to performing the strictures of modern femininity.

Frankel's inclination to expose all parts of her personal life testifies to the new regimes of mandatory disclosure and transparency that epitomize reality television, a development that I discuss in the next chapter and that Alison Hearn terms a "monetization of being."[69] Though the field remains glutted, Frankel nevertheless stands out as one whose romantic, maternal, and professional trajectory provided excellent television fodder in a neoliberal climate interested in the question of female self-actualization, and she has been handily rewarded for her professionalization of housewifery. To repeat, Frankel's narrative played out against the backdrop of wifedom even when Frankel's actual time as a wife was dramatically short-lived, a reality that speaks directly to my argument that under the capacious umbrella of the moniker housewife fall all traditionally feminized events, tensions, and negotiations. Moreover, in this cultural milieu, struggles with work and family, the quest to find and keep love, and the pressures of successful professionalism serve as the fabric of American female lives.

A second and yet vitally important legacy of Frankel's fame trajectory is her demonstration that the housewives' public perch grants them the access, right, and legitimacy to turn their professionalization of wifedom into a profitable business enterprise. Specifically, the housewife's history as a consumer, purchaser, and domestic architect has been translated in the twenty-first century into her role as a purveyor of luxury, high-end, high-status goods. Though Frankel is by far the most successful and accomplished professional to have launched a brand while on *The Real Housewives*, almost every housewife *since* Frankel has tried her hand at product development and marketing. (Bravo obliges housewives to grant the network a cut of the products developed during their tenure—a contractual clause that Frankel sagely refused to sign.) According to a *Huffington Post* article, 42 percent of the Bravo housewives had their own product lines and brands in 2012, and this percentage has surely grown in the years since.[70] These product lines run the gamut and include, but are by no means limited to, clothing, makeup, shoes, handbags, perfumes, beauty products, advice books (particularly in the realm of diet and exercise), memoirs, cookbooks, wines and spirits, food, vacation sites, and workout accessories. Though varied, these products nevertheless remain tethered in some way to the concept of aspirational femininity, connecting the sort of appearance or activity that a well-heeled woman would enjoy to a marketable product that allows purchasers to indulge in the fantasy of a high-end life. As June Deery clarifies, "If the participants don't have a business to publicize when a series starts, most eventually do. Hence, the show in part creates the wealthy lifestyle it portrays . . . some participants afford their lifestyle in part by selling its props (clothing, cosmetics, alcohol) to others."[71] Housewives commodify their status as women, in essence selling femininity. Moreover, they earn the right to do this by appearing as exemplary or iconic women, as did mediatized 1950s housewives.

While Bravo's housewives phenomena might seem to be a rarified cultural happening, I want to close with the observation that it represents a larger trend in the cultural trajectory of wifedom. As Chocano observes of the Bravo housewives, not only does their "housewifeliness exist almost entirely outside the parameters of marriage," they have also "turned the role of the housewife into a job—one that sells a lifestyle brand to a generation at once ideologically opposed to and functionally cut off from such a lifestyle."[72] The housewives in this way remain both ordinary and extraordinary, and their housewifery exists as both aspirational and cautionary. As the purveyors of luxury goods associated with femininity, the housewives increasingly trouble the already blurry line between their status as producers and consumers. Televised housewives produce the image to be consumed and also lend their names to products that ostensibly allow for their lifestyle to be approximated and aped. At the same time, the housewives are the consummate consumers—specifically of brand-name clothes, expensive accessories, flashy cars, fancy homes, extravagant meals, upscale vacations, and even cosmetic surgeries. In the next chapter, I delve more deeply into how these products and their purveyors fit with Bravo's larger network brand.

The housewife's disruption of the boundary between producer and consumer also usefully clarifies the shadowboxing match between the housewife and the working woman, a division that has been so central to much contemporary and even feminist thought. There was a time as recently as 2010, when former governor and vice presidential candidate Sarah Palin called herself a "housewife," a move that I read as emphasizing maternity and domesticity in order to disavow the unappealing image of the calculating female professional and, implicitly, the feminist.[73] Yet, if the housewife was recently feminism's other, she is today merely the aspirational everywoman, one who has figured out how to render her interests, emotions, families, and friendships profitable. What is striking about the trajectory of the housewife is the extent to which feminized media culture is saturated with her afterglow. This transition speaks to the professionalization of femininity, the reach of neoliberalism, and the oft-remarked-upon fact that in the current phase of late capitalism it is difficult to find any sphere of existence that is not imbricated in a market economy. In this way, it is unsurprising that the housewife's status as exempt from or outside of corporate logics would give way to a reality wherein some of the most affluent and professionally successful women featured in contemporary media are housewives. While this eventuality is in alignment with current modes, it is still important to recognize the overdetermined and gendered nature of this trajectory. While the housewife may have realized the supposed liberation that comes from having a career, it is merely the professionalization of the cosmetic aspects of feminized identities that have found a place in the market. To thoroughly professionalize femininity, as I will explore in the next chapter, involves turning a complicated person into a wife, a transition that is perhaps as constricting and emotionally dangerous as being a traditional housewife was once thought to be.

4

From Basketball Wives to Extreme Cougar Wives

Niche Marketing the Wife Brand

Since 2006, Bravo's so-called housewives have been joined by basketball wives, mob wives, governor's wives, football wives, Nashville wives, sister wives, and extreme cougar wives, and the shows in which they appear are perhaps most famous for reveling in the wives' outspoken and bad behavior. This chapter examines the glut of wifely programming on reality television in terms of the niche appeal wives lend to their respective networks, their class and racial politics, and the emotional labor that professional wives perform on their shows. Because reality wives navigate complicated and often hostile group dynamics, their status as wives is often less important than their positioning as friends or (more routinely) as enemies. This positioning serves as yet another testament to the work of wifedom—wherein, under the auspices of being a wife, women receive compensation for appearing on television as exemplars of contemporary femininity.

This chapter continues chapter 3's investigation of the labor of being a wife on reality television. Whereas the previous chapter investigated the increasing nebulousness of the term housewife and specifically examined how women professionalize their wifedom in service of personal brands, chapter 4 takes a more broadly industrial approach. Reality wives, I argue, work for their networks, distinguishing these networks' interests as well as segmenting their intended audiences. The shows themselves, as well as the extra- and paratextual offerings featuring their celebrity stars, explore the disappointments of love, the nuances of sexuality, the stresses of family life, the pressures of money, and the dynamics of female communities. These offerings are typically racially and regionally inflected, characterizations that help to particularize the brand identities of their respective broadcasters.

After a brief discussion of the prevalence of emotional labor on wife shows, I focus specifically on three case studies. First, I examine Bravo's flagship *Real Housewives* franchise, arguing that the brand identity now associated with the network, particularly its identification with upscale luxury, high fashion, and trendsetting lifestyles, can be traced directly to this programming. The housewife has been of seminal and foundational importance to Bravo's courting of its self-styled "affluencers." Bravo's *Real Housewives* also set the terms for wives shows that followed on other networks, specifically by focalizing on female competition as operationalized through fighting. I close this section with an investigation of *The Real Housewives of Atlanta*, a program that bears a different representational burden thanks to its racial makeup and whose introduction of racial diversity to the franchise has proven to be a boon for Bravo.

The influence of Bravo's *Real Housewives* series can obviously be felt in my second case study, which concentrates on VH1 and its spate of wifely programs, specifically *Basketball Wives* (2010–13), *Football Wives* (2010), *Basketball Wives LA* (2011–16), and *Mob Wives* (2011–16). In total, these offerings call on Bravo's tradition of foregrounding acrimonious female relationships. At the same time, they quite self-consciously speak back to Bravo and to the assumption of whiteness and privilege that has circumscribed wifely discourse. In this way, VH1 intervenes in a televisual landscape that has typically ignored the intimate lives of women of color. Specifically focusing on *Basketball Wives* and *Mob Wives*, the discussion highlights how these shows bring together women whom men have betrayed and whose fissures stem primarily from sexual competition. Observing that many of VH1's reality stars continue to relive their romantic disappointments, I argue that the network's wifely brand puts patriarchy at the center of its investigations, offering a female perspective on what have historically been male-dominated realms.

The chapter ends with a brief discussion of TLC's *Sister Wives* (2010–), *Extreme Cougar Wives* (2012), and *My Five Wives* (2013–14), offerings that align with TLC's unofficial status as a "freak show" network featuring anomalous families and domestic tensions. These offerings distill and intensify the sort of pressures and representational codes that this book has traced throughout. Specifically, I discuss how *Extreme Cougar Wives* engages in conversations about parity in marital economies, while *Sister Wives* and *My Five Wives* echo wifely television's focus on female communities, highlighting the implied sexual competition between women.

Emotional Labor and Wifely Reality TV

By way of an extensive rhetorical analysis of *The Real Housewives* reunion specials, Lauren Squires reminds us that "disclosure is normative." More pointedly, participating in a reality show means at least to some extent forgoing one's private life. Faced with a fellow New York housewife who refuses to characterize the nature of a relationship with a certain man ("Whether I'm dating someone or not is really none of your business"), the other housewives correct her, stating, "We're on a *reality television* show."[1] In a different exchange, this one with the Beverly Hills cast during a reunion show, cast member Brandi Glanville says, "I think when you sign up for a reality show you don't get—you don't get to *have* a secret." Both exchanges express cognizance of a set of work rules underpinned by compulsory transparency; as these wives understand so well, refusing access to one's personal life constitutes a violation of the terms of employment.

This section will look at the type of labor required of a reality television wife, beginning with the identification of reality television as a genre with unique implications for female communities. Noting that women's culture was the first "mass-marketed intimate public in the United States of significant scale," Lauren Berlant describes what she terms "the sentimental bargain of femininity": "The emotional labor of women places them at the center of the *story* of what counts as life, regardless of what lives women actually live: the conjecture of family and romance so structures the emergence of modern sexuality, with its conflation of sexual and emotional truths, and in that nexus femininity marks the scene of the reproduction of life as a project."[2] Berlant's claim that feminine emotions become the centerpiece of "life as a project" reverberates with wifely television and specifically the foregrounding of affect on these shows. The requirement to place emotions at the center of the display serves as something of a feedback loop, where the requirement of being a professional female necessitates performing as a female is already thought to act. Put another way, the sort of histrionics that characterize wifely television reproduce and circulate the ascriptions typically attached to women, namely, emotionality, irrationality, and an inability to distinguish between a perceived slight and an actual injustice. Reality television also pointedly sutures the emotional life of women to sexual and romantic realms, as if to suggest that these experiences most deserve hand-wringing (and often rancor), and are the predominant concern of female lives. What Berlant terms the "conflation of sexual and emotional truths" anchors wifely television. In these myopic worlds, displayed emotions tend to be the only ones that carry currency—hence, the incessant attention paid to how the women feel about themselves, one another, and their primary domestic connections.

To be sure, women's emotionality structures the reality format writ large and is not confined to wifely television per se. As Katherine Sender asserts, also calling on Berlant, "With its domestic location, use of the close-up shot, and emphasis on women's discourse and concerns, reality television is a 'technology of intimacy' particularly well-placed to construct this sense of an intimate public in prime time."[3] Similarly, Beverley Skeggs suggests that women's emotional labor fundamentally animates the genre: "Reality television is premised on spectacularly visualizing women's affective labor through its focus on relationships, dispositions, and emotional performance."[4] Emotional management of relationships likewise circumscribes the narrative arcs that do exist on wifely shows wherein women navigate love, friendship, and child rearing in public terms. Moreover, the relationships between women organize the content of wife shows as wives doggedly and oftentimes treacherously negotiate relationships with one another.

Despite a nomenclature that suggests otherwise, reality wife shows prominently visualize the emotional work of female friendships, even at times more so than they engage with issues of romance or sexuality. In this rendering, friendship registers as a bond comprising a network of affections, resentments, and jealousies. Participation in these circuits of emotion therefore requires putting one's own life in conversation with those of the other women featured on the show. As Emma Lieber observes, *The Real Housewives* grants each cast member her own story line via the confessionals, where the women privately self-disclose to the camera how they are (or were) feeling about a certain event. This structure offers the wife the opportunity to articulate her own point of view. Yet, her simultaneous appearance in another woman's plot "counters this self-regard by making her, for that moment, merely a character in another protagonist's story . . . In all these cases, the structures serve as architectural embodiments of the ethical necessities and unavoidable difficulties of cosmic space-sharing."[5] More than merely a philosophical exercise, reality shows interrogate whether various embodiments of femininity can coexist. Taken to extremes, these shows raise the question of whether and why it is worth attempting reconciliation.

The drama of these negotiations is, indeed, the bread and butter of wifely television. It would nevertheless be disingenuous not to place wifely television in the realm of market economics. Despite the salient issues these programs raise about love and friendship, women appearing as wives receive compensation for this work, with their employability premised on how adroitly they can meet the demands of their producers and publics. Characterizing workers on reality television as "hybrid person-characters," theorist Alison Hearn charges that their "work/lives are, apparently, one seamless flow of value generation . . . being *is* labor and produces value, both for the individual person-characters and for their producers and networks, such as MTV or Bravo."[6] It is difficult to know, of course, the extent to which a reality wife has been exhorted to behave in a certain way or coaxed into playing up a certain character type or trait. For Hearn, reality show stars "perform to a 'format'; their performances of selfhood are completely conditioned by the show's narrative conceits, aesthetic concerns, production exigencies, and sponsorship imperatives."[7] Hearn's characterization of the industry forces cognizance of how routinely formats and franchises determine content. Though various reality wives claim to be presenting their authentic selves, the women construct their performances under the auspices of a network that likely already has a wifely brand. Likewise, as cable markets segment according to gender, taste cultures, racial and ethnic identity, and particularized interests, the need for wives to perform in ways that comply with their network's specific brand profile grows ever more acute.[8]

Encouraged to manufacture drama, wives know the parameters for performance and attempt to meet producers' expectations. I borrow this notion from Laura Grindstaff who, after her observation of the filming of an MTV college reality show called *Sorority Life* (2002–4), wrote that

Figure 4.1. Literally laboring for wifedom on season 8 of *The Real Housewives of Orange County*, Gretchen Rossi staged a surprise marriage proposal to longtime partner Slade Smiley. Rossi was nevertheless let go the next season. Photograph courtesy of Bauer-Griffin.

producers construct the "contexts of performance."[9] The producers' desire to fan the flames of conflict between young women seems analogous to the conditions of production for wifely shows, and Grindstaff notes that producers stage scenarios in order to maximize the opportunity for charged events to happen. Although the women appearing on *Sorority Life* did not receive exact instruction about how to act, they nevertheless experienced tremendous pressure to appear interesting and provocative, which manifested in excessive drinking and partying.[10] The women knew the cultural scripts for females their ages and vocalized a desire to comply with dictates, which, according to Grindstaff, include "behaviors like cattiness, competitiveness, and back-stabbing."[11] The same could well be said of reality wives who, in the words of Jane Feuer, "structure their lives to follow the formula."[12]

As I began to explore at the end of the previous chapter, reality wives understand that being expressive and even controversial constitutes part of the job. Consider the following admission by original Orange County housewife Vicki Gunvalson, gathered by Martina Baldwin, who interviewed Gunvalson as part of Baldwin's dissertation research: "If there's no drama, there's no show. So we know that. We all call it 'camera balls.' When we turn the camera on, it's go time. . . . So we know we have a job to do when those cameras turn on. That's it. We have to talk about somebody, we have to throw the bomb, we have to be doing something, we have to be. That's why I've been on it 8 years. So, camera turns on, I gotta do my job, camera turns off, I go back to work."[13] Gunvalson suggests that in essence she has two jobs: her reality star appearances and her work as an insurance agent. Because wifely reality television has tended to promote a catfight mentality, wives face pressure to manufacture fights in order to legitimize their presence on their respective shows and meet network expectations.

Moreover, the requirement for wives to be inflammatory and controversial exists as something of an open secret, particularly for casts where fights and drama represent a significant portion of narrative content. As Terry Nelson argues, specifically as it relates to reality television shows featuring African American women like *The Real Housewives of Atlanta*, "Passive and docile demeanors and boring and annoying personal lives are not rewarded in shows such as these that strive for and survive off the explosive and volatile personalities that are typified by the African American women."[14] Anecdotally, a number of women have specifically been dismissed from *The Real Housewives of Atlanta* for being too interested in peacekeeping or not interested enough in bullying, including Deshawn Snow and Lisa Wu (formerly Wu-Hartwell). The pressure to perform in salacious ways even apparently fueled Orange County housewife Peggy Tanous's decision to quit the show: "We started meeting with producers to discuss story lines . . . I started getting anxiety thinking about all the forced drama that does happen on occasion."[15]

If financial rewards and job security incentivize fighting, wives who do not perform in this manner risk their own irrelevance and the loss of what may be a lucrative profit stream. "They continually have to convince their producers that they have storylines and, to some degree, a measure of wealthy accoutrements that make them interesting enough to film," observes Kristen Warner. Atlanta housewife Kenya Moore, for example, reportedly faked a romantic relationship to secure a place on the show and misrepresented her economic status to producers, attesting to wealth she did not have. These women must "raise the stakes time and again, often making themselves look quite foolish in order to maintain their financial livelihoods on their respective programs," Warner explains.[16] Often, women need their job on reality television in order to finance the lifestyle that legitimates their appearance on television in the first place.

Like many other jobs, the role of being a reality wife offers perks and risks alike. One of the risks common to many of the shows I examine is that they trade on female relationships, attempting to make them profitable even though these recalibrations may jeopardize affective bonds. To choose one representative example, New York housewife Jill Zarin claims that she staged a fight with Bethenny Frankel for ratings during season 3 of the show, yet she never told this to Frankel. The women's relationship suffered irreparable harm and Zarin was subsequently fired. Examining this episode as an illustration of the delicacy of negotiating emotional bonds within a system of profit and financialization, Jacquelyn Arcy argues, "Blurring the boundaries between affective ties and capitalist exchange, the *Housewives* bring into focus the tensions between irrational emotional behavior and rational entrepreneurial practices. . . . The popularity of the *Housewives'* brands signals their success in parlaying reality television fame into commodity capital, however their failing relationships suggest the contingent and unpredictable effects of administered emotional labor."[17] Despite the exaggerated and patently outlandish events that take place on wifely television, women's participation in this realm can destabilize professional outcomes and personal relationships alike.

Though this section has concentrated primarily on emotional labor, rigid notions of beauty and youth also predominate wifely programming. Surveying myriad scenes where Bravo's housewives undergo cosmetic surgery or merely express angst about their aging bodies and describe the lengths they go to in order to defy the passage of time, Ruth Wollersheim notes, "Body maintenance and disciplining is a key topic in the confessionals as the housewives narrate over footage of spa treatments and cosmetic surgery."[18] Wives labor not only in emotional realms but also in physical ones, clarifying the fact that women put real bodies and real relationships in service of their work on reality television. Whereas these women might undergo such procedures anyway, doing so on reality television undeniably shores up normative ideas of femininity. Likewise, embodied norms tend to bespeak class status. If women who are essentially professional females partake in these activities, female audiences learn that body surveillance and discipline constitute a cornerstone of the bargain of femininity. This ethos doubles, of course, as postfeminist dogma.

Through the case studies that follow, I stress that wives work for their networks in both physical and emotional terms. They also provide a service to female audiences who have flocked to these shows in droves. In each section, I keep this duality in mind. I do not want minimize the women appearing on these shows by framing them as cultural dupes who sell their emotional labor for low wages, nor do I seek to criticize the viewers of these shows. Wife television would not be a widespread global phenomena if it were not in some ways enjoyable and thought provoking. This chapter therefore foregrounds how various networks profit from wives' labor and interrogates why these portrayals carry cultural resonance. Specifically, I believe that various wife shows echo a reality television landscape that has become increasingly segmented, and that these fractures are etched on and indicated by the bodies and appearances of women.

The Real Housewives: Bravo's Juggernaut

In a televisual landscape wherein traditional broadcast and cable networks are quickly losing ground in the face of technological change, the NBC-owned Bravo network has maintained a stronghold in the market, offering advertisers a dedicated and highly coveted audience base. To give one representative statistic from a 2016 Bravo specifications sheet: Bravo was the number one cable network for affluent and educated adults between the ages of eighteen and forty-nine, and nearly one-third of the viewers in this group have a household income of over $100,000 a year.[19] Though there are manifold reasons for Bravo's success, the network in part owes its staying power to its signature brand, *The Real Housewives* franchise. In this section I more precisely quantify the importance of *The Real Housewives* to Bravo, identify the franchise's hallmark features (which have in turn influenced wifely programming on other networks), and investigate the specific value of *The Real Housewives of Atlanta*, Bravo's most popular housewives iteration.

Bravo's status as the go-to network for upscale audiences interested in lifestyle issues has a long history. Beginning initially as an arts channel, most famous for *Inside the Actors Studio* (1994–), Bravo was purchased by NBC in 2002 and quickly tried to find its footing in this larger roster.[20] Known for the sort of highbrow content that appealed to older audiences, Bravo signaled a shift in tone with its introduction of *Queer Eye for the Straight Guy* (2003–7), a makeover show where five gay men gave grooming, manners, housewares, and fashion advice to a hapless straight man, often at the behest of his long-suffering wife or girlfriend.[21] With this program, Bravo indicated an evolution in its network identity, one that would eventually crystalize into a distinctive brand focusing primarily on lifestyle content. *Queer Eye* nevertheless retained the network's upscale ethos, specifically via the inclusion of fashion-conscious gay men. "Bravo tapped into the association between gay men and affluent, high-class style in order to attract audiences to cheap reality programming without risking the low-rent association that reality makeover shows have," argues Katherine Sender. At the same time, and as Sender also reports, gay men tend to appeal to women viewers thanks to "their historical association with taste and fashion, their status as straight women's best friends, and their availability as objects of desire (however unattainable)." Sender calls this "dualcasting" and asserts that gay men's appearances were instrumentalized to attract young, female audiences to this heretofore somewhat stodgy network. Gay men served so well in this capacity because in Sender's rendering they are "trend-setting, affluent, female-friendly, and newsworthy,"[22] an ascription that serves as an apt encapsulation of Bravo's program content and brand appeal. Since this metamorphosis in tone, Bravo has virtually cornered the market on upscale, lifestyle programming.

In 2007, Bravo commissioned a self-study to more fully capture the contours of its audiences and to better comprehend how its turn toward glossy, reality television programs was enticing advertiser-coveted demographics. Subsequent to this study, Bravo coined the phrase "affluencer" to suggest the sort of audience member that it most actively sought to court. The term connotes the union of "influence" and "affluence" and underscores the equal significance of the two. Affluencers exhibit financial prowess and serve as influential brand ambassadors, acting as tastemakers and trendsetters. By codifying its intended market appeal in order to be not only descriptive but also prescriptive, Bravo extended and expanded what was already a recognizable niche. *The Real*

Housewives franchise was in turn instrumental to this effort, crystalizing the Bravo brand by clarifying its values, aesthetic, and appeal.

The Real Housewives franchise both precipitated and reified the affluencer as Bravo's target demographic. Bravo considers itself a premiere lifestyle destination for "food, fashion, beauty, design, digital and pop culture,"[23] and *The Real Housewives* franchise epitomizes such currents, offering itself as a sort of real-life *Sex and the City* wherein fashion, style, makeup, and fancy dining coalesce to provide an aspirational vision of a feminized high life. At the same time, and also like *Sex and the City*, the series purports to focus on female groups. Unlike its predecessor, however, tension and acrimonious exchange characterize these relations.

Bravo's *Housewives* focalize the network's brand and exist as the ground zero of wifely reality television. Perhaps foremost, Bravo's conception of wifedom entails living a life of luxury and privilege, or at least appearing to do so. The women appearing on the shows present audiences with an aspirational vision of femininity that valorizes consumerism, celebrates body modification, and revels in conspicuous consumption, argue Nicole Cox and Jennifer Proffitt.[24] Wealth provides both the mise-en-scène and the narrative impetus for the *Housewives* franchise, which offers viewers the pleasure of being granted access to upscale public spaces, taken inside palatial homes, invited to gala events and high-profile charity auctions, and skirted off to vacations in tropical locales. These public forays are in turn matched with private confessionals wherein housewives offer reflections and comments, and specifically dish on their feelings about the other housewives. Confessionals represent standard fare in reality television, of course, but the fact that these confessionals so closely mirror the franchise's more general aesthetics still merits consideration. Heavily made-up, lavishly accessorized, and elegantly dressed, housewives film confessionals in the plush surroundings of their own homes: "The housewives' professional hair and makeup and the luminous lighting . . . glamorizes the banality of the domestic," observes Pier Dominguez.[25]

Housewives exhibit interest in donning the most stylish and expensive clothes, makeup, and accessories, and testify to their elevated class status through the employment of a cadre of professional assistants, including fashion designers and stylists, publicists, home managers, event coordinators, nannies, and personal assistants. While a number of Bravo's housewives did experience financial troubles, particularly in the wake of the 2008 recession, they rarely moderated their behavior to reflect these struggles. "On the housewife series, even crises can be good spending opportunities. The gals in Orange County are still riding in limos, getting plastic surgery, and going on shopping sprees," Vicki Mayer commented in 2010.[26] This aesthetic dovetails in every way with the affluencer viewer who fashions herself accessing, or deserving access to, similar luxuries. Similarly, the network stresses the quest for opulence as an unassailable prerequisite—the housewives routinely assert their desire to possess lavish houses, enjoy high-end vacations, throw extravagant parties, buy designer clothes, and purchase top-of-the-line cars. In this way, a sense of competition over material goods as well as the status and visibility that such access affords organizes their lives. Similar desires also apparently motivate and inspire Bravo's core viewers.

In a less material sense, Bravo cultivates a demand for perfection vis-à-vis the operationalized existence of success. In the previous chapter, I surveyed the rise of Bethenny Frankel, who served as an example of the sort of upwardly mobile entrepreneur to whom Bravo viewers gravitate. Indeed, reports indicate that the network awarded Frankel her own spin-off series thanks to the popularity she enjoyed with audiences.[27] Frankel's rise is but one testament to Jorie Lagerwey's observation that the network offers "a complex celebration of female economic power and entrepreneurialism." The women on the network devote personal labor to the creation of "self-as-brand," which Lagerwey dubs the "Working on Me Tendency."[28] This ethos represents a common theme in *Housewives* programming since women typically strive for some goal, be it greater fame, a more fulfilling relationship, or simply a bigger house. Though fractured by their fallouts, Bravo's housewives unite in their desire to accumulate money, love, or professional accolades. As Jane Feuer puts it, Bravo's programming is "about lifestyle desire and its vicissitudes."[29] As affluent, educated, social connectors, Bravo's viewers are likewise ambitious about their lives, their looks, and their social capital, attributes the housewives consistently model.

The housewives' respective narratives incorporate their roles as style moguls and trendsetters—many plotlines revolve around their businesses, products, or fund-raising efforts. Recognizing that the housewives sell not only a series of products but also a sense of a glossy lifestyle,

Peter Bjelskou calls the women "branded socialite entrepreneurs."[30] In the previous chapter, I surveyed the housewife's historical designation as a consumer of household goods. Bravo's housewives serve as a direct extension of that legacy in a neoliberal age. Toasters, refrigerators, and washing machines—that is, objects that serve the family—have in turn been replaced with objects that serve the self. Accessing glamour and luxury via personal goods exists as the housewives' raison d'être, as does making that sensibility available for the viewer's consumption via the programs and the housewives' associated product lines. In 2015 *E! News* (also owned by NBC) ran an only somewhat satirical article titled "I Went 24 Hours Using Only *Real Housewives* Products and Life Became a Lot More Fabulous."[31] It chronicles the foods, drinks, accessories, stores, restaurants, books, and advice that the housewives purvey and offers the tongue-in-cheek thesis that by using these products the consumer, too, becomes chic and fabulous. While this article serves primarily to advertise the housewives' manifold goods, it likewise highlights their implicit promise of affording the consumer a seemingly more rich existence.

Some have argued, of course, that the pleasure of watching *The Real Housewives* programming derives not from aspirationalism but rather that viewers enjoy the opportunity to deride the housewives' more abject qualities. *Real Housewives* executive producer Andy Cohen confirmed that the network intentionally shows the housewives in a less-than-flattering light, specifically focusing on their hypocrisies: "We do something with the editing that is called the Bravo wink. We wink at the audience when someone says 'I'm the healthiest person in the world' and then you see them ashing their cigarette. We're kind of letting the audience in on the fun."[32] The network frequently undercuts its housewives, showing them to be vain, catty, superficial, or materialistic. Bravo, explains Jorie Lagerwey, "simultaneously promotes its performers, their products, and the luxurious lives they appear to lead, while conspiring with middle- and upper-middle-class consumers to mock and discipline their out-of-reach consumption and out-of-bounds behavior."[33]

This strategy also dovetails with the presentation of the housewives' now-notorious fights by granting viewers a chance to take a bird's-eye view of the women's foibles. "The show's mockery and prosecution of tremendously wealthy women may also let the merely affluent Bravo audience off the hook," speculate Michael Lee and Leigh Moscowitz. "In their role as viewer-judge, they may conclude that some rich people do their class comically wrong."[34] A distanced perspective also allows viewers to better position themselves as savvy observers who are in on the joke. This perspective, I have argued elsewhere, is a hallmark of the post-feminist mediascape, and here I would suggest that the fights do serve this purpose. At the same time, they also allow viewers to witness these women suffering from affective disappointments and gain insight into the vagaries of female groups.

In a nuanced reading of the prevalence of fighting on the *Housewives* franchise, Pier Dominguez argues that "the docusoap genre works by offering disorienting and anxiety-inducing explosions of affect that are then followed by cathartic discussions of emotion (focused on understanding the previous outbursts), creating for viewers a sense of connection with the program and its cast through their ability to witness these moments of intimate discord." Situated as bystanders to the emotional immediacy of these disagreements, viewers are invited to consider the affective weight these encounters carry. Moreover, thanks to the franchise's intense focus on personal relationships, scholars have placed *The Real Housewives* within the tradition of melodrama, which "publicizes and spectacularizes the private and the everyday."[35] Read in this light, the housewives' fights serve to negotiate feminine emotions and domestic identities in formats that have typically appealed to female viewers.

Melodrama offers exaggerated caricatures and prioritizes intimate bonds. As a result, critics deride the form for being too emotional, too sensationalized, and too overwrought, a charge also leveled at *The Real Housewives*. Yet, much as melodrama's excesses belied serious occasions of repression, abuse, and othering, housewives do navigate emotionally fraught issues, struggling with waning finances, failed business ventures, strained marriages, fractured families, and parenting challenges. The pressures undeniably influence the show's battles, which have featured, among others, divorcing spouses, allegations of partner abuse, attempts to save a marriage after infidelity, revelations of alcoholism, and insults between feuding family members. While these skirmishes may at the same time involve petty slights, invented injuries, and salacious gossip—typically, these are the sort depicted between female cast members—the housewives' altercations testify to a willingness to acknowledge, in classically melodramatic terms, the secrets that lie beneath the surface of manicured lives. (This observation again highlights the link between the fictionalized melodrama *Desperate Housewives* and *The Real Housewives* franchise.)

At the same time, these disputes are taken decidedly outside the context of the domestic. In this way, wifedom exists as a public identity, as this book has been arguing throughout. Not only are these injuries, slights, and divisions filmed, often in public places, but they are also in turn inflamed by the paratextual materials associated with the show, and relived during the show's airings, reunion shows, and the Andy Cohen–helmed *Watch What Happens Live* (2009–).[36] Housewives keep these feuds alive via social media, specifically by tweeting (including during the show's broadcast), writing in the Bravo-sponsored blogs about each other, and granting interviews where they discuss these fractures. This description elucidates the sort of emotional labors that I wrote about previously and confirms how closely the show hews to soap opera formats wherein drama is prolonged, reconciliation is promised and then deferred or reneged, friendship and relationships are interrupted and disrupted and often never fully healed. Moreover, social media, reunion shows, and real-time occurrences (including calls and questions from viewers) on *Watch What Happens Live* provide a sense of immediacy to squabbles that may have occurred months ago, as Martina Baldwin argues.[37] The mediatization of these fissures serves to reinflame tensions and prolong the quarrels' drama, hence cultivating viewer engagement and investment. In this way, Bravo circulates a continuous affective register of hope, betrayal, aspiration, and disappointment.

This section closes with a meditation on *The Real Housewives of Atlanta* because it is the most popular Bravo *Housewives* series, has inspired the highest number of spin-offs, and also serves a niche function with respect to the network's programming. Developed in 2008, *The Real Housewives of Atlanta* represented the third installment in the Bravo franchise, following *The Real Housewives of Orange County* and *New York*, respectively, both of which featured all-white casts. Bravo's introduction of a predominantly black *Housewives* series complied in troubling ways with a pattern in media representation where black casts or characters serve merely as token additions or mirror already established formats, argues Catherine Squires. The solution to the "problem" of the *Housewives* all-white casts, she acerbically notes, was the Atlanta spin-off, "with an almost all-black cast, with one white wife. Problem solved!"[38] The show delivered Bravo another lucrative market—black women—and participated in the franchise's already established heuristics and optics.[39] At the same time, the inclusion of the white Kim Zolciak (who nevertheless claims to be "a black woman trapped in a white woman's body") suggests the network's interest in retaining and performing outreach to its white audiences.[40]

Filmed in what has been called "Black Hollywood," the show focalized on Atlanta's elite women and continued the franchise's normalized configuration of hurt feelings, insults, and misunderstandings set against the backdrop of public outings and functions such as lunches, shopping, and party planning. It also continued Bravo's interest in female entrepreneurs, featuring luminaries like songwriter and music producer Kandi Burruss, model Cynthia Bailey, and entertainment attorney Phaedra Parks. Yet, the show drew attention to race in a way that none of its predecessors did, once again calling on black lives to be the standard-bearers of race coding. "In the premiere episode, the words *African American* or *Black* are mentioned no less than three times in the first thirty seconds, all before the opening credits. The background music common to all of the *Housewives* shows was given a pronounced drumbeat for the Atlanta edition, adding a tinge of hip hop flavor to its various scenes," Racquel Gates points out.[41] *The Real Housewives of Atlanta* transparently invokes racial histories, tensions that pointedly animate interpersonal conflicts. During a group holiday to South Africa, a black cast member tells the white cast member, Kim, that another of the housewives said that she couldn't see Kim "holding any black babies," as Catherine Squires documents. The women have to work through the misunderstanding, and Squires observes that telling on people for saying racially, sexually, or class-charged things is a favorite driver of drama "on the 'wives'-type shows."[42]

While all the *Housewives* installments have a local flavor and highlight certain regionalized attributes in a cosmetic sense (e.g., in their opening credits the Orange County housewives hold oranges, the New York housewives hold apples, and the Atlanta housewives hold peaches), only the Atlanta show is called on by Bravo to arbitrate American race relations. For example, whereas the whiteness of the cast in other *Housewives* iterations goes largely unremarked on, the need to make blackness visible and legible directly informed the introduction and presentation of housewife Porsha Williams, granddaughter of civil rights leader and philanthropist Rev. Hosea Williams, who had close ties to Martin Luther King Jr. Williams's first confessional on the show cuts in historical photographs of King and Hosea Williams and features her donating $10,000 to and volunteering with the Hosea Williams Feed the Hungry Foundation. "This introduction to Porsha, through her history, deliberately positions her within a trajectory of the history of race in America," Ruth Wollersheim contends.[43] It was doubly scandalous, then, that during a filmed group holiday in Savannah and a visit to the iconic First Baptist Church, Williams betrayed her ignorance of the fact that the Underground Railroad was not actually a running train. Much like Jessica Simpson's infamous "chicken of the sea" question,[44] this was seen as a moment of shocking ignorance. It was also a sequence Bravo happily exposed using the Bravo wink.

To be sure, all the *Housewives* shows in some ways lampoon their casts and feature women who behave in ways that register as rude and outrageous. Nevertheless, only the Atlanta cast's outlandish behaviors exist in a realm of racialized signification; many have accused the program of reifying stereotypes of black women. As Gretta Moody documents in her audience study of black female viewers watching season 3 of *The Real Housewives of Atlanta*, viewers exhibit awareness that producers frame narratives within a racialized matrix that highlights the women's assumed character flaws. As Moody writes, "Discussion of perceived stereotypes—black women are angry, controlling, or gold digging, have no use for men, and contribute to dysfunction in families—emerged across focus groups." Moody's viewers nevertheless rejected these attributions, pointing to their constructed nature: "Black viewers in this study built racial boundaries to separate themselves from producers, who were perceived as outsiders . . . for all the participants, the 'producers' represented an outside force that pushed the housewives beyond the 'proper' boundaries of blackness."[45] In keeping with the notion that the producers invite and reward certain types of racialized performances, it also bears noting the show's stars are known for their famous quips and dismissive one-liners ("Whose gon check me, boo?"; "I'm rich, bitch!") and for introducing new compounds like "boughetto" ("bougie" meets "ghetto"), identifications that comply with a generalized stereotype of the sassy black woman and are born out of a discriminatory racial imagination. Finally, it has been argued that Atlanta's housewives are more sexualized and depicted as more violent and aggressive than are other *Housewives* casts.[46]

On the other hand, some believe that the show participates in a trajectory of racial uplift and material success and that the net effect is to model the attainability and desirability of wealth. Speculating that *The Real Housewives of Atlanta*'s popularity can be traced in part to its "narrative of urban success, echoing *Sex and the City*," Cynthia Davis observes that the show consistently depicts the entrepreneurial achievements, philanthropy, and family relations of women who are "educated, articulate, affluent, aspirational, fashionable, and family oriented."[47] This description illustrates how successfully the show complies with Bravo's brand, yet it is also true that the primary cast members' blackness and their representability in a larger arena of respectability politics remains inescapable.

As a black offering on a predominantly white network, *The Real Housewives of Atlanta* has from its inception been in dialogue with the white imaginary. For one, and as I documented in the previous chapter, whiteness circumscribes the housewife ideal regardless of the housewife's status as a real woman and or media creation. "White women are the face of traditional housewifery," Robin Boylorn points out.[48] Bravo's casting of the Atlanta show after the parameters of its franchise had largely been set by white women only served to participate in and propagate this exclusionary legacy. While speaking to a black cast member who began appearing on the show a few years after she did, Leakes articulates this tension: "You had an opportunity to watch us. When I came on this show I didn't have anything to watch. We had the [*Real Housewives of*] *Orange County* girls but they are white with blonde hair, and I am a brown girl, and we didn't have anything to watch."[49] Lacking role models, and appearing on a network that reaffirms whiteness as the upper-class standard, Leakes usefully points out the disenfranchised position in which Bravo placed her and her original cast mates. At the same time, Leakes has been savvy in her understanding that *The Real Housewives of Atlanta*'s success relies in part on its diversification of Bravo's roster, and she has used this difference as a platform to bolster her own celebrity. In a 2012 interview with *The Insider*, she attributed the popularity of the show to its centralization of what she called "brown girls," asserting that thanks to their honesty and lack of plastic surgery, the Atlanta wives are "keepin' it real" in a way that the other housewives are not.[50] Here, Leakes seems to call on the long-standing and yet troubling perception that it is "cool to possess the vitality, originality, and magnetism black people as a whole seem to imbue."[51]

The Real Housewives of Atlanta's reputation as the most affectively engaging show in the Bravo *Housewives* lineup (which is no small feat given the oversized personalities that pepper all its offerings) should be credited at least in part to this segregated racialized imaginary. More bluntly, Bravo benefits from the wives' willingness to act in ways that both echo and ratchet up the intensity of the other programs. Noting how the show engages a logic whereby outbursts are followed by explanations and recontexualizations that serve to preserve and yet defer "thrilling anxiety," Dominguez writes that "Bravo uses the performance and affective labor of black women to mark black racialized gendered excess as 'trashier,' more embodied, more excessive." Bravo therefore profits from what Dominguez calls "the affective excess of black femininity."[52] The use of black programming to confer on predominantly white networks a differentiated identity via an altered affective register has been helpfully parsed by Jennifer Fuller, who asserts that "cable channels' uses of blackness should be understood as a method of cultivating brand identities with transracial appeal."[53] Fuller speaks mainly about quality television shows intended to convey edginess and urbanity, and thus Bravo's deployment of blackness is a variation on that theme. Specifically, the Atlanta cast's blackness amplifies qualities already associated with the franchise such as vulgar materialism, solipsistic self-interest, and frank putdowns of other women. In this way, blackness registers not so much as distinct but simply as more intense.

Black female viewers have also greeted the show with genuine enthusiasm, excitement recorded in their viewership and via their social media habits. Black women represent a loyal and engaged viewership, buttressing Bravo's profile as a network that cultivates dedication via social media. In an article where they coin the term "black social TV," Sherri Williams and Lynessa Williams argue that black women exist as a cornerstone to salvaging real-time television viewership thanks to their enthusiastic and frequent use of social media technologies. Black au-

Figure 4.2. NeNe Leakes at the Golden Globes in 2013, her celebrity image having transcended her stint on *The Real Housewives of Atlanta*. Photograph courtesy of Bauer-Griffin.

diences watch more television than do other demographics, and black Internet users have a particularly strong presence on Twitter, where trending topics often reflect black-themed shows, they assert. Williams and Williams point specifically to the controversial Atlanta second season reunion special, which "generated seven trending topics on Twitter including the phrase 'Poor Kandi,' in reference to viewers' feelings about housewife Kandi Burruss' mother meddling in her relationship." The Atlanta housewives also received extensive treatment as the subjects of Instagram memes.[54] While Bravo does not separate out the racial demographics of its audience members, and therefore it is impossible to know the extent to which black viewers account for Bravo's popularity, Atlanta's visibility in the terrain of social media is undeniably helping to bolster the network's profile.

In his memoir, Andy Cohen notes of *The Real Housewives* that "every series has its own flavor; OC is cul-de-sac normality. Atlanta is campy and over the top. Jersey is hot-tempered and clannish. DC was thoughtful and provocative. Beverly Hills is image-conscious and *this* close to Hollywood. Miami is spicy and tele-novelic. New York is aggressive and controlling."[55] Cohen's words atomize the juggernaut that is Bravo's *Real Housewives* franchise, suggesting that female cast members' bodies, interests, ethnicities, and attitudes have been commodified in service of audience segmentation. Through a savvy blend of regional specificity, anchored by an underlying consistency of affluence, the *Housewives* franchise epitomizes Bravo's interest in presenting an aspirational femininity that is heavily stylized. If anything, the women themselves are like the fashions and accessories featured on the show, whereby they serve to convey a regionalized and racialized image and affect. This winning combination has in turn inspired a number of copycats.

VH1's Wife Franchise

Beginning in the early 2000s, the Viacom-owned VH1 network transformed itself from the soft-pop sister of MTV to a more racially and culturally diverse channel anchored by a nostalgic approach to pop culture as well as numerous reality offerings. Hitching its wagon to "celebreality," a term the network coined to describe a programming slate comprising "celebrity" "reality" television, during this period shows such as *The Surreal Life* (2003–6), *Flavor of Love* (2006–8), and *Celebrity Rehab with Dr. Drew* (2008–12) branded the network as the go-to site for celebrity meltdown, sensationalized behavior, and carnivalesque dating. It was during this phase that VH1 began to make irony a defining feature of its nostalgia, notes Jon Kraszewski. This branding effort also invested heavily in the notion of hip hop's broad demographic appeal. When CEO Tom Calderone took over the network in 2005, "he envisioned hip hop as a sincere nostalgic experience that could bring in viewers from various racial backgrounds," Kraszewski reports.[56] Nostalgia for hip hop became instrumentalized as a vehicle for VH1 to market to a broad, racially diverse audience; at the same time, hip hop's incorporation into the wider capitalist marketplace was accompanied by a flattening of its racial and cultural politics. This strategy also coincides with Jennifer Fuller's observation that "blackness operated on cable as a signifier for 'quality' and 'edginess' in the 1990s and early 2000s."[57]

Flavor of Love, which I discussed in chapter 2, was likewise a defining show in VH1's brand trajectory and an important precursor to the wife shows that now dominate its roster and represent some of the network's most profitable and popular offerings. As a black-centered dating program, *Flavor of Love* spoke back to NBC's *The Bachelor*, self-consciously flipping the racial profile of the cast. Writing in 2008, Rachel Dubrofsky and Antoine Hardy pointed out at the time that "*Flavor of Love* is the only version of a love story about Black people in the RTV [reality TV] landscape."[58] *Flavor of Love*'s popularity, as well as that of its spin-offs *I Love New York* (2007–8) and *Flavor of Love Girls: Charm School* (2007), confirmed the existence of a sizable audience of viewers interested in campy drama, outsize personalities, and performative animosity, all of which VH1 would later mine for its wife shows. VH1's ability to attract attention for its programming slate spoke also to a dearth of programming about and for women of color, particularly African American women.

Much as it did by revamping *The Bachelor* into the campy *Flavor of Love*, VH1's development of its *Wives* franchise was a self-conscious reboot of Bravo's predominantly white *Real Housewives*, turning a popular and yet exclusionary format into a more populist and exaggerated offering. Borrowing the *Housewives* form and format, VH1's wifely programs concentrate on groups of female friends who engage in catty interplay, generally against the backdrop of glamorized surroundings. I include *Basketball Wives*, *Mob Wives*, *Love and Hip Hop*, and their various regionalized spin-offs in my conceptualization of VH1's *Wives* franchise, though my discussion here will focus primarily on *Basketball Wives* and *Mob Wives*, the two offerings that blatantly use wifely terminology. (VH1 also quite distinctly organized its reality programing around heteronormative life phases for black women, including in its repertoire dating shows, wife and girlfriend shows, couple shows, and marriage and family shows. At the same time, the cast members in these shows rarely follow that scripted and prescriptive ordering that demands dating or even monogamy exist as precursors to commitments like marriage and childbearing.) VH1 also significantly upped the ante on Bravo by diversifying its shows' casts and concerns and inflaming their conflicts. Whereas the disputes featured on various Bravo series read primarily as verbal skirmishes, in many of VH1's wifely programs verbal and physical fights constitute a majority of a show's airtime. At the same time, VH1's wifely offerings far more acutely narrate the disappointments of patriarchy, presenting a treatise on sexual competition and sexual betrayal, at times to poignant effect.

Basketball Wives investigates the wives, girlfriends, and ex-girlfriends of famous basketball players, commenting on the relationships between them and implicitly showcasing the competition that a scarce marital economy creates. From the very opening when star and producer Shaunie O'Neal reveals that after seven years married to Shaquille O'Neal she has filed for divorce, the show foregrounds a melancholy ethos. O'Neal's opening salvo states, "Beyond the bling, we deal with all kinds of craziness, from cheating, to groupies, to loneliness." An early shot in the pilot episode features her putting a lone duffel bag into an SUV. In addition to invoking the basketball player's iconic gym bag, the prop serves a metonymic function with respect to the idea of leaving a bad marriage, suggesting that the departure exists as a solitary and unglamorous pursuit. *Basketball Wives* quickly offers a remedy in the form of female groups, claiming that women can weather these personal storms together. Whereas Bravo's housewives typically use intro sections to emphasize their wealth, independence, and/or blustery bravado, *Basketball Wives* ostensibly brings together women who have in some way been hurt by men and who continue to relive the trauma of those betrayals. Their communal sense of the emotional turmoil generated by

Figure 4.3. The placement and stance of the cast of VH1's *Basketball Wives* mimics the publicity surrounding Bravo's *Real Housewives* franchise. Photograph courtesy of Photofest.

their proximity to the men who inhabit the realm of professional athletics stitches together this otherwise disparate group.

The specter of male philandering and the toll it takes haunts the series, inflecting and infecting the relationships between the women. Defined by their relation to each other in what might be termed an economy of adultery, the featured wives on *Basketball Wives* have been cheated on, fear being cheated on, have been a party to someone else's cheating, or are suspiciously appraised by the other women to be the type of woman that their husbands or boyfriends might cheat *with*. Where a woman falls on this spectrum has a deterministic effect on her status in the group. One of the most fractious members of the first season of *Basketball Wives* is Gloria Govan, a woman who vocally and often arrogantly reaffirms her relationship's imperviousness to these temptations and whose sister allegedly slept with Shaquille O'Neal, realities that immediately place her at odds with the other wives and specifically ring leader Shaunie O'Neal. Govan's self-righteous assertions of her loyalty to her sister, as well as her repeated insistence of her situational distance from the other women because she enjoys a relationship with her fiancé, Matt Barnes, characterized by trusting openness repeatedly garners exasperation from the other wives. Similarly, the young, unapologetic Royce Reed elicits suspicion and even rebuke from the older wives. Reed formerly worked as a dancer for the Orlando Magic, and she is repeatedly scripted as a threat or an outcast for her suggested sexual provocations.

In her writings about female publics, Lauren Berlant has coined the term "the female complaint," which she refers to as a "discourse of disappointment." Specifically, Berlant points out the coexistence of fantastical ideals with harsh realities, observing that "the fantasy dictum that love ought to be the gift that keeps on giving is a fundamental commitment of female complaint rhetoric. The position of the depressive realist who sees that love is nonetheless the gift that keeps on taking is the source of complaint epistemology." Berlant also speaks of the bargaining that women do to "stay in proximity to the work of love at the heart of normative femininity," zeroing in on the "utopian and pathetic impulses behind this bargaining, and its costs and pleasures."[59] This definition provides an explanatory heuristic for the conflicts on *Basketball Wives* since love's many broken promises feature prominently in the narrative. It should not go unacknowledged, of course, that wives typically fight with each other rather than the men who have cast them in positions that they clearly find humiliating and belittling. Wives often accuse each other of putting on airs, of not being authentic, of lying to, humiliating, backstabbing, or disrespecting each other. Yet, in an ontological sense, they rail against their devaluation in a sexual economy where increasing age works against them and where the imposed distance between them and their partners provides ample physical and psychological space for betrayal.

As the wives see it, other competitors in the form of other women are all too eager to assume their positions, a usurping that would carry both emotional and financial consequences. Indeed, for many of these women financial security comes from their proximity *to* famous men. They owe their casting on the show, for which they are clearly being paid, to their romantic involvements with basketball stars. Though many of VH1's wives have mounted businesses that rely on their newfound celebrity positioning, at stake in these brawls with other women might be nothing less than these women's livelihoods. As I discussed earlier, not being contentious enough can be cause for dismissal from a show.

Basketball Wives stages uncertainties regarding the supply and devotion of eligible men, insecurities that in actuality organize a larger swath of heterosexual culture, as I outlined in chapter 1. Wives demonstrate cognizance that, simply put, if there are not enough quality men to go around, marriageable men with solid financial futures merit the competition they engender. Though men are in various ways absent from VH1's wifely programs, their presence haunts the conflicts and fortifies the resentments between women. In Berlant's terms, the broken promises of normative heterosexuality underpin these fractures, yet what gets discussed and cathected are these women's broken promises to and betrayals of each other. Unstable marriage economies nevertheless have a particular resonance in communities of African American women, where shortages of eligible men have meant systemic exclusion from the institution. This reality translates on *Basketball Wives* into deep divisions between women who are legally wed; those who are fiancées, girlfriends, or ex-girlfriends; and finally the groupies, with the latter appraised as failing to carry the former's legitimacy.

All the cast members are nevertheless called "wives," a nomenclature that intervenes in a racialized trajectory. "Perhaps the reason that the women on *Basketball Wives* cling so tightly to their 'wife' status is because black women have usually been excluded from an understanding of what it means to be one," speculates Racquel Gates, who also suggests that "it might be productive to view it as an attempt to appropriate the signifiers associated with wifedom that are typically denied to black women: security, legitimacy, and respect."[60] It is crucial to differentiate the term "wife" on *Basketball Wives* from the "housewife" moniker. Whereas chapter 3 examined the loosening of the term "housewife" and argued that it began to signify feminine concerns writ large, *Basketball Wives* manifests a different dynamic, placing black women's sexual and romantic hopes at the center of narratives that have historically excluded them.

Specifically, *Basketball Wives* uses the term "wife" to signal a concern with love, sexuality, and intimacy, and to insist on the importance and relevance of this topic for a group whose concerns rarely register in the popular lexicon. This is not to say that the series features happy or uplifting content. If anything it is quite the opposite, since the shows give voice to insecurities and disappointments that limit, cripple, or curtail the female romantic imaginary. Moreover, there is some evidence that

these difficulties register more distinctly in media that features and is designed to reach black women. Discussions of male infidelity, instruction
about how to accommodate scarcities of well-educated and financially
stable men, and meditations on negotiating men's children from prior
relationships feature more prominently in advice directed toward black
women as opposed to advice targeted for whites, argues Sanja Jagesic.[61]
Given this disparity, VH1's interest in the tribulations of romance and
sexuality offers a different and seemingly quite welcome intervention into
a televisual landscape that has typically ignored the intimate lives of black
women. In offering a capacious reclamation of the moniker of wife, VH1
signals an investment in stories that are, broadly, about love and loss.

This interest in the vicissitudes of black female experience extends
throughout VH1's wifely franchise. *Love and Hip Hop: New York* (2011–)
begins with a female voice-over claiming that "behind the Bentleys and
the bling, hip hop is a brutal boys club; and for a woman trying to get
hers, it can be a real grind." *Love and Hip Hop*—now a franchise of its
own including *Love and Hip Hop: Atlanta* (2012–) and *Love and Hip
Hop: Hollywood* (2014–)—collectively frames the struggles of women to
break into the hip hop industry or to be recognized, appreciated, and/or
wed by its notoriously noncommittal men. At the same time, the women
are typically taken advantage of, lied to, and routinely humiliated, and
they lash out against the men who have hurt them and the women they
perceive to have been party to that hurt. As Gates writes of both *Basketball Wives* and *Love and Hip Hop*, they explore "the joys and tensions of
messy interpersonal relationships," and "present the raw emotions that
black women experience in these situations."[62] VH1's wifely franchise
also tends to rehearse difficulties that have emotional, physical, and financial consequences such as child support, single parenthood, romantic disappointment and betrayal, and sexual competition. In this, VH1 is
again raising the stakes on Bravo. Whereas the slightest social injury (oftentimes a catty insult directed toward one real housewife from another)
can extend into a weeks-long feud on Bravo, VH1's wives negotiate issues that often have deep financial and emotional consequences. This
casting of women who struggle, often violently, nevertheless carries risk
insofar as they participate in an American media sphere that unfairly
situates portrayals of African American women as representative and
totalizing rather than individual and situational.

Many have made the argument that by illustrating black women at odds with one another in toxic and sometimes violent ways, shows like *Basketball Wives* only reify troubling stereotypes surrounding black women's sexuality. To provide one of many representative examples, consider a chagrinned *Essence* magazine writer who charged that "these shows seem to feature one type of woman most prominently: She's irrational, unreasonable, oversexed and violent, and more often than not she's so lacking in self-regard she's willing to be humiliated publicly by the man she claims to love. In short, the women on these shows often represent the worst stereotypes ever hurled at us. Tacky. Violent. Ho."[63] Dismissals like these largely fail to take into account these programs' appeal to black women or their intense popularity. Building on the assertion that mediated representation offers African American women a site of belonging and pleasure, Kristin Warner suggests that though the outcomes may be bruising, "the issues causing the fights, such as jealousy or rivalry, are central to communal conversations among black women, which must deal with not-so-gentle issues." Moreover, "in between those moments of foolishness lay questions for black women about how they viewed themselves and their worth."[64] Warner's assertions about the serious and all-too-real issues at play in offerings like *Basketball Wives* help to explain their appeal. "Shows like *Love and Hip Hop, Basketball Wives*, and other unapologetically trashy reality television programs provide a safe space for emotional and psychological catharsis and for the exploration of complicated, messy, or 'negative' feelings," explains Gates.[65] VH1 has in this sense capitalized on the relative dearth of representations of black women's love lives and on audiences' hunger for real conversations about betrayal, disrespect, and humiliation in the areas of both romance and friendship. This hunger is in turn fed by shows like *Basketball Wives, Love and Hip Hop*, and the aforementioned *The Real Housewives of Atlanta*.[66] Wives work for their networks and also for audiences, offering them a cultural touchstone in what was heretofore a rather bereft landscape. Both Bravo and VH1 have profited from these representational voids.

This is not to argue that all African American audiences have willingly embraced these divisive portrayals. As *Essence* reports, Shaunie O'Neal was quite distressed by the direction of *Basketball Wives*, especially in its later seasons when the brawling became even more sensationalized.

"*Basketball Wives* was supposed to highlight us as strong, independent women," she asserted. "I went to VH1 and said, 'We need to be more positive,' and showed them viewer e-mails." According to O'Neal, she was reminded of her status as a businesswoman and told to continue. She claims, "The problem is that at the end of the day, the network decides what it wants."[67] After a controversial fourth season, the fifth season of *Basketball Wives* attempted to rehabilitate the show's image, stressing the women's solidarity rather than their fractures. Perhaps not incidentally, this was also the show's last season. Without giving the network a pass, I locate a repetition compulsion with respect to these shows insofar as they work out black women's positions in a system where the gender and racial politics often do not favor them. To offer one more example of how the abuses of patriarchy register on the bodies of wives, in 2012 *Basketball Wives* star Evelyn Lozada filed for divorce a mere forty-one days into her marriage with football star Chad "Ochocinco" Johnson, after he head-butted her in a parked car and left a three-inch gash on her forehead. Part of the appeal of the *Wives* franchise, I suspect, is its availability as an outlet for female anger and injury, a way to reject the status quo and fight back—however inconsequentially—against the frustrating realities of obsolescence, invisibility, and even abuse. As Gates describes it, "These shows provide viewers with pleasures stemming . . . from the collective experience of being systematically denied access to the aspects of the American Dream and/or neoliberal notions of success that most mainstream media offer."[68] Underpinned by an attempted display of agentic self-valuation on the part of their featured women, VH1's shows nevertheless sadly reinforce these women's relative powerlessness.

Blacks and whites face different representational burdens, a reality that also divides and segments the viewing public. In a quote captured in an audience study of *Love and Hip Hop: New York*, one young black woman articulates, "*Real Housewives of Beverly Hills* and all that, they be having drama! And it be over like the smallest thing! And they fight too, sometimes. But for some reason, their fighting is okay, but our fighting is not okay [even] when it's about like, our Baby Daddy's and stuff like that. Fight over a ticket at a hotel—from a restaurant is okay. [They] can fight over that, but we can't fight over some girl like, messing with my Baby Daddy."[69] This reaction evidences a larger recognition that black women's fights receive criticism whereas white women get a pass for acting badly. As the speaker rightly points out, black women's anger is typically pathologized as deviant, excessive, and out of bounds. Explicitly comparing the reception that black and white women, respectively, receive when they engage in conflict throws into relief the fact that black women face unfair stigmatization. Moreover, the women on VH1 fight over issues largely spawned by their being at the mercy of a system that is sexist and racist. Here, the viewer describes the implicit competition between herself and a woman presumably having a sexual relationship with the man who fathered the speaker's child, a conflict that renders the sorts of fights depicted on *The Real Housewives of Beverly Hills* trivial by comparison. Finally, though the manifest content of the dispute the speakers references is between women, it testifies primarily to a system wherein women experience a consistent lack of male support and have little recourse for rectification.

Mob Wives, another hallmark in the VH1 roster of wife shows, depicts a similar set of gender divisions whereby women rail against the broken promises and hurts promulgated by the men to whom they entrusted their lives. *Mob Wives* features wives, ex-wives, and daughters of men known to be involved in organized crime and billed itself as an investigation of their family lives, often as single parents. Faced with men who were incarcerated or otherwise absent, the mob wives deal with the realization that these men have their own share of secrets both criminal and sexual. It is not uncommon, for example, for mob husbands and fathers to have lied to the featured women about their crimes, the extent of their involvement in these acts, and/or their extramarital activities. As well, the men on the show are largely spectral, appearing primarily via recollections from the women or as disembodied voices on telephones calling from prison. Inspired by the idea of showcasing women who were contending with unfortunate realities, *Mob Wives*, like *Basketball Wives*, used women who have been in some way betrayed by patriarchy to anchor its appeal, showcasing female perspectives in what are otherwise male-dominated arenas.

Sometimes referred to as "The Real Housewives of Staten Island," *Mob Wives'* debt to the Bravo franchise was apparent from its pilot episode: "The show takes the core elements that made the 'Real Housewives' series on Bravo a cultural phenomenon (warring cliques, alcohol-fueled lunches and camera-ready catfights) and combines them with actual

Mafia set pieces of men getting caught up in sweeps, men spending much of their married lives in prison, men with girlfriends on the side," claimed the *New York Times*. The brainchild of Jennifer Graziano, a daughter of famous mobster and former consigliore Anthony Graziano and sister to cast member Renee Graziano, Jennifer Graziano sold *Mob Wives* to VH1 with the claim, "This isn't about the men . . . It's really how the lifestyle itself affects the ladies. And when men go to jail and leave their families behind, what the woman needs to do to support themselves and pick up the pieces."[70] Again, we see a focus on and intent to foreground female concerns, a notion that has proven a consistent drumbeat for VH1. Yet, despite Graziano's measured tone, *Mob Wives'* knock-down-drag-out brawls rival and maybe even outdo the ferocity featured on *Basketball Wives*. At the same time, *Mob Wives'* skirmishes did not garner as much censure as those depicted on *Basketball Wives*. Also unlike *Basketball Wives*, *Mob Wives* drew accolades for its honesty and rawness in large part, I suspect, because the mob serves as a compelling trope for white American audiences thanks to iconic offerings such as *The Godfather* films and quality television shows like HBO's *The Sopranos* (1999–2007). *Mob Wives* benefited from the fact that the sufferings of Italian American women call on a rich, deep, and respected representational tradition.

The way *Mob Wives* frames its female characters also invites a sympathetic gaze. "Each scene begins like a frame taken from an FBI surveillance tape, complete with a 'click, click' sound effect and the occasional time stamp, as the character is caught in freeze frame and identified with salient details, like 'Carla Facciolo. Ex-husband: Joseph Ferragamo. Time served: 6 years,' even as the women do something as banal as heading off to the manicurist or carrying a fruit plate to a friend's party."[71] By illustrating the women as having been criminalized by association, the setup intimates their unwitting participation in the mob lifestyle, a framing that stands in stark contrast to *Basketball Wives*, which frequently portrays the women as jockeying for fame, as gold diggers, and as posers. The popular press likewise tended to take seriously the difficulties mob wives face, suggesting that their travails point out the superficiality of Bravo's housewives by comparison. Referring to "those other real housewives franchises," the *Hollywood Reporter* gushed, "their endless squabbles and social climbing antics are rendered rather trivial

Figure 4.4. The mob wives arriving for their appearance on *Good Morning America* in 2011. Photograph courtesy of Bauer-Griffin.

after you watch the first five minutes of *Mob Wives*."[72] Importantly, *Mob Wives* earns privilege thanks to its association with mob history and because of the women's whiteness. Whereas it can be argued that the mob wives lack a certain class status, as evidenced by their regional affiliation with the working-class borough of Staten Island as well as their often out-of-control brawls, crass language, and exaggerated, surgically enhanced bodies, they rarely risk being taken as racial exemplars as the *Basketball Wives* often are.

The show is nevertheless consistent with VH1's legacy of employing women who build celebrity brands grounded by their connection to famous men. Indeed, the stars of *Mob Wives* admit outright to the professionalization of wifedom and its ancillary benefits. As Renee Graziano did publicity for the show's final season in early 2016, she blatantly invoked empowerment as a perk of having appeared on television, vocalizing a sort of neofeminist rhetoric: "I learned how to be Renee . . . Not just Anthony Graziano's daughter, not Jr.'s ex-wife, just Renee."[73] Ironically, Graziano argues that being cast as a "wife" assisted her in jettisoning that very identity. Appearing on the show clearly afforded Graziano the chance to exert herself over and above male-dominated realms even as she leveraged those connections to foment her own celebrity. More broadly, and as evidenced by their elevated cultural profiles, active Twitter accounts, and appearances in periodicals like *Us Weekly* and *Life and Style*, the mob wives have translated their celebrity into lucrative profit streams. Mob wives pack clubs and parties and are available for bookings as celebrity appearances. This professionalization in many ways rehearses the sort of monetization of wifedom that I examined in chapter 3, though *Mob Wives* serves a distinct function with regard to VH1 since it is highly consistent with the rancorous tone that has come to characterize female relationships on the network.

Putting these wifely offerings in conversation illustrates VH1's strategic interest in exploiting the profitability of women's lives. If foregrounding hip hop represented a targeted appeal to racially diverse audiences, wifely programming represents another tactical move, one that gives voice to gender and racial disenfranchisement. VH1's women face obstacles that are manipulated but not necessarily manufactured. Instead, real issues fuel the fractures on these various series, such as trying to overcome relationship dissolution or abuse, growing up in a crime family, or being the behind-the-scenes partner of a famous hip hop star who does not publicly acknowledge you exist, much less that you are the mother of his children. The intervention into this realm of silence and secrets, the sometimes brash way that the women have clawed their way out of obscurity, and the loyalty of their fans all suggest the financial exigencies and consequences at stake in these portrayals.

This reality also helps to explain the lack of real narrative or narrative progress on VH1's most contentious shows. Instead, the shows revolve around what Misha Kavka calls "setting up encounters between people who have fallen out."[74] Pointing to the importance of the sensate or the embodied in reality television, Kavka suggests that the genre offers "an exemplary form of materialized affectivity," and notes that these are "bodies in the midst of or on the verge of an encounter but without any immediate payoff in the realm of signification."[75] Seen in this light, VH1's brawls materialize female anger spurred by these women's positions of perceived marginality, though this anger lacks a productive outlet. As I have argued, hurt stems from a state of disenfranchisement and a sense of the injuries promoted and propagated by patriarchal organizations. At the same time, women's bodies do the work of making these affective injuries visible, meaning that female stars must put their bodies in service of reproducing and replaying VH1's now-notorious brand of skirmish. Albeit overwrought and amped up, the vestiges of anger, betrayal, and striving that VH1's wifely reality programs illustrate are perhaps all too real.

TLC and Extreme Wifedom

Initially an educational channel anchored by a cinema verité ethos and featuring benign series such as *A Wedding Story* (1996–2005) and *A Baby Story* (1998–2007), in the early 2000s The Learning Channel began to focus its programming on documentary-style reality shows with a more outlandish bent. (In 1998 it began referring to itself simply as TLC.) The channel predominantly treats subjects whose bodies, interests, or families push the boundaries of normalcy. Diagnosable disorders feature prominently in TLC's reality palette (*Hoarding: Buried Alive*; *My Strange Addiction*), as do families who are unconventional in some way (*Jon and Kate Plus Eight*; *19 and Counting*; *Little People, Big World*) and people with entertainment aspirations gone awry (*Toddlers and Tiaras*; *Here Comes Honey Boo Boo*). As Moya Luckett writes, TLC "merges the conventional and extraordinary."[76] The same sensationalistic ethos has guided the network's approach to the topics of marriage, wives, and domesticity. From its gimmicky dating shows (*Love at First Swipe*; *Love at First Kiss*; *Married by Mom and Dad*) to its revelry in unconventional pairings (*Extreme Cougar Wives*) to its polygamous family exposés (*Sister Wives*; *My Five Wives*), TLC spectacularizes and exaggerates wifedom. Admittedly, wifely programming on TLC represents but a sliver in its wider panoply; wifely programs do not represent the market cornerstone that they do for Bravo or VH1. TLC's wifely offerings nevertheless illustrate what happens when representational codes are put under pressure, such that a study of TLC serves to distill marital trends, including the institution's circulation and replication of market calculations and conventions. I will focus on *Extreme Cougar Wives*, *My Five Wives*, and *Sister Wives* in order to propose that they foreground marital logics of competition and resource allocation while at the same time offering a perspective unique to TLC's brand of exaggeration.

Extreme Cougar Wives was a three-episode miniseries that focused on heterosexual couplings between women in their fifties, sixties, and seventies and men in their twenties, with each episode featuring three different couples. The majority of these relationships were serious but not institutionalized by marriage, though one couple holds a "handfasting" ceremony to pledge their commitment, much to the chagrin of the man's family, especially his mother. The show unsparingly focuses on the more salacious details of the pairings (the admission that one couple met at a high school dance, where he was a student and she was the chaperone; another man previously dated his now-girlfriend's daughter years ago), and their quirkier elements (the couple that enjoys Civil War reenactments). In keeping with a network brand whereby gratuitous voyeurism legitimates itself with educative condescension, *Extreme Cougar Wives* instantiates a disapproving gaze through the use of dissonant music and the derisive looks and judgmental comments of friends and bystanders. After ogling a bartender whose cougar girlfriend is also in the bar, a group of attractive white, twentysomething women express dismay at learning that he is dating a woman thirty-seven years his senior: "That's not normal, I don't think," one says, clearly annoyed that he has chosen his girlfriend "when there are women like us, who are beautiful and they go for like a sixty-five-year-old woman." The tone is meant to appeal to the aghast viewer who is perhaps secretly titillated but outwardly horrified, again a staple of the sort of viewer TLC courts. This framing also lays bare the often-unspoken rules of necessary complementarity in age, income, and status that tend to animate marriage choices, and reveals the symbolic discipline that ensues when these rules are violated. As I discussed in chapter 1, selective mating habits consolidate wealth and power, a practice referred to as assortative mating. If transgressed, as they are here, the transgressor becomes subject to a regulating gaze.

At the same time, the show testifies to the existence of a sexual economy that resides outside these calculations. While the cougar is typically thought to have money whereas her young lover specializes in sexual prowess, *Extreme Cougar Wives* features women who do not enjoy extreme wealth but rather demonstrate a genuine enthusiasm for their young lovers and an appreciation for their own vivacity. One exceptionally lively cougar in her seventies laughingly divulges to a blind date that she recently slept with an eighteen-year-old. Another talks earnestly about the way her sexual life has taken forms she never thought possible, and suggests that she never was as open with her former husband about her wants and desires. Routinely, the cougars testify to their contentment with this phase of their lives as well as their affection for, and compatibility with, their partners. Because it grants agency and selectivity to the cougars, the show exhibits a rather dissonant attitude toward them, whom it both judges and celebrates. While the show on the one hand features optimistic confessionals from the cougars, at the same it sensationalizes their relationships.

This mixed tone interestingly and perhaps surprisingly also confirms the representational dominance of Bravo's housewives. The second episode rather awkwardly begins with the same sort of opening proclamations one would find on Bravo: "I am one tough cougar" and "I am a cougar, and I am at the *top* of the dating food chain" (the latter slogan accompanied by a shot of a scantily clad cougar being lifted out of the pool by her sculpted boyfriend). Whereas the bravado rings false, it does confirm the extent to which female representational culture is delimited by the affective parameters that demand a posture of self-confidence, as

I discussed in chapter 1. *Extreme Cougar Wives* is in this sense both a continuation and a distillation of representational trends.

I utilize the long-running *Sister Wives* and the lesser-known *My Five Wives* to make a similar argument regarding the polarity of camaraderie versus competition on which so many wives texts depend. These TLC offerings comply with the network's focus on unconventional families and grant viewers the opportunity to enter heretofore-unexperienced worlds. Whereas polygamy and its practitioners are beset by the charge that the practice creates dangerous male demagogues and exploits vulnerable women, these shows seek to self-consciously normalize the parties to polygamous marriages. Wives in these programs tend to appear as agentic, introspective, and articulate, and do not comply with the sorts of sister wife images typically brandished in the media, what Brenda Weber calls "scores of downcast women wearing big bangs, long braids, and even longer pastel dresses."[77] The families depicted on TLC spend considerable time negotiating intimate partnerships even if the topic of these negotiations is a bit far afield (e.g., whether and how to bring on an additional wife, or whether the family will be considered a viable candidate to adopt a child). The families are also in the process of navigating tight financial times, especially thanks to the burden of caring for, in the case of *My Five Wives*, twenty-five children. Like many of the reality show participants discussed in this chapter, the wives and their partners clearly consent to appearing on television at least in part for a modicum of financial relief. Also like the housewives, the sister wives featured on the eponymous show launched a business inspired by their celebrity: My Sisterwife's Closet, an online retail outlet.

If sexual competition is, as I have argued, an animating force in a number of wives' portrayals, *Sister Wives* and *My Five Wives* bring this topic to the forefront. The notion that multiple women must content themselves with the affections of a man they all share inexorably circumscribes the show's narrative content. On the pilot episode of *My Five Wives*, the women talk about the loneliness they experience between their chosen nights with husband Brady (he rotates among them), and a tense exchange occurs over the question of with whom he will share his birthday. The wives admit to having difficulty seeing him behave with physical affection toward the other wives. One wife, for example, does not want to flaunt her attempts at pregnancy because it will confirm to the other wives that she and Brady are having sex during each of her nights. Another wife admits after production that she did not watch the show because she did not want to see the bedroom exchanges between Brady and the other wives. Yet, unlike the aforementioned reality wives for whom sexual competition represents a largely unacknowledged but animating force, the polygamous wives negotiate and contend with their jealousy, generally treating each other with respect and even love.

In this way, the polygamous wives realize the promise of camaraderie that is offered but largely rings hollow on shows like *The Real Housewives* or *Basketball Wives*. If anything, the relationships between these women constitute their primary affective bonds. As Moya Luckett argues of what she calls the "female group text," which includes *Sister Wives*, "evoking the multiplicity of female identities, the female group text further extols women's capacity for fulfilling relationships with each other—relationships that help them to self-nurture and develop as individuals."[78] When the women featured on *Sister Wives* acquiesce to bringing on a fourth wife, it occurs after a prolonged negotiation. Moreover, as the series has continued through its now-fourteen-season run, the relationships between the women (which admittedly undergo ups and downs) constitute primary narrative content. In many ways, these bonds are as important as their relationship with husband Kody. Their collective mothering of the clan's eighteen children also testifies to the women's sense of collective responsibility. In 2014, first wife Meri agreed to a divorce from Kody so that he might legally marry fourth wife Robyn, a transition that was largely motivated by the need for Kody to adopt Robyn's three children from a previous marriage. This investment in the bonds of sisterhood is so foreign to the type of acrimonious exchange that characterizes most wifely programming as to render it anomalous.

This dissonance was acutely on display in *My Five Wives'* pathetic attempt at a reunion show following season 1, where the host kept prodding the women to engage in confessional-type behavior that would reveal their true animosity, even retuning to moments of tension during the season via flashbacks. Sitting uncomfortably, the wives refused to divulge anything mean-spirited or even admit that conflicts were ongoing, inadvertently emphasizing the distance between this flat offering and Bravo's always-incendiary *Housewives* reunion specials. In only this way, perhaps, does TLC exhibit more restraint than its contemporaries do. Again, this example is illustrative of how ill fitting formulaic parameters are for women who share genuine bonds of caring and affection, and highlights how the wives phenomena rewards certain types of wives and emotional registers while rendering others invisible. At the same time, the conceit of the polygamous marriage participates in TLC's larger brand of the sideshow.

As this chapter has surveyed, to be a professional wife entails a willingness to sell and commodify both one's intimate life as well as manifold products. If the *Real Housewives* franchise and its spawn are taken as exemplary, popular depictions of female identity in the current era tend to showcase the many sustained contradictions that surround American wifedom and work. Being a reality wife is a job where, paradoxically, one gets to be oneself according to someone else's rules. Not insignificantly, all the wives surveyed in this chapter ultimately work for a white man, including *Housewives* executive producer Andy Cohen, VH1's CEO Tom Calderone, and Discovery Communications (the parent company for TLC) president David Zaslav. Wives help these networks achieve the goal of market and channel segmentation; this formula works so well because, as Squires says, this programming tends to "leverage racial difference or conflict to generate drama and spectacle."[79] Whereas the wives glean cultural and financial rewards for their participation on reality television, they typically do not helm their own broadcasts nor do they set the representational parameters for their appearances. In the next and final chapter, I look at the specter of the professional wife who attempts to emerge from the shadow of patriarchal limitations, focusing specifically on political wives motivated by raising their own cultural profiles.

5

Good Wives

Public Infidelity and the National Politics of Spousehood

You were with him 24/7 for months and you missed the most fundamental thing about the man. Peter Florrick is not number one. Not nationally. She is.
—Eli Gold, explaining why Alicia Florrick, Peter's wife, is the better candidate on *The Good Wife* (2016)

I need to make some plans for my political future, and I do have a bright, bright political future. The sweet lawyer who gave up her career for her husband, suffered a miscarriage, and had a late in life baby while first lady . . . That's gold. That's a future president. That's a hell of a second act, and America loves a second act.
—Mellie Grant, diagramming her political aspirations in *Scandal* (2012)

Some twenty years after American audiences were titillated by the lurid image of a sitting president receiving oral sex from an intern in the Oval Office, and mostly chagrined by his ambitious wife who did not leave in the wake of that scandal, the figure of the wronged political wife looms large in the national consciousness. Thanks to a disturbingly common-place stream of twenty-first-century adultery scandals featuring modern politicians, American media is again replete with a set of iconic and evidentiary items that recall Monica Lewinsky's infamous blue dress, among them Carlos Danger's (aka Congressman Anthony Weiner's) tweets of himself in his tighty whities. The erring politicians names are by now all too familiar (John Edwards, Larry Craig, James McGreevey, Christopher Lee, Arnold Schwarzenegger, Eliot Spitzer, Mark Sanford, David Petraeus, Anthony Weiner), but so, too, increasingly, are their wives (Hillary Clinton, Elizabeth Edwards, Jenny Sanford, Silda Wall Spitzer, Maria Shriver, Huma Abedin). Political wives have begun to take their own turn in the spotlight, an ascension which reveals that their typically assumed victimization is both a misnomer and an oversimplification.[1] Such a paradigm shift in turn elucidates the surprisingly instrumentalized function that marriage has come to play in twenty-first-century politics and popular culture.

The attention trained on political wives reminds us that for public figures there are myriad benefits to having a good marriage and even (if not more) dangers in not. Related is the role that, in a still largely male-dominated political arena, wives play in maintaining a requisite image for the men whose lives, campaigns, and children they support. Before the current onslaught of sexual controversy, media coverage of infidelity typically degenerated into an echo chamber of hysteria about the deviant prurience of powerful men, including armchair psychologizing about men's need to risk danger and assert their prowess and inviolability. Tales of misbehaving male politicos tempt us into binaries where "bad husbands" hurt "good wives," simplistic schemas that tend to disempower the women cast as gatekeepers of morality and virtue. Yet, it is precisely these well-meaning but ultimately damaging mythologies that a number of today's wronged wives resist.

As this chapter will argue, the wronged political wife has been reimagined in the post-Clinton era as a figurehead of a very different sort: one with her own ambitions and goals, whose implied victimization does not capture the complexity and calculation of her position. Foregrounding marriage as an act of visible labor that in many ways benefits wives as much as their spouses, political wives—both in practice and in mediated representation—have opened up a space in which to talk about marriage as a platform for female achievement and professionalism. Though once understood as little more than a passive sufferer, the political wife as a figurehead has matured and evolved in such a way, I contend, as to provide insight into how marriage operates as a business. In such a realm, "wife" is a job title. Beginning with a section that addresses the legacy of Hillary Clinton, who assures a very different script for this seemingly tired role, this chapter offers an investigation of how current discourses have reimagined contemporary wifehood, arguing that political wives help to reorder the national politics of American marriage.

The Clinton Blueprint

Organized around a "ripped from the headlines" premise, the CBS drama *The Good Wife* (2009–16) began its pilot episode with a press conference that replicated a number of real-life instances. Brought down by a sex scandal involving charges of high-end prostitutes, bribery, and corruption, disgraced politician Peter Florrick (Chris Noth) resigns from the state's attorney's office as his blindsided wife Alicia (Julianna Margulies) stands silently beside him. Quiet and stone-faced until the couple goes backstage, once there Alicia forcefully slaps her husband across the face. This impulsive yet strident action lays bare the show's interest in scripting a wronged wife whose passivity is not a foregone conclusion, a fictionalized assignment of agency that circumscribes her characterization.

In keeping with this attitude and in the wake of her husband's incarceration and the family's ensuing financial difficulties, Alicia returns to a long-abandoned legal career, accepting a position at a law firm co-led by a former law school friend. As the series creators explained, Alicia's profession was designed to resonate with the real-life women who have faced similarly sensationalized circumstances; showrunners Robert and Michelle King explicitly credit the genesis of *The Good Wife* to their witnessing of disgraced politician Eliot Spitzer's resignation press conference in 2008 during which Silda Wall Spitzer, his accomplished, Harvard Law–trained wife, stood miserably beside him. Like Alicia, Wall Spitzer gave up a promising career to raise children and returned to a prestigious job in the wake of her (now ex-) husband's scandal.[2] While the Kings often reference Wall Spitzer in accounts of their inspiration for the show, Alicia Florrick's resonance with multiple wronged wives is nevertheless striking: shortly after the show's premiere, *People* magazine quoted Jenny Sanford saying that she finds it "creepy" that Alicia is, like her, a Chicago native and Georgetown grad.[3] As the Kings also noted, a surprising number of wronged wives have legal backgrounds. Hillary Clinton graduated from Yale Law School and practiced while her husband was the governor of Arkansas, and Elizabeth Edwards went to law school at the University of North Carolina (where she met John Edwards) and actively practiced well into their marriage. A similar pedigree is claimed for first lady Mellie Grant (Bellamy Young) in the ABC

Figure 5.1. *The Good Wife*'s first conciliatory press conference. Photograph courtesy of Photofest.

drama *Scandal* (2011–18). As Mellie notes, she was at the top of her class at Yale Law, which included her future husband, President Fitzgerald "Fitz" Grant (Tony Goldwyn), whom she outperformed.

The Good Wife established its dialogue with its real-life counterparts early in the series proper: in the pilot episode, senior law firm partner Diane Lockhart (Christine Baranski) gestures to a picture of herself with Hillary Clinton and says to Alicia, "If she can do it, so can you." The act of self-consciously invoking a woman whose career has soared since her husband's affair was broadcast to national audiences enunciated the terms by which a scorned wife could emerge as a capable laborer, a recognition that *The Good Wife* made its centerpiece throughout its tenure. The line also served to establish Hillary Clinton's role in the series writ large, and Clinton has repeatedly served as a muse both for Alicia and for Diane, a law partner whose gender (and liberal politics) in her often male-dominated profession served as a stumbling block.[4] As this line confirms, Hillary Clinton's role as a suffering wife has been largely erased in the national consciousness, replaced with an image of resilience that has come not only to ground portrayals of political wives but also to set new terms by which such figures claim agency.

According to this precedent, wronged political wives do not fade into shameful obscurity but rather triumph in professional spheres. To give just a brief overview of Hillary Clinton's trajectory: after enduring Bill Clinton's numerous extramarital dalliances, including the Monica Lewinsky affair that was revealed in 1998 and rocked the last term of his presidency, Hillary Clinton ignited her own political career soon after her husband left office. (That she had her own agendas was made clear long before this time, and was particularly evident in a nationwide health care initiative that she spearheaded during her husband's first term.) After leaving the White House, Clinton served for eight years as a senator from New York. A longtime frontrunner for the 2008 Democratic presidential nomination, her candidacy was ultimately eclipsed by relative newcomer Barack Obama, under whom she served for a term as secretary of state. She was widely favored to win the presidency in 2016, though she suffered an almost wholly unforeseen defeat at the hands of real estate tycoon and reality television celebrity Donald Trump.

Despite this somewhat stunning turn of events, Clinton's legacy and specifically her transition from supposed victim to powerful agent augured a revised emotional template for the wronged wife. Most saliently, Clinton remained stoic and largely impassive in the face of sensational-ized media scrutiny, and said very little about her husband's multiple and humiliating missteps, her decision to stay married to him, or their marriage's many compromises. With this behavior, she became an icon for self-possession in the face of media chaos, a stalwart posture she likewise encouraged in fellow aggrieved wives. In her 2007 memoir *Silent Partner*, Dina Matos McGreevey, now ex-wife of former New Jersey governor Jim McGreevey, writes that following her husband's public admission that he had been unfaithful with a male former staffer and was in fact a "gay American," she reached out to Clinton, who recommended a crisis manager. During their conversation Clinton advised Matos Mc-Greevey to keep her focus on herself and her daughter, procure her own advisers rather than rely on her husband's, and consider the media "an intrusion and a distraction and not the point."[5]

Clinton was likewise a strong supporter of Huma Abedin, who was her friend and State Department aide at the time that Congressman Anthony Weiner's first sexting scandal broke in 2011, as well as a close confidante in the ensuing years when Weiner mounted a comeback attempt to be New York City mayor, before a second sex scandal ended his candidacy in all but name.[6] (Weiner's multiple sexual indiscretions and criminal online behaviors may have been partially responsible for costing Clinton the 2016 election, which I address in some detail shortly.) In addition to an eerie similarity in their marital woes, the ties between the two women run deep: Abedin began as an intern for Hillary Clinton during the same period as Monica Lewinsky, and has spent the lion's share of her professional career laboring under the former first lady. Often referred to in press reports as Clinton's "surrogate daughter," Abedin's saga also unfolded in a manner not unlike her mentor's in terms of the way the story was reported and the supposed timing of the wives' recognition of their husbands' assignations.[7] For the Clintons, the then-new website *The Drudge Report* broke the news of Bill's affair, alleging that *Newsweek* was sitting on the story. In Weiner's case, it was new media source *Big Government*, the website of the late conservative blogger (and former *Drudge* assistant) Andrew Breitbart, that first accused Weiner of using social media to send sexually suggestive content (including lewd pictures of his barely cloaked penis) to a variety of young women. Likewise, Weiner's second scandal broke when an obscure gossip website called *The Dirty* released sexually explicit messages sent between him (Carlos Danger) and the likewise apocryphally named Sydney Leathers. Both Clinton's and Weiner's scandals point to the power of new media sources to trump print media outlets in terms of reporting political sex peccadillos, and underscore how the interweaving of gossip and personality now constitutes a mainstay of American political enterprise.[8] Relatedly, they illustrate the extent to which the media arbitrates public opinion and the fact that formerly tabloid fodder has taken its place in the ranks of legitimate journalism.[9]

For Weiner the third time around was when the *New York Post* broke the story in August 2016 that he had continued his sexcapades, this time sending a Republican operative a suggestive picture of himself, visibly aroused, while his sleeping son lay beside him. Abedin quickly announced that the couple was separating, amid reports that as a result of the photo the New York City Administration for Children's Services was investigating Weiner. Shortly thereafter, the *Daily Mail* announced that Weiner had also sexted a fifteen-year-old girl, prompting a federal investigation into Weiner's online activities and the eleventh-hour revelation in late October 2016 by FBI director James Comey that Hillary Clinton's e-mails were again under investigation, based on information found on Weiner's computer and involving Abedin since they shared the device. Mere days before the presidential election Comey announced that no new material incriminating Hillary Clinton had been discovered, though many Clinton supporters felt that the damage had been done since questions about her credibility and specifically the e-mail scandal dogged her 2016 campaign since its inception. In May 2017, Weiner pleaded guilty to a federal obscenity charge for sexting an underage minor. The same day, Abedin filed for divorce.

I want to spend a bit more time parsing out the similarities between Clinton and Abedin and their respective marriages, because they speak not only to the women's shared ethos and ambition but also to new paradigms for wifedom. Like Bill Clinton's assertion that he "did not have sexual relations with that woman," Anthony Weiner initially obfuscated the terms of his involvement with the 2011 sexting scandal, maintaining that the lewd pictures sent from his phone were the result of a hacker, media conspiracy, or both. Both wives were also at least initially con-

vinced of their husband's innocence and believed that his foes were behind the vicious rumors. Both men eventually confessed. In Weiner's
case, the sequence followed a script that has now become de rigueur:
he called a tearful press conference to publicly acknowledge the rumor's
truth and apologize, and ultimately resigned from Congress. Abedin in
turn was noticeably absent from this event—when asked where she was,
Weiner churlishly told reporters, "She's not here." This question of the
wife's role vis-à-vis conciliatory press conferences, and particularly the
Abedin-Weiner marriage, will be an ongoing source of investigation for
this chapter. Here, however, I will assert that Hillary Clinton likely inspired Abedin's absence from this first press conference. Much like Clinton's exile during the Lewinsky debacle, Abedin initially maintained a
steadfast silence about her marriage when, days later, the press revealed
that she was pregnant with the couple's child. Abedin was working as
(then secretary of state) Clinton's deputy chief of staff during that time
and left for a tour of Africa with her boss the week after her husband's
apology. Though Abedin has not revealed the content of those conversations, she admits to having sought her mentor's advice during the trip.[10]
Clinton and Abedin's comportment—and their reticence—in the face of
their respective scandals indicates the symbolic power that wives have
even in situations that seem to enforce the opposite, and also confirms
these wives' positions as the more sure-footed and capable members of
their marital unions. Though Abedin eventually distanced herself from
Weiner, she was a key player in his failed bid to become New York City's
mayor in 2013, as I will discuss.

In addition to making a case for stoicism and self-reliance, Clinton's
legacy has much to say about the healing and rehabilitative powers of
work. In her 2000 autobiography *Living History*, Clinton divulged that
her decision to run for the Senate provided a path to reconciliation. "Bill
and I were talking again about matters other than the future of our relationship," she writes. "Over time we both began to relax."[11] The media
coverage of Silda Wall Spitzer similarly invoked the idea that work can
function as a palliative that lends wronged wives a renewed sense of
public worth. Though remarkably reticent, Wall Spitzer did capitulate
to a *Vogue* spread in 2009. The profile focuses almost exclusively on her
professional accomplishments, from the founding of a children's charity
to her position, post-scandal, as managing director of a hedge fund run

by women. Besides an oblique gesture to having faced "challenges" and the need to use one's "internal power to move forward," Wall Spitzer says nothing in the interview about her marriage.[12] In keeping with the fierce defense of their privacy, the Spitzers quietly announced the end of their marriage on December 24, 2013, subsequent to Eliot Spitzer's failed attempt to be elected New York City comptroller and after numerous reports that the couple had long been living apart.

Media portrayals focusing on wronged political wives similarly position professionalism as a personal salve. In *The Good Wife* season 1 episode "Running," Alicia's now-exonerated husband asks how she would feel if he were to run again for the office of state's attorney. She tells him that she does not want their children involved and adamantly asserts, "I want to work." The same mantra underpinned the 2012 USA network miniseries *Political Animals*, which likewise patterned itself on Hillary Clinton. Starring Sigourney Weaver as Elaine Barrish, the series took some telling liberties. As a former first lady who decides to divorce her philandering blowhard husband on the night she loses her presidential bid, Barrish subsequently becomes secretary of state under the president to whom she lost in the primary.[13] The six-episode series narrates the period during which she holds this post and yet imagines another presidential effort for Barrish, centralizing the question of whether she will run again and attempt to unseat a president who has yet to have a second term. Importantly, Barrish serves as a synecdoche for the legacy of second-wave feminism. Unwilling to abide her husband's multiple infidelities, she leaves him to pursue a demanding job where she is repeatedly marginalized as a result of her gender and aggressively stands up to myriad male counterparts. When the White House is faced with an overseas hostage crisis, for instance, Barrish is not brought in until hours later because, as the White House chief of staff says in condescending tones, he assumed she was busy with her son's engagement party. The sexism of this statement and its explicitly gendered understanding of what constitutes an important event is made clear when Barrish insists that as the nation's foremost diplomat her attendence at the meeting should have been unquestioned. The commanding presence of Sigourney Weaver, who brings with her a legacy of memorable film roles as a battle-scarred warrior (e.g., the *Alien* franchise), provided an extratextual resonance to the miniseries, and Weaver publicly conceded that *Political*

Animals was conceived with Clinton in mind and designed to showcase how capable a woman in politics could be.[14] The conceit of the series, whereby Barrish must consistently negotiate her famous family—and appearances by a charming, still-amorous ex-husband, whose drawl is clearly meant to mimic Bill Clinton's—nevertheless confirm the difficulty for wives of escaping their marital legacies.

To the extent that she has transcended marital scandal—and again, this history repeatedly reared its head, especially during her presidential run—and crafted her own professional identity in its wake, Clinton serves as a potent reminder that wives are aided by their marital legacies yet hampered by them as well. Clinton's political rise in many ways mimicked her husband's insofar as it, too, was rife with potent and lucrative corporate networks and power-brokering opportunism, scandals that continued to dog her campaign in the form of the accusation that the Clinton Foundation traded political favors for financial support from well-heeled donors (exchanges that have troubling resonances in the context of Clinton's previous position as secretary of state). Similarly, Bill Clinton's history of extramarital dalliance was consistently referenced by Hillary Clinton's opponent, Donald Trump, who repeatedly suggested that Clinton aided her husband's philandering by publicly discrediting the women who accused him of sexual dalliances, hence calling into question Clinton's commitment to women, a cornerstone of her campaign. And, in a series of stunt-like moves, Trump suggested via Twitter that he might invite Bill Clinton's former mistress Gennifer Flowers to attend his and Hillary's first presidential debate. Though that threat never materialized, prior to their second debate Trump called a press conference with women who claimed to have been in some ways sexually victimized by the Clintons—including Paula Jones, who accused Bill Clinton of harassment in the 1990s—and brought the women to the debate as his guests. Arguably, this was also a move designed to divert attention away from Trump's own history of sexual assault, epitomized by his "Grab 'em by the pussy" comment to Billy Bush in 2005, reports of which broke days before the second debate.

This image of the political wife as a shrewd operator and at times rule-bending opportunist has also been used to productive effect in a number of popular culture offerings. In *The Good Wife*, steely ambition informs the morally questionable ways that Alicia's career advances thanks to backdoor deals greased by her husband's political connections, and the fact that her triumphs are often at the expense of friends, mentors, and even lovers. Her capacity for cutthroat maneuvers is exceptionally clear during a season 1 story line in which Alicia secures a permanent job at her law firm by calling in a connection; a season 4 story line in which she accepts a partner position, even after pledging solidarity to other associates who were, like her, initially passed over for promotion; a season 5 story line in which she leaves her employers to begin her own firm, snatching a number of their high-profile clients in the process; a lengthy season 6 sequence in which she repeatedly plays dirty politics in her own bid to become state's attorney; and finally, a sequence in the incendiary series finale in which she sabotages Diane, blindsiding her with evidence of Diane's husband's infidelity, a move designed to exonerate Peter from legal charges and effectively illustrating that Alicia's primary allegiance is to the Florrick dynasty. As if having presaged this betrayal, seasons earlier Diane characterized the power couple as "Bill and Hillary on steroids" after Peter, then the governor-elect, uses his bully pulpit to assist his wife's new firm in poaching her old firm's clients. *The Good Wife* cocreator Robert King echoed this description, explaining in a 2013 interview that the show "started as an exploration of the cipher who stands by her man, but now Alicia is 'more like Hillary is to Bill.'"[15] Alicia's own son makes a similar comparison, telling his mother "You and dad are playing Bill and Hillary . . . Anything we do is a family issue. The Florricks is a family business." As if to further underscore the connection between the Florricks and the Clintons, in *The Good Wife*'s seventh and final season Peter runs for president and the show explicitly names Hillary as Peter's opponent in the race and voices his hopes of being named her vice president.

Similarly opportunistic maneuvers impel the repeatedly cuckolded Mellie Grant in the ABC drama *Scandal*. Frustrated by her trivialized role as first lady—after being vomited on by a child while filming a public service announcement, Mellie screeches, "Top of my class at Harvard, top of my class at Yale Law, and this is what I've been reduced to?"—Mellie insists on playing a bigger role in governing the nation. Always on the lookout to advance her own position, and incensed that her husband characterizes her as "ornamental" and "not functional," Mellie inserts herself in national conversations that force her husband's

Figure 5.2. "I don't know why everybody says little girls dream about weddings," says *Scandal*'s Mellie Grant. "I always wanted this," referring to the presidency.

hand in both domestic and foreign policy. In the episode that features her outburst, she publicly consoles a bereaved family whose daughter's killer has diplomatic immunity and essentially forces her husband into tense relations with Russia. When her husband is shot and lays comatose in a hospital bed, Mellie forges his signature on a letter testifying to his good health and demanding his reinstatement. In a statement that forecasts her intentions, she tells the president's top adviser, "Woodrow Wilson's wife ran the country for two years after his stroke and no one was the wiser." Given these political ambitions, and the show's repeated positioning of her as both ruthless and relentless, it came as no surprise that season 5 featured Mellie's own presidential run, and the eventual inauguration of her as president in the season finale.

The same ruthlessness can be claimed for *House of Cards'* (2013–) imposing Claire Underwood (Robin Wright), since her political scheming assists both her diabolical husband's ambitions and, pointedly, her own. Well understanding that an advance in Frank Underwood's (Kevin Spacey) position also guarantees one for her, Claire enlists the nonprofit environmental firm that she runs to propel her husband's designs on the White House, and she purposefully turns a blind eye to his philandering when it involves a political reporter her husband is both bedding and using for his own gain. (He later murders the reporter, as well as another male politician who becomes inconvenient.) After her husband secures the presidency, Claire deploys her position as first lady to strong-arm him into appointing her UN ambassador, until he makes her resign at the behest of the Russian president. Agitation over her sidelined role, coupled with her growing awareness that she is a gifted campaigner with a bright political future in her own right, Claire leaves her husband and explores embarking on a congressional run. When her husband and his cronies sabotage those efforts, she ups the ante again by threatening to derail her husband's presidential campaign if he does not make her his vice president.

In a plotline not unlike Mellie's, Claire also usurps her husband's power after he is shot by a reporter whose life the couple previously ruined. In fact, Frank's near-death offers Claire a golden opening: instead of sitting by her husband's hospital bed, she essentially runs the country for the duration of his illness. Coyly manipulating the feckless vice president—who stays behind while the president receives a liver transplant—and mercilessly blackmailing would-be opponents, Claire travels to Europe, sidelines the secretary of state, and negotiates a Russian bailout, a deal that involves a partnership with China and is credited with ending an American oil crisis that has wreaked havoc across the country. The Underwoods later tout Claire's seminal role in negotiating this deal as proof of her political prowess, which the couple uses to productive effect in securing for her a nomination for vice president. The couple rigs that election and eventually takes office, but Frank is dogged by ongoing ethics investigations, leading him to acquiesce to impeachment. Claire assumes the office of president, and in the season 5 finale breaks though the fourth wall to convey a simple but steely message: "My turn."

This image of the wife not as victim but rather as political operative is the most widely circulated image of her in the twenty-first century. Admittedly cynical, it purposefully employs the Clinton legacy to assist wronged wives in escaping victimization and instead offers the image of a woman with professional competence, enduring resolve and, often, a pragmatism that slips into pathological ambition. As this section has detailed, rehabilitating wronged wives often involves claiming agency through tenacity and aspiration, whereby wives recognize the need to double down to secure their own professional futures, a trope identifiable in both real-life trajectories and popular culture products.

Infidelity and Celebritized Media Circuits

Validating the old "hell hath no fury" adage, in the appropriately titled episode "A Woman Scorned" Mellie Grant tearfully goes on television and reveals that her husband, the president, has been unfaithful. Mellie in fact implements a plan she has long threatened:

> I will walk out in front of the press and I will explain to them that my marriage is over because, while I was pregnant with his child, my husband was having an affair with Olivia Pope. I will leave him and I will take his children with me. I will take every penny he has in the bank and every dollar of political capital that he has in this town. I will court feminist groups and mother's groups and religious groups. I will bury him, and I will dance on his grave. And then, I will run for office.

As these words attest, Mellie ingeniously and indiscriminately plans to utilize her position as a wronged wife—and, significantly, mother—to mobilize supporters from various and even opposing corners. Negotiating her relationship to the public is of paramount importance both for her future and for her husband's because, as Mellie well knows, both careers rely heavily on the narrative crafted around scandal. Their image in this respect falls squarely under the media's purview, which determines whether a wronged wife is a guileless victim or deserving of comeuppance, whether a mistress was conniving or merely naive, and whether a straying husband was plotting or taken off guard.

Mellie's seething rage represents a refreshing addition to a media circuit that only recently included the side of the scorned wife in its calculations. In fact, erring politicians have long had at their disposal press conferences and televised interviews in which to either deny wrongdoing or make their public mea culpas, with the latter typically legitimated by rumors of private spiritual counsel with religious leaders. Long before the Lewinsky scandal and while on the campaign trail in 1992, Bill and Hillary Clinton sat for a *60 Minutes* interview where, facing allegations

Figure 5.3. After this 1992 interview with *60 Minutes*, Hillary Clinton was pilloried for defending her marriage and insulting cookie-baking, stand-by-your man types.

of an extramarital affair with Gennifer Flowers, Bill Clinton admitted "wrongdoing" and that he "caused pain" in his marriage. Tellingly, Clinton refused to say whether he had an affair, staking his fitness for office on having been exceptionally candid with the public already: "I mean, you know, this has become a virtual cottage industry. The only way to put it behind us, I think, is for all of us to agree that this guy has told us about all we need to know." He asserted that the Clinton marriage is not an "understanding" or "arrangement," a perception that has nevertheless clung to the couple ever since, and particularly in the wake of his subsequent infidelities. Yet, despite these important admissions (and telling omissions), the interview is remembered less for Bill Clinton's evasion than for Hillary Clinton's assertion that "I'm not sitting here—some little woman standing by my man like Tammy Wynette. I'm sitting here because I love him, and I respect him, and I honor what he's been through and what we've been through together." Hillary Clinton's attempt to assert her own power and choice in the situation was roundly criticized. Her commentary drew flack, even from legendary songstress Wynette, a flogging that displays how little cultural tolerance wronged wives were afforded if they tried to assert anything other than victimhood.

In contrast and paradoxically perhaps, ready-made circuits for the mistress to tell her side of the story exist in easy abundance. Appearances in *Penthouse* and *Star Magazine*, on *A Current Affair*, and on television in Spain and Germany, for instance, netted Gennifer Flowers approximately $500,000.[16] These pathways correspond in important ways to twenty-first-century developments in celebrity culture where, thanks in large part to the domination of reality TV and the rise in online celebrity news and gossip, ordinary people are routinely plucked from obscurity and have a multi-mediated landscape on which to dot their exposure.[17] One notable harbinger of the current zeitgeist can be found in the trajectory of Jessica Hahn, the church secretary who, after a sex scandal in 1987 involving televangelist Jim Bakker, posed for *Playboy*, had a cameo on the television show *Married . . . with Children* (1986–97), and made frequent appearances on the *Howard Stern Show*. Hahn's transmedia successes have in turn been aped by a number of more modern mistresses. Monica Lewinsky, for instance, sat for an interview with Barbara Walters, cooperated with Andrew Morton on a book titled *Monica's Story*, served as a spokeswoman for the Jenny Craig weight-loss program, participated in the HBO documentary *Monica in Black and White* (2002), and appeared on the short-lived reality dating show *Mr. Personality* (2003).[18] As recently as 2014, Lewinsky penned a story for *Vanity Fair* where she writes, " It's time to burn the beret and bury the blue dress."[19] Following the piece, Lewinsky embarked on a round of high-profile speeches and launched a campaign against cyberbullying.

Celebrity mistresses nowadays enjoy and have access to multiple outlets for exposure, which include book contracts and magazine spreads, appearances on radio and talk shows, starring roles on reality television, and endorsement deals, all of which attempt to capitalize on the salacious aspects of their stories. To name some of the most prolific of these in recent times, Eliot Spitzer's mistress Ashley Dupré parlayed her experience as a high-end prostitute into media fame by conducting a high-profile interview with ABC's Diane Sawyer, posing for *Playboy*, writing a sex column in the *New York Post*, and appearing as a contestant on VH1's *Famous Food* (2011). John Edward's former mistress Rielle Hunter followed a similar script, appearing on the *Oprah Winfrey Show* (1986–2011), rehashing the affair to *GQ* and posing for suggestive pictures, and authoring a tell-all memoir titled *What Really Happened: John Edwards, Our Daughter, and Me* (2012).[20] Finally, Sydney Leathers, paramour of "Carlos Danger" (aka Anthony Weiner), became a pitchwoman for the dating site

Arrangement Finders, a site that sets up affluent men with young women, and she figured prominently in a 2013 seasonal ad campaign, appearing on billboards that proclaimed, "Get a Mistress for Christmas." She also, as the documentary *Weiner* (2016) revealed, attempted a public run-in with him on the night he lost the mayoral election, an outlandish stalking scenario that occurred at the urging of shock jock Howard Stern, whose radio show she had appeared on earlier that day.

As these instances confirm, a celebrity branding circuit exists for the former mistresses of high-profile male figures, though these women often reside on the fringes of respectability.[21] In its fictionalized exploration of this reality, *The Good Wife* episode "Threesome" begins with a television sequence that features Peter's former mistress Amber Madison, a name clearly meant to evoke AshleyMadison.com, appearing with talk show host Chelsea Handler.[22] Later in the episode reference is made to Madison's radio appearance with Stern, the controversial male figure with whom many mistresses (including the aforementioned Hahn, Dupré, and Leathers) have also spoken. However, Madison's appearance in these venues is hardly celebrated or condoned. Instead, media portrayals frequently villainize the mistress character in order to invite empathy for the wife. When made aware of how Madison's media circuit has excoriated Alicia as sexually inhibited, Alicia begs her estranged husband to "make it stop." Audiences are then invited to applaud Peter and his handler's threatening that if Madison goes ahead with a planned tell-all book, they will sic on her a previous boyfriend, a reputed mob boss. The plotline promotes unsettling class implications that underline the wronged wife's relative refinements when compared with the mistress's tawdry excesses.

These examples attest to the veracity of Bill Clinton's observation that political scandal has become its own cottage industry, though up until recently, wronged wives have not enjoyed the media exposure afforded to either errant politicos or unrepentant mistresses. I explore this development in the next section, arguing that a new strain of "scorned wife media" now insists on the wife's possession of capability, fortitude, and self-possession, a perception aided by the mediums in which she appears. These products—which often come in the form of book-length memoirs—gain symbolic capital by setting themselves in contradistinction to the more tabloid-oriented media that tends to favor the mistress.

In this way, female media culture codifies and underscores the assumed respectability of the wife and the assumed disrespectability of the mistress, as evidenced by wives' appearances in venerated venues that play up these women's sympathetic qualities.

Redefining Victimhood in the Wronged Wife Memoir

On the tenth anniversary of the revelation of her husband's relationship with Monica Lewinsky, and while running in a tight primary race against then-underdog Barack Obama, Hillary Clinton sat for an interview with Tyra Banks on Banks's eponymous talk show. When asked why she stayed in her marriage, Clinton answered, "I really had to dig down deep and think hard about what was right for me, what was right for my family." Though she claimed she never doubted Bill's love, "I had to decide what I ought to do. I think it is so important to be able to hear yourself at a moment when it is hard . . . there are so many times when you really have to listen to yourself."[23] The commentary was, I suspect, meant to humanize and soften Clinton during a difficult and often nasty campaign season. During the interview she also noted that women who have been through similar trials frequently seek her counsel, a comment that sought to establish her approachability and legitimize her accessibility, a posture that nowadays represents a necessary element of political identity. Clinton's demeanor stood in stark contrast to the tight-lipped treatment of the affair that appears in her memoir *Living History*. There, she speaks in clipped tones, noting that during a chilly family vacation to Martha's Vineyard, "Buddy, the dog, came along to keep Bill company. He was the only member of our family who was still willing to."[24] This comparison between Clinton's various rhetorical voices speaks to the strategic resonance of the shape-shifting narrative that is the tale of the wronged wife in twenty-first-century culture.

As this section will explore, wronged wives have recently laid claim to their own female media circuit, intentionally making use of female-oriented genres like the memoir in order to tell their side of the story. I refer here to four specific texts: Dina Matos McGreevey's *Silent Partner: A Memoir of My Marriage* (2007), Elizabeth Edwards's *Resilience* (2009), Gayle Haggard's *Why I Stayed: The Choices I Made in My Darkest Hour* (2010), and Jenny Sanford's *Staying True* (2010), all of which detail the difficulty of negotiating private scandals in public arenas. Though pastor Ted Haggard was not a politician, his downfall as a result of a sex scandal with a male prostitute and his subsequent removal from the evangelical mega-church he founded garnered national media attention. I include Gayle Haggard's memoir in my analysis because like any wronged political wife, she served as an object of public fascination.

Because they use first-person, autobiographical formats in which to tell their stories, these narratives resonate with popular culture portrayals that provide the wife's oft-eclipsed point of view. Employing the memoir genre, these women achieve a sense of vindication (and maybe even outright revenge), a posture that plays into feminist understandings that self-disclosure can be an act of empowerment.[25] The larger mediascape echoes and reinforces similar understandings: *The Good Wife*'s decision to narrate from Alicia's point of view was one key reason for its heralding as a "feminist show."[26] From a marketing standpoint, wronged wife memoirs are also surprisingly good business. According to a 2011 *Variety* story on sexual scandal and Hollywood, filmmakers generally shy away from sexual scandal, believing that tabloids and television shows present more suitable storytelling venues than do feature-length films. Executives make a strong distinction, however, between wives and mistresses. They regard mistresses' tell-alls as forgettable, whereas first-person accounts from wives present marketable and profitable opportunities, especially if she is a sympathetic public figure, as Elizabeth Edwards was. If Maria Shriver (wronged wife of California ex-governor Arnold Schwarzenegger) were to write a book, "it would have a lot of appeal," according to the literary agent quoted in the article.[27] In keeping with this logic, it was reported in April 2017 that Huma Abedin was seeking a book contract, asking $2 million for her story.[28]

Investing in the rhetorical act of sharing stories of strained (and sometimes broken) marriages with an audience of presumably female readers, the wronged wife memoir exists in a mode that Lauren Berlant has termed "the female complaint," which she identifies as founded on "witnessing and explaining women's disappointment in the tenuous relation of romantic fantasy to lived intimacy."[29] Berlant argues that complaint genres "associate femininity with the pleasures, burdens, and virtues of emotional expertise and track its methods in different situations" as well as "focus on the sacrifice of women's emotional labors to a variety of kinds of callousness, incompetence, and structural inequity."[30] While each of the texts studied here possesses different tones and details varied outcomes, each uses the memoir form to explicate emotional and other forms of labor and to negotiate its own relationship to interested audiences. In each case, the wronged political wife demonstrates cognizance of her role as a public figure and of the fact that she may have contributed to propagating falsified narratives. The memoir, I argue, serves as her exoneration and justification, legitimization that often comes through the gesture of asserting herself as a marital laborer. In short, these narratives reveal the details of public family making. It should perhaps be acknowledged that these memoirs do participate in a wider pattern of what Nathan Rambukkana calls the "adultery industry," a term he uses to describe a whole field of discursive production surrounding adultery.[31] While these texts certainly do not condone or endorse the practice of adultery, they do participate in its larger sensationalization.

Wronged wife media reinforces the assertion that women's efforts on behalf of their husbands—and especially on the campaign trail—were performed in good faith. Jenny Sanford's memoir *Staying True* expressly makes this point as she details the events leading up to June 2009 when her husband, South Carolina governor Mark Sanford, disappeared for five days to Argentina to reconnect with his longtime mistress, a woman he famously called his "soul mate." Returning from the unplanned trip to face a barrage of questions about his marriage and his whereabouts, Sanford called a press conference where he spoke for over eighteen minutes, elaborating on his feelings, detailing his infidelities, and making multiple apologies and excuses. Tellingly, Jenny Sanford did not appear at the press conference, a move that has been credited with changing the terms by which wronged wives may operate. In a think piece about Huma Abedin's absence from Anthony Weiner's first press conference, pollster Cecelia Lake is quoted as saying, "Jenny Sanford really liberated a lot of these political wives," teaching them that "I don't have to put up with this anymore."[32] Mark Sanford eventually resigned the governorship and the couple divorced in 2010. Sanford then reunited with his mistress, Maria Belen Chapur, and regained public office, securing a South Carolina congressional seat in 2013. Given this history, it should come as no surprise that fractures in this relationship also occurred in uncomfortably public terms: Sanford outed a breakup with Chapur in

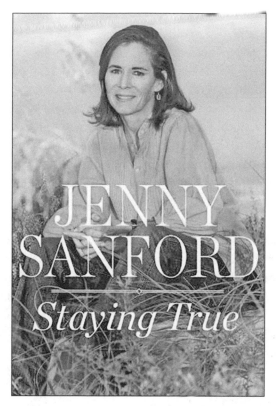

Figure 5.4. Jenny Sanford emphasizes that she remained committed to wifedom even after her husband abdicated his role as husband.

a rambling 2014 Facebook posting where he in part blamed his ex-wife for hindering his new romance. Chapur had no previous knowledge he planned a public revelation of their trials, and expressed as much to the press. In 2015, it was reported that Sanford and Chapur had reunited.

Given her saga, Jenny Sanford's book is perhaps understandably rich in the details of her husband's multiple hypocrisies, including the accusations that he breached his faith, neglected his children, acted as a tightwad with her but a spendthrift with his mistress, and treated her coldly during the period when he was attempting to break off the affair. In this way, the memoir establishes rhetorical authority in Jenny Sanford's suffering. Effecting a tone of Christian and charitable goodness, she positions herself as a giver, in contrast to her husband's relentless and insatiable quest for self-gratification. Sanford writes, "I was proud to conclude that giving and doing more for our marriage than I had received in return had been the right thing to do for our family," a sentiment that suggests she understands marriage as a kind of citizenship.[33]

In addition to the palpable sense of betrayal and anger caused by this marital rupture, Sanford's memoir contains a serious indictment of how her labor as a political wife was exploited. While she stalwartly defends her choice to give up a job as a New York investment banker early in her marriage when the couple moves to her husband's boyhood home in South Carolina, and speaks proudly of being a full-time wife and mother to the couple's four sons, she notes with frequency that they all worked on Mark's behalf. She discusses running his first campaign for Congress ("I gave it my all, and improbably, I became the wife of a politician"), and describes writing letters, making speeches, and participating in campaign appearances to establish his beliefs and policies. One of Sanford's biggest complaints is that while her husband used their family to publicly buttress his candidacy and to prop up the family values campaign he ran ("Mark was a man who spoke often about living according to principles and values, and our family was part of his appeal, evidence of character") he privately neglected them. Sanford also writes with a wearied tone of the labor it took to keep their family in a photo-worthy condition: "I always needed to be aware of how I looked or how our children looked or acted in public." In contrast to the patience she displayed in the face of unrelenting demands, Mark was short-tempered and uncompromising, as evidenced by his annoyance with her when one of their sons was photographed looking bored during a speech by George W. Bush. As if to discipline her unsympathetic husband rather than her all-too-human son, Sanford divulges, "Mark was disappointed in me for not coaching the boys to look interested, but I myself was proud of their good behavior. There's only so much you can ask of a child, and sitting through a political speech was the limit!"[34] Sanford's sense that her husband treated her children more like employees than offspring aids her indictment that he had lost touch with the affective realities of family life. As well, it speaks to the emotional disciplining imposed by their position as public figures.

This often-uneasy relationship between domesticity and politics—and specifically the necessity of laboring to keep one's true feelings in check while under public scrutiny constitutes another hallmark of wronged wife media. Of the books surveyed here, Sanford's presents the most biting critique of the deleterious effects of this performance. Specifically, she laments the porousness of their family life insofar as the public had almost constant access to it. Confirming an observation made by a former governor's wife, Sanford repeats the previous first lady's contention that residing in the governor's mansion is "like living above the shop" since the family could hear events and tours below.[35] By comparing her home to a shop, Sanford is in effect characterizing the machinery of her marriage and family as a production process.

Dina Matos McGreevey likewise makes note of these requirements, but has a more nuanced view of their costs and benefits. She describes how her courtship with Jim McGreevey was performed under the auspices of the public eye, even from the beginning: "Our dates often took the form of campaign stops: breakfasts with senior citizens, football games at high-school athletic fields, church picnics, dinners at catering halls." Matos McGreevey theorizes that this public show of intimacy was not so foreign for her because, though for most children "family life is a private matter, it's a life lived at home," as the sister of a chronically ill brother "some of our most important and powerful activities as a family took place in the public sphere of hospitals and doctors' offices, as my parents tried to protect and provide for my brother . . . once the usual boundaries separating private life from public life had been, for me, removed—or at least redrawn—the political had become the personal." Matos McGreevey's framing of advocacy work as a joint endeavor and acquiescence to having that work supplant a private life in fact brings her to a prescient reformulation of the public sphere. As she writes, "Political action was a passion, and the public arena was an intimate space." To explain the functioning of the public sphere in this way, she reiterates the couple's shared belief in the promise of public service and notes that even before meeting her husband she was a strong advocate in the Portuguese community where she grew up. In a story that underscores the extent to which her family life was defined by similar efforts, she describes how the couple's baby joined them on stage during Jim's swearing-in ceremony for governor, and writes, "I couldn't help but think, with a bit of a twinge, that this public moment was also our most moving family moment since Jacqueline's birth."[36] Given what she would

later find out about her husband's secret sexual proclivities, it is not surprising that she would look with some dismay on this event. Yet, hers is
actually a keen insight into shifting definitions of family life. In an era
in which private moments now take place in the public eye—photos of a
new baby are, for example, posted almost immediately on Facebook and
Instagram—Matos McGreevey's family life anticipates the sort of mediatized existences that most Americans enjoy. It also underscores the need
to examine marriage as a form of labor that functions on increasingly
public terrain, a point that this book has been making throughout. In
this respect, though political wives would seem to be a rare breed whose
public negotiations of their domestic lives have little traffic with those of
everyday Americans, in fact their stories simply throw into starker relief
such exigencies.

Given the new normalization of wifely labors, it can perhaps be better understood why Elizabeth Edwards describes campaigning for her
husband's presidential bid, even after learning of his affair, as a gesture
she did not view as an act of prevarication but rather as a decision that
testified to one of their marriage's most cherished strengths. As she details, urging her husband to remain in the 2008 presidential race was
not a way of hiding their struggles, but was rather meant to save the
marriage by reminding them both of the larger goals of their partnership. Edwards writes, "We were lovers, life companions, crusaders, side
by side, for a vision of what the country could be, and we were an old
married couple . . . And that part about crusading together, it was the
glue . . . I grabbed hold of it. I needed to. I needed him to stand with
me, and although I no longer knew what I could trust between the two
of us, I knew I could trust in our work together."[37] As her statements
suggest, the couple's "work together" was an asset rather than a liability,
providing both a reason and a means (at least momentarily) to preserve
their marriage. Recasting the partnership as work was a perception that
paradoxically offered a means to salvage it.

By stressing the extent to which the work of wifedom was integral
to both their personal and professional lives, wives' memoirs usefully
complicate easy divisions between public and private. These memoirs
suggest that even after the revelation of a personal betrayal, wives see
the work of their marriages as both meaningful and a source of pride.[38]
Because marriage exists for reasons beyond the immediate partners—

and is cast, instead, as more of a national responsibility—scorned wife memoirs achieve the paradoxical feat of affirming a politics of spouse-hood that transcends the scandal that precipitated the memoir. Far from partaking in a false performance, these wives suggest that neither their marriages nor the work they did in the public eye was misleading. (If anything, Matos McGreevey's memoir suggests that her efforts were not properly recognized. If her title *Silent Partner* is to be taken literally, she was behind the scenes supporting the endeavor yet also lacking the requisite credit for it.)

This recasting of marriage as a partnership that both husband and wife knowingly operationalize also helps to explain why wives frequently characterize the fallout from these marital breaches less as a loss of in-timacy and more as a loss of work. Gayle Haggard writes with poignant sadness that when she and her husband were exiled from their evan-gelical church after his sex scandal involving a male prostitute, she was forced out of a paid position as the full-time director of Women Belong, a women's ministry. After her eventual separation from John Edwards, Elizabeth Edwards similarly describes feeling that she lacked both a per-sonal and a professional identity ("Now I have to find the person that I was—or might have been—had I not fallen in love with John thirty-five years ago.") She describes, in turn, how she opened a small furniture store: "In this world, I am not John's wife. My name is not in a tabloid. I am Elizabeth buying for a small store in Chapel Hill."[39] Here a crisis in marriage reads, tellingly, as a crisis of identity, a point that suggests an ineluctable association between intimate lives, personal commitments, and professional obligations.

Larger national conversations on marriage and politics also increas-ingly describe wifedom in occupational terms. A *Newsweek* cover, em-blazoned with the words "The Good Wife, 2012," features a smiling, pearl-wearing blonde in a red suit. The story then includes the follow-ing assertion: "With women empowered to do more than nurture their husbands, political wives—in whom women often seek a more polished version of themselves—are increasingly expected to be more than just the perfect helpmeet. (Though, make no mistake, that is still required.) Standing beside your man with an adoring gaze remains a part of the job, only now you need to exhibit goals and interests of your own—a passion if not exactly a portfolio."[40] It is not incidental that the article deploys the phrase "remains a part of the job"; as this book has traced throughout, wifedom's status as a job is integral to its contemporary resonance. *Scandal's* Mellie Grant explicitly receives analogous counsel: in a flashback sequence reflecting the early days of her marriage, and while Mellie is still working at her law job, an adviser counsels that if she hopes to help her husband win a governorship, she must make *him* her profession: "He is your charity work. He is your full-time job. You're the wife. Help him." Similarly, after the tragic and sudden death of her son emotionally paralyzes Mellie, she is lured back to making public appearances as first lady not by her husband's cajoling but rather by the words of his press secretary, who tells her, "Children die. . . . Do your job." These sentiments are echoed in *House of Cards* by an acrimonious season 3 exchange between Claire and Frank Underwood. Refusing to appear with her husband in public after she realizes that her husband has benefited more from her support than vice versa, Frank responds in kind by pointedly explaining his expectations for her, which involve traveling to New Hampshire to campaign for the next day's primary election: "I'm doing my job . . . now it's time for you to do yours."

The requirement that women turn wifedom into a profession nevertheless tends to invite public disapprobation, a discomfort we might trace to the fact that when women's work exists as an extension of her marital or maternal role, it resides on the margins of recognizable economies. Profiting either economically or emotionally from personal relations—or using intimate bonds as the basis for advancing a personally meaningful agenda—immediately makes a woman vulnerable to the accusation that she labors solely for the purpose of selfish gain. These anxieties affirm the symbolic stronghold of the idea that wifehood and motherhood exist solely and ahistorically in the realm of the domestic, cherished notions that have a somewhat awe-inspiring ability to persevere even in the face of their largely illusionary status. We can see similar unease in the wariness with which American media culture approaches the position of the "political wife," a label that memoirists like Sanford decisively shun for its suggestion that it involves profiting from family life, hence polluting a sacrosanct set of bonds. In these discursive realms, the figure of Hillary Clinton serves as a cautionary tale, thanks to her identification as a wife who has remained in a marriage that appears to be most saliently a powerhouse professional partnership. The assumption that Clinton willingly sacrificed love in exchange for influence and access has come to symbol-ize the personal costs wrought by extreme opportunism.

The specter of ruthless ambition run amok expressly haunts Matos McGreevey, who uses her memoir to rebut the claims that she knew all along her husband was gay: "Some took gratuitous swipes at Hillary Clinton while taking swipes at me, saying that, like her, I was an oppor-tunist, and that I'd married Jim knowing he was gay because I wanted to be first lady and advance my own political future." Matos McGreevey adamantly refutes this accusation: "I would have never married Jim knowing that he was gay. And, as much as I'd enjoyed politics before I married him, I wouldn't have married him as a way of advancing my own chances of becoming a successful candidate for office myself either. Who needed Jim? I would have done it on my own if I'd wanted to."[41] Matos McGreevey's disclaimer illustrates the influence that figures like Hillary Clinton have had on the cultural discourse. Rather than needing to avow agency, Matos McGreevey feels compelled to disavow oppor-tunism. Her comments confirm a wider cultural understanding of the logics this book has been tracing insofar as she acknowledges that mar-riage is increasingly viewed as a commitment undertaken for personal gain. Matos McGreevey's statements also illustrate how life experiences are filtered by and lived in dialogue with the press—the term "political wife" even has a place in her book's index.

In contrast, Jenny Sanford's repeated assertion that she hated the work of wifedom emphasizes her essential femininity and seemingly in-oculates her from this critique. Repeatedly professing her investment in old-fashioned notions of traditional gender identities and testifying to her efforts to shield familial labors from the ugliness of market forces, Sanford exculpates herself from the sorts of suspicions that plague Matos McGreevey. The aforementioned *Newsweek* cover story describes Sanford as one who "endured" fifteen years of political wifedom, and she is quoted as saying, "I could not wait to get out of the job."[42] Sanford has also earned something of a reputation as the go-to pundit for describ-ing the punishing aspects of political wifedom. She also appears in 2013 *Washington Post* piece that ran after the revelation of Weiner's second scandal: "As a person and as a woman and as a wife, I've been through the painful reality of marriage with a troubled individual and having it in the press. My heart goes out to her."[43]

According to wrong wives' memoirs, their images exist in direct dialogue with the mass media; as a result, the women feel compelled to dispute unfair mediatized depictions. As Elizabeth Edwards writes, "I was never as good, or as bad, as the shifting image portrayed." It is important to her to be known as herself, especially in the face of the increasingly toxic descriptions voiced by Andrew Young (whom she never names), the sycophantic staff assistant who helped her husband hide his affair. In his book *The Politician* (2009), Young describes claiming paternity for John Edwards's daughter with Hunter and excoriates Elizabeth Edwards for the wrath she exhibited after finding out the truth. As she confesses, "I never was Saint Elizabeth. I never pretended to be. I never was a monster. I certainly don't want to be. I was simply a person, incredibly fragile, who became more and more afraid of what tomorrow would tell me about my health, about my family, about my life."[44]

Invoking her own media troubles, Haggard laments how her husband was misrepresented in the film *Jesus Camp* (2006) and ambushed on CNN's *Larry King Live*, misrepresentations that in turn impelled their collaboration with an HBO documentary *The Trials of Ted Haggard* (2009), a more sympathetic narrative that highlights Haggard's difficult efforts to build a new life after he is exiled from his former church and from the state of Colorado. In the documentary, Gail Haggard answers questions about her decision to stay with her husband, but does it while walking beside him, his presence a silent but potent reminder of how his interests are framing her words and sentiments. For his part, the man with whom Haggard had a long-standing sexual relationship granted a radio interview to Sirius XM radio host Michelangelo Signorile, a circuit that again suggests how many avenues exist for the intentional participants in a scandal, and how relatively few there are for those who are only collaterally involved in it.[45] Gail Haggard's memoir is the only place where she tells her story on her own terms. Relatedly, the couple's appearance in 2012 on the sensationalized reality show *Celebrity Wife Swap* (2012–15), where they trade with the family of erratic actor Gary Busey, seemed to be motivated by an attempt to rehabilitate Ted Haggard's tarnished reputation in Colorado Springs after he returns to begin a new ministry, yearning for a fresh start. On the show, Gayle Haggard reads as centered, poised, and articulate, even as she trades on her wifedom to aid her husband's career (and possibly earn the family some money).

As these examples demonstrate, wronged wife memoirs make deliberately strategic use of media platforms, texts that also inadvertently reveal the increasingly dialogic nature of marriage. One need not be on the campaign trail to recognize that marriage and its lived realities are public acts or to see that wifedom is performed on multiple stages. Blurring lines between what constitutes work and what constitutes marriage, scorned wife media reveal ineluctable slippages between intimate labors and public efforts.

Instrumentalizing Marriage and "America's Baby"

Undeniably borrowing from these real-world cases, CBS's *The Good Wife*, the ABC drama *Scandal*, and Netflix's *House of Cards* all feature political wives who respectively utilize the perch of wifedom for political gain. This section will thread a discussion of Alicia Florrick, Mellie Grant, and Claire Underwood alongside real-life wives, explicating how these characterizations encapsulate the new rhetorics of wifedom that this book has been tracing throughout. Specifically I will examine the professionalization of marriage and the instrumentalization of children, explicating the benefits that accrue to women prepared to make their family lives a centerpiece of their public images.

According to the strictures of the American political process, the quality and performance of a candidate's marriage bespeaks his or her personal character. According to this paradigm, the functionality of a candidate's partnership (a designation that rests to an extraordinary degree on sexual fidelity) fundamentally testifies to his or her true nature. Conversely, if that partnership undergoes stress or fracture, it becomes the responsibility of the other partner—and almost always, the wife—to assure the public that faith in the candidate or politician is again warranted because the union has been rehabilitated. *The Good Wife* has been particularly eloquent on this matter: post-scandal, Alicia's (largely falsified) testaments to their marital reconciliation undeniably aid Peter's political comeback. When Peter runs for state's attorney, for instance, Alicia consents to a live on-air interview televised the night before the election. Despite the couple's still-rocky relationship, her appearance helps him to win the post. Tellingly, the interview also plants what will be the first seed of many, when the female interviewer asks

Alicia about her political aspirations and frames Alicia as the more well liked of the two. Harnessing this theme, the show repeatedly returned to the idea that Alicia, not her husband, deserved a political future.

The Good Wife also repeatedly revisited the deliberate instrumentalization of media forms in order to create the appearance of marital harmony. In season 3, after a television appearance in which Alicia (identified in the caption as "politician's wife / lawyer / mother") appears on *Charlie Rose*, attesting to Peter's commitment to his family, Peter's chances at the Illinois governorship—and his stature in the eyes of coveted women voters—rise markedly. Increasingly, however, *The Good Wife* illustrated how this necessity cuts both ways; as Alicia's own aspirations intensified, so, too, did her need to maintain the appearance of marital conviviality. In seasons 5 and 6, the couple is estranged in all but name, yet Alicia tells Peter, "I'm not going to divorce you. You are too valuable to me professionally, just like I am to you. But we are not going to see each other anymore, not unless we have to."

When Alicia decides to run for state's attorney—a decision that comes at the behest of none other than feminist paragon Gloria Steinem—she, too, becomes the mouthpiece for why her marriage to Peter represents a crucial component of their respective professional lives. When Peter balks at introducing her when she makes the announcement of her candidacy, she sketches out a number of distasteful consequences for him should he refuse: "Your favorables will plummet through the floor. On the day you want to be talking about pensions, every question will be about the state of your marriage. Yes, I may need you, Peter, but you sure as hell need me, too." As both Alicia and Peter come to realize so intuitively that it becomes second nature, political futures depend on the perceived stability and normalcy of a candidate's connubial relations. Rehearsing the extent to which the Florrick's marriage does not simply support the spouses' respective careers, but exists as merely another arm of them, Alicia informs Peter that if he desires her presence at a political event, he is to call her office: "My assistant will put it on my calendar." Alicia thus dispassionately rehearses the transactional nature of the Florricks' marriage; performing it represents simply another professional obligation.

The Good Wife hence coldly and explicitly articulates the terms of the couple's marital arrangements, and suggests the extent to which political futures rise and fall on a couple's perceived unity. This same understanding organizes the presentation of the Grant marriage on *Scandal*, the televised offering that most consistently atomizes the machinations it takes, as a handler says, to "spin a dead marriage." *Scandal* also adroitly articulates the political gains that accrue when spouses effectively launch such a public relations campaign. Attending parent-teacher conferences, jovially sharing ice cream cones, and performing the sort of gentle teasing that reads as affection, Fitz and Mellie follow a familiar playbook as they seek to repair their strained relations. In a sequence that underscores the incredible power that perceptions of marital authenticity wield, the series showcases what can best be understood as a "Hail Mary" marriage move. Faced with polling numbers that report Fitz will lose Super Tuesday thanks to a lack of connection with female voters, Mellie uses a cozy pie-eating photo-op in a Georgia diner to spin a poignant yarn.[46] She interrupts the proceedings, sharing with the amassed group of southern women a fabricated story about having recently suffered a miscarriage, a loss she attributes to the stress of campaigning: "Even though it was only eight weeks, it was a baby, and it was a member of our family, and I have grieved for the loss of our child every day since," she tearfully confesses. Using the pain of their shared trauma, and Fitz's supposed willingness to quit the race so that the couple could have "time to take care of each other," Mellie's cover story explains what she notes has likely been perceived as their distance while on the campaign trail. This stunningly opportunistic move accomplishes a number of goals, humanizing their marriage (and implicitly affirming a continued sexual connection), asserting the maternal impulse as common ground shared with female voters, and reframing marital disruption as grief rather than estrangement.

In contrast, one of Claire Underwood's greatest liabilities is that she has had multiple abortions, a fact that she goes to great lengths to hide. In this way, *House of Cards* emphasizes that motherhood remains a sacrosanct aspiration for wives, insofar as it immediately confirms their supposed relatability and warmth. Worse than never having children is, of course, deliberately and intentionally prohibiting their existence, as Claire did on multiple occasions. The Underwoods' primary rivals in the presidential race are in turn a fecund young Republican couple with two small children, a fact that again highlights the Underwoods' sterility and coldness. (The comparisons between the Underwoods and Shakespeare's Macbeths are, in fact, vast and multiple.) In keeping with this ethos, the Underwoods' own "Hail Mary" move is far grimmer and has more dire consequences than does Mellie's false miscarriage. In an effort to deflect attention from a damaging exposé of their improprieties and illegal maneuverings, and to salvage a sputtering presidential campaign, the couple decides to sacrifice an American hostage and take the country to war.

As these cultural offerings account for, political wives reside in a landscape where motherhood remains an unquestioned and yet pivotal aspiration. Into this milieu enters Mellie's pièce de résistance, what the press terms "America's baby." In a brilliantly lucid articulation of how family and marriage may be operationalized in an American culture whose widespread cynicism somehow does not extend to the revered mythology of the family, Mellie views the baby as both a weapon and an asset. Having announced to the American public that she is pregnant (again, another lie) in an effort to distract from the allegation of a presidential sex scandal with an intern (another way in which the show borrows from the Clinton legacy), Mellie and Fitz get down to the task of procreation ("We'll have to start trying right away, of course," Mellie says with curt efficiency). Visibly pregnant in the season 2 opener, and in response to her husband's plaintive plea that "everything is not a political move," she diagrams for him exactly under what circumstances this child was conceived, and the baby's larger significance in terms of their joint political aspirations:

> Honey, you are not some toothless mechanic from Indiana and I am not some chunky girl from a trailer park. We didn't fall in love, get drunk, and do it in the back of a pickup truck. This baby, bless its heart, is not ours. This baby is our patriotic duty. This baby was conceived in service to our country. This is America's baby, and Kimberly Mitchell is coming to watch us find out whether it's a boy or girl because you are the leader of the free world and you couldn't keep your pants zipped and your hands to yourself. This baby is my way of giving you a little political bang for your buck.

Mellie in turn uses the interview where the sex of "America's baby" is revealed to strong-arm her husband on a sensitive foreign relations issue. Suggesting that he should send troops to East Sudan to protect its children from genocide (but really hoping that a popular war will sew up his reelection chances) Mellie comments after the fact on how she used her pregnancy strategically: "I struck just the tone that you needed with the public. Both hands on my belly, I shared my concerns."

This sequence coldly articulates the maternal as a performance ripe for manipulation and showcases the maternal body as a serviceable entity. As Cyrus Beene (Jeff Perry), the president's chief of staff, says to Mellie, "You and that belly have done enough for Fitz's reelection chances already." Asserting that women's reproductive capability serves as a powerful asset in the image wars, the plotline suggests a keen understanding of how gendered ideals can themselves be exploited, presenting a biting rejoinder to the belief that maternal capabilities somehow exempt or extract women from crass calculations. Mellie clutches her son, though only when the press is watching; "Nobody likes babies," she says matter-of-factly in one of her more honest moments. Though Mellie is fond of reminding her husband that she gave up her career for him and had children for him, the America's baby plotline suggests that this child serves *her* and she blatantly instrumentalizes the baby for her own political advantage.

In a telling reversal of the baby's birth as a humanizing gesture, and again in homage to the show's many Shakespearean undertones, *House of Cards'* Claire unflappably administers a mercy killing to her dying mother the night before her appearance at the Democratic convention, where she is locked in a tight battle to secure a nomination for vice president. Displaying a steely will that clearly has passed through the generations, Elizabeth (Ellen Burstyn) essentially urges her daughter to sacrifice her for the political boost it will provide. As Elizabeth says, "It'd help you win. Having your mother gone." In the wake of her mother's death, Claire mobilizes sympathy precisely as her mother would have wished. Accepting the nomination for vice president, Claire prevaricates about their relationship, attesting to a relation of warmth and encouragement that is largely falsified.

Collectively, these shows demonstrate the bald insight that America's investment in the narrative of the happy family is ripe for exploitation and manipulation. Not only must the wife play a germane and integral role in presenting the family as such, but she also holds incredible power to rehabilitate or tank the family brand. *Scandal*'s cognizance of this reality in fact cuts across multiple plotlines. In a first season story line, fixer Olivia Pope (Kerry Washington) tries to convince a South American dictator to let his unhappy wife leave and keep her children because, if he does not accede to her demands that she retain primary custody, Olivia predicts the wife will wage her own public relations offensive. Smart and powerful women "strike back," Olivia says, "by writing memoirs, and appearing on talk shows, and at benefits and on red carpets, talking about women's rights in the developing world, and how babies were ripped from her arms by a ruthless dictator who can't run a family much less a country." As Olivia tells him, he best think carefully because his decision is a matter of "political survival": "This woman can either be the mother of your children or the face of your opposition." Pointing out the power and prevalence of female media circuits—an observation that this chapter has also been emphasizing—*Scandal* adeptly illustrates the symbolic value of the wife.

House of Cards echoes this sentiment in very similar terms. In large part thanks to Claire Underwood's tactically timed disappearance from the campaign trail, Frank Underwood's presidential campaign flails. Specifically, she refuses to celebrate her husband's victory in Iowa, does not go to New Hampshire, which he then loses, and deliberately sabotages South Carolina. Reminding him of these failures, she leverages her own position and utility: "Your race is in real trouble. You need me, Francis. My approval ratings are higher than yours. I can help you win Texas." Claire's offer of help nevertheless comes with various strings attached, including her demand that he put her on the ticket as his vice president. To convince him, Claire articulates her value to him and the implicit threat she will pose if he does not concede to her demands: "You can't win without me . . . I can be a part of your campaign, or I can end it. I'll do whatever it takes . . . but I will not let this go."

Scandal, *House of Cards*, and *The Good Wife* offer important lenses through which to view actual political marriages and the scandals that have rocked twenty-first-century media. A testament to the wife's power to use her motherhood as a syllogism for ethics is clearly found, for instance, in Maria Shriver's participation in Arnold Schwarzenegger's bid for the California governorship in 2003. Defending him from damaging rumors that he inappropriately groped a number of women, and using her own reputation as a strong and principled woman as collateral, Shriver's support effectively salvaged his candidacy when she gave a series of speeches (aptly titled "The Remarkable Women's Tour") that testified to her husband's character and his support for female accomplishment.[47] After she yoked her own credibility to his, Schwarzenegger's betrayal—fathering a child with a longtime member of his household staff but not revealing this fact for over ten years—seemed all the more cruel, a sentiment that turned the tide of public opinion very much in her favor. Likewise, though it arguably did not have the same rhetorical force, in October 2016 Melania Trump mounted a defense of her husband after incriminating tapes emerged of him talking lewdly about groping women. Melania Trump asserted that "I don't know that person that would talk that way," and suggested her husband was egged on by "boy talk," defenses that arguably allowed Americans already planning to vote for him to look the other way.[48]

However, the instrumentalization of wifedom and motherhood among real-world figures is perhaps nowhere on better display than in the example of Anthony Weiner's comeback attempt to run for New York City mayor in 2013. A little over a year after the sexting scandal that forced his resignation from Congress, Weiner and Abedin began their public relations offensive, sitting for a story in *People* magazine carrying the treacly title "Anthony Weiner, 'I Feel Like a Different Person.'" Beginning with a cozy two-page photo spread featuring the couple with their infant son, the article includes a still from Weiner's tearful first press conference, and begins with the following sentence, "The former congressman from Queens, wearing seersucker shorts, black socks and a Mets cap, is crooning 'Joy to the World' as he shampoos his 6-month-old son Jordan's hair."[49] This sentence is telling, for Weiner speaks enthusiastically and lovingly about fatherhood, playing up his role as a house husband, in contrast to his career-minded wife. The article postulates that the now-humbled man spends his time catering to a child, an image that represents a significant recasting since Weiner's reputation in Congress was that of a brash and bold egoist. This sentiment was echoed in a *New York* magazine article which claimed that Weiner's domestication softened him: "With Huma often still traveling with Hillary, the once peripatetic Weiner, a man who'd schedule ten events on a single Sunday, had become a house husband, giving his son a bottle, changing his diapers,

Figure 5.5. Testing the waters for a return to public life after Anthony Weiner's resignation from Congress, the couple sweetly testifies to the life-changing effects of parenthood.

watching him grow."[50] Supposedly a better person post-scandal, Weiner and his comeback narrative fit snugly with the notion that becoming a parent serves as a maturing transition. Adding to this story of a late-life reform, Weiner became a first-time father at age forty-seven.

Weiner's instrumentalization of his status as a parent is well evidenced in the repeated rehearsal of his excitement over witnessing Jordan's "first steps," a familiarly monumental turning point in parenting. The milestone is referenced in *People* ("I'm not doing anything to plan a campaign . . . The only next dramatic steps I'm planning on are Jordan's first")[51] and provides the opening salvo in a *New York Times Magazine* cover story about the couple timed to correspond with Weiner's announcement that he would seek the position of mayor of New York City ("The first thing Weiner said when I sat down was that their 13-month-old son, Jordan, had just moments ago taken his first step"). The author describes Weiner and Abedin as both "giddy, kvelling with baby-pride, especially Weiner."[52] Given that in the midst of these gauzy interviews Weiner continued sending sexually explicit correspondence to a variety of young women, using the alias "Carlos Danger," it is hard not to read his and Abedin's invocation of their son as an "America's baby"–type calculation. In this regard, the obsession with Jordan's first steps provides the sentimental equivalent of Mellie putting her hands on her belly. In the press coverage, the baby was also repeatedly used as an explanation for why Abedin stayed with Weiner for so long.[53]

Despite Weiner's casting as a *Mr. Mom* figure in multiple publications, Abedin occupies an essential role in this full-court press. In fact, *People* magazine credits her as the one who brought the press in because, though normally "press shy," she is "proud to be married to him." In the piece, and as she will in later portrayals, Abedin refers to the work of their marriage: "It took a lot of work to get to where we are today, but I want people to know we're a normal family."[54] In this rehearsed narrative, Abedin casts herself as a loving wife who forgave her husband after much deliberation. Weiner's first mayoral campaign video, in which Abedin plays a prominent role, also perfectly encapsulates the logics of repentance and reform on which these performances depend. Beginning with a bustling breakfast scene that features the couple feeding their child, Weiner says in voice-over, "Every day starts here, and it's the best part of my day." While Weiner talks about his history with and commitment to the city, Abedin brackets the video, appearing in the beginning and in its closing moment. She sits beside her husband on the stoop of a brownstone apartment—rather than at the Park Avenue luxury building where they actually live, a $3.3 million apartment owned by a longtime backer of the Clintons. In close-up Abedin says, "We love this city, and no one will work harder than Anthony to make it better," before she casts a brief sidelong glance at him.

Abedin's appearances on the public stage on behalf of her husband in fact had a remarkable consistency. All emphasize the work of marriage; stress the power of individual choice ("It was the right choice for me. I didn't make it lightly");[55] and offer the assertion that Abedin committed to her marriage after being assured that Weiner—whom she refers to as Anthony—is reformed. These invocations adeptly utilize the logics of female media forms, which tend to reinforce neoliberal, postfeminist teleologies of personal growth. Making this case in the *New York Times Magazine* profile, Abedin tellingly invokes Hillary Clinton by name when she explains how she, too, was forced to make a very personal choice: "I think she would be O.K. with my saying this because she has said this before: at the end of the day, at the very least, every woman should have the ability and the confidence and the choice to make whatever decisions she wants to make that are right for her and not be judged by it."[56] (Clinton was reportedly, however, not so "O.K." with these references; the Clintons were cited twenty-one times in the Weiner-Abedin profile, a point about which they were not happy.[57] Abedin and Clinton's defenses of their respective marriages nevertheless have incredible consonance.) Abedin makes a typically postfeminist assertion of the right to personal choice and privacy, yet it exists primarily as a sleight of hand. Asserting privacy, Abedin courts publicity. Abedin's marital struggles in fact provide excellent fodder for female media forms keen to circulate neoliberal notions of self-help individualism, a fact that Abedin and Weiner capitalized on in order to bolster their relatability and, presumably, enhance Weiner's chances of winning the mayoral race.

Identical understandings of the need to choose the best path for oneself anchor the 2013 op-ed Abedin wrote for *Harper's Bazaar*, tellingly titled "The Good Wife," in which she calls her husband "a better man" and writes that "New Yorkers will have to decide for themselves whether or not to give him a second chance. I had to make that same decision for myself, for my son, for our family. And I know in my heart that I made the right one."[58] Ironically, by the time the story ran the second scandal was widely known and the publication wrote a new introduction to the piece that acknowledged the transgression. Abedin's decision to make a public plea for her husband's candidacy in a high-end fashion magazine likewise deftly underscores her image as a glamorous jet-setter. Years before marrying Weiner, Abedin was written up in a 2007 *Vogue* profile that praised her style sense, sophistication, and maturity; overall the piece framed her as an international sophisticate.[59] Abedin's comfort with female media forms and the extent to which she has been willing to deliberately court them speaks to the range that she displays, traversing as she does elite publications and those, like *People*, that have a more middlebrow appeal.

Demonstrating a remarkable ability to work within the affective paradigms that female media culture favors, Abedin's "stand by your man" appearance at her embattled husband's press conference after his mayoral race became mired in scandal called on similar rubrics of personal agency and choice. Divulging to the crowd that this was her first press conference, and that she was "very nervous" and wrote down her remarks as a result, Abedin read, "Our marriage, like many others, has had its up and its downs. It took a lot of work, and whole lot of therapy,

Figure 5.6. Appearing by his side to defend her husband during the final weeks of his embattled 2013 mayoral campaign, Abedin divulged that staying in her marriage "was a decision I made for me, for our son, and for our family."

to get to a place where I could forgive Anthony." Pausing on the brink of tears, she says, "It was not an easy choice, in any way. But I [with emphasis] made the decision that it was worth staying in this marriage," and smiles at her husband. "I didn't know how it would work out, but I knew I wanted to try." Abedin goes on to reference the "horrible mistakes" her husband made, both before he resigned from Congress and after: "But I do very strongly believe that that is between us and our marriage." While Abedin's appearance did not prove game-changing enough to garner her husband a win in the mayoral election, it did serve to establish her believability, legitimacy, and credibility at exactly at the moment when her husband was losing what was left of his.

Abedin's reaction to her husband's second public humiliation may well have, in fact, only heighted her appeal. As Hinda Mandell rightly reminds us, the visage of an unhappy wife at a politico-done-wrong press conference typically affords the press license for public pity: the act of calling a woman out for "standing by her man" underlines a publication or author's own progressive stance, positioning them on the "side" of the wronged wife.[60] Such postures assert that a publication or author is thinking of the woman's best interests, a viewpoint that can slip into the accusation that supporting one's fallen husband amounts to false consciousness. We would be remiss, however, to read today's wronged wives—or their media participation—through this lens. Cogently and often calculatingly harnessing the power of female media forms, wronged wives instead often use the declaration of personal choice as a strategy to deflect criticism and preserve their own images. Abedin's more public negotiation of her husband's second humiliation was perhaps more savvy than her first absence, in that it begged for her to be compared to her husband and to emerge, unilaterally, as the more likable and principled of the two. In the final section, I consider the larger notion that the Weiner-Abedin marriage became impossible to maintain given her brand image, and the suspicion that their failed union may very well have denied the United States its first female president.

When He's Bad for the Brand

That Abedin was able to negotiate her public image with more savvy than her husband and retain an image of being media-shy rather than fame-hungry was also rehearsed in the publicity surrounding the release of the 2016 documentary *Weiner*, which carried remarkable backstage footage of Weiner's failed mayoral campaign. In addition to catching the pair in awkward, quotidian moments (her telling him "I'm not crazy about those pants"), the documentary captured and filmed what was clearly *another* painful and humiliating chapter in the Weiner-Abedin marriage, a nadir encapsulated by footage of Weiner on election night sending Abedin home alone (after spending the day appealing to her to appear in public with him), arriving at his concession party, and then running through a McDonald's restaurant to avoid an awaiting Sydney Leathers, code-named "pineapple" by Weiner's handlers.

Many viewers wondered why a supposedly laconic Abedin would participate in a documentary, a choice seemingly antithetical to her fiercely maintained privacy. Yet, as I have argued here, Abedin consented to considerable publicity, particularly in moments where her wifedom and her glamour promised to pay professional dividends for both her and her husband. The documentary nevertheless trades on trumping her supposed inaccessibly: hearing her voice on camera, Weiner says, is "like hearing Charlie Chaplin in the talkies for the first time." Heightening this sense of mystique, Weiner revealed some four months after the film's release that they had not given permission for the footage of Abedin to be used in the final cut.[61] The filmmakers did not substantiate this allegation, but it did serve to suggest yet again that Abedin was not courting publicity, and did not deserve to be tarnished by association. In the documentary, Abedin does however reveal herself as a cool political operator: she woos a major donor over the phone, hangs up, and tells Weiner, matter-of-factly, "Alright, he'll max. His wife is going to max out."

Abedin's (at least) initial agreement to appear in the film suggests that both spouses predicted a different outcome to Weiner's mayoral campaign, and that given a happier result, her participation would have bolstered them both. Similarly, there is reason to believe that had Weiner not failed so publicly again in August 2016 and thereafter, the marriage might have survived. Two weeks prior to the third scandal, when Weiner sent a scantily clad photo of himself perched near his sleeping son to a woman with whom he had been corresponding, Abedin was the subject of a glowing *Vogue* profile, with accompanying photos by Annie Leibovitz. While the piece concentrated mostly on her responsibilities as Hillary Clinton's top aide (and, it was intimated, likely chief of staff were Clinton elected), as well as her impeccable fashion sense, a portion of the article was predictably focused on Abedin's juggling act as a working mother. In the midst of a frenetic election season, Abedin gives Weiner considerable credit for managing the domestic front, saying, "Many working moms feel this way—there is a lot of guilt . . . I don't think I could do it if I didn't have the support system I have, if Anthony wasn't willing to be, essentially, a full-time dad."[62] Given this glowing endorsement of Weiner, it is particularly ironic that the lasting fallout from his behavior was that it spurred the revived e-mail investigation that may have ultimately cost Clinton (and Abedin) the presidency. Perhaps portending this damaging potentiality, the Clinton campaign reportedly long viewed Abedin's marriage as a liability. The couple's separation was announced mere hours after the pictures were revealed, and coverage of the split suggested that the couple had been estranged and living apart for some time, though the *Vogue* profile, which covered a time period merely weeks beforehand, offers no such intimations. In truth, it appears that Abedin was willing to publicize and even compliment her troubled marriage until its very last hours. (In fact, amid rumors that the couple might still reconcile, Abedin filed for divorce only when it became clear that Weiner could go to jail. The divorce petition was brought to court the same day that Weiner pleaded guilty to a federal obscenity charge, a sentence that ultimately led to Weiner's incarceration.)

When the split was announced, Donald Trump suggested that Abedin might have shared sensitive information with Weiner, alleging that she may have violated national security. What seemed at the time like hyperbole—clearly designed to remind voters of Hillary Clinton's own troubled marital history and issues with her credibility—in turn quickly escalated into reality when an investigation began into Weiner's alleged sexts with a fifteen-year-old girl and the FBI reopened its investigations into Hillary Clinton's e-mails just days before the election. Though there is clearly no single cause for Clinton's largely unpredicted defeat, there is reason to think that the reinvigorated e-mail investigation and the suspicions it raised about her trustworthiness did not help her candidacy.

Taking into account these developments in an effort to conclude this chapter and *Wife, Inc.* as a whole, it bears acknowledging that this chapter was largely written with a different outcome in mind. When Clinton's victory seemed all but assured, I planned to end with a discussion of the wronged political wife as a thoroughly reimagined figure, one transmuted into a savvy operator who knows how to formulate domestic narratives and craft them in service of professional gains. It is still true, of course, that in real-life cases as well as media portrayals wifely victimhood frequently gives way to a compromised and often calculating resilience. With regard to the Clinton-inspired character of Alicia Florrick, it is undeniable that Alicia's stomach for moral compromise grew stronger with each passing year of the series, and her political aspirations intensified at the same rate that she lost ethical integrity. In the series finale, with her soon-to-be-ex-husband embroiled in yet another scandal, it is verbalized that Alicia's electability is the future of their brand. Similarly, both *Scandal* and *House of Cards* twin a political wife's decision to run for elected office with her desertion of her marriage, a confluence which suggests that political futures do not hinge on husbands—and may in fact be hampered by them. *House of Cards* does, however, capitulate to a one-two ticket, after Claire makes it known that she will stop at nothing to derail her husband's presidential campaign if he does not include her in it. However, when she secures the presidency, it is intimated that she will again distance herself from Frank.

The signal that wives can exist without husbands—and are at times better off for it—is also underscored by the reality that all the fictional wives featured in this chapter in some way embark on extramarital sexual activity. This behavior takes many forms, from casual encounters to outright affairs, from quiet understandings between estranged spouses to consensually nonmonogamous arrangements. In all, however, these tales of sexuality suggest not only that marriage fails in many capacities to regulate or contain desire, but also that its historical status as playing this role is almost entirely beside the point. Instead, in the new national order sexual activity is merely one more facet of intimacy that is up for negotiation.

As this chapter and book have argued, female representational culture has turned with increasing focus to the wife's aspirations. Though the term wife may be mired in histories of subordination and minimization, in practice she is more likely an icon of fortitude and a figure of pragmatism, one whose skills and competencies are being put to self-interested use. The collapse of the domestic and the professional and a weary, savvy knowingness on the part of wives suggest in turn that the public role now eclipses the private moment. All that said, it is instructive to remember that the sorts of wives who fall into such a categorization are those who enjoy extreme cultural privilege, as does Hillary Clinton. If, as I have been arguing, female media forms tend to replicate and buttress class inequalities, and use the figure of the wife to do so, the rejection of Clinton's candidacy could well signal an exhaustion with these hierarchies. A generous reading of Trump's victory might emphasize that his appeal was precisely to the vast numbers of Americans of whom I spoke in this book's introduction, those who cannot afford to marry because they lack financial stability, for whom his campaign slogan to "make America great again" afforded the promise of the sort of economic prowess that would enable worry-free marriages, home purchases, and offspring.

At the same time, I would be remiss not to read Clinton's defeat in the context of gender and wifedom. For many Americans, a rejection of Clinton was also a rejection of the dynastic nature that American politics has taken since the second Bush presidency. In addition, it confirms that Hillary Clinton could never wholly escape her marriage to Bill Clinton, and the complicated commingling of business, politics, secrecy, intimacy, and family that is their practice and legacy. Perhaps, then, Clinton's status as a wife is the final rub, one this book has tried hard to suggest is changing. Clinton's defeat illustrated that things have not altered as rapidly or as permanently as I forecasted. For all the nuanced meanings of the term, wives are women, and women remain disadvantaged by the very fact of their gender. Despite the myriad ways in which real-life and fictionalized wives have jettisoned domesticity, trivialized marriage, and monetized their femininity, popular culture will never entirely let them escape their status as a member of a disenfranchised group. Without shedding this constraint, wives might be brands, self-starters, franchises, and conglomerations, but in the wider scheme of mass culture, they have sadly yet to be CEOs.

ACKNOWLEDGMENTS

It would perhaps appear that I have never been interested in anything *but* wives and marriages. First captivated in 1981 at age eight by the wedding ceremony of Diana Spencer and Prince Charles, I watched the event live as it was broadcast from London. Subsequently, I devoured Diana's image in every medium willing to deliver it. I particularly remember pouring over the photos of her wedding, and later her new babies, in *People* magazine. What I have come to realize since that time is that the mediation of Diana's wifedom *was* the story. Perhaps the first signal of the zeitgeist to come, this cultural happening paved wave for what I diagnose in this book as contemporary wifedom's saturation in, and dependence on, female media cultures. The people I thank here have encouraged and fortified this long-standing fascination, supporting me with lots of love and little judgment.

This project began in earnest in 2013 during a one-semester sabbatical from Simmons College. Since that time, I have benefited enormously from the generous support of the college's professional development funding, which has allowed me to refine many of these ideas at conferences, particularly the annual gatherings of the Society for Cinema and Media Studies, as well as the intimate and collegial settings of Consoleing Passions International Conference on Television, Video, Audio, New Media, and Feminism. I have also been bolstered by the support of my wonderful colleagues at the college. I thank Kelly Hager for her enthusiasm and attention to detail, Sarah Leonard for her quiet wisdom, Lowry Pei for always taking the long view, Catherine Paden for her steadfast sanity, Colleen Keily for always bringing color to the conversation, Renee Bergland for modeling careful reading and lively writing, Pamela Bromberg for sharing her bounties, Cathie Mercier for her discerning eye (and palate), Mary Jane Treacy for her passionate investments, and Leanne Doherty for helping me to laugh through it all. I also owe a huge debt to Rachel Lacasse for her efficiency, competency, and help with tasks both cerebral and mundane. Other colleagues at Simmons have led by example, modeling decency, humanity, and pedagogical rigor, particularly Stephen Berry, Carole Biewener, Jim Corcoran, Katie Conboy, Eduardo Febles, Greg Feldman, Sheldon George, Ellen Grabiner, Diane Grossman, Jennifer Herman, Heather Hole, Valerie Leiter, Briana Martino, Steve Ortega, Laura Prieto, Jyoti Puri, Saher Selod, and Richard Wollman. I also want to recognize the students I have had the pleasure of teaching at Simmons over these many years, without whom my career as an academic would not have been possible.

Though this book was written long after I finished my doctoral degree, I still benefit in innumerable ways from the examples set by my mentors at the University of Wisconsin–Milwaukee, particularly Gregory Jay, Jane Gallop, and Vicki Callahan (now at USC). All respected scholars, caring teachers, and rigorous critics, they taught me what it means to be an academic. I also want to recognize the friends I made at UWM as a doctoral student, particularly Andrea Deacon, Maureen McKnight, and Zoran Samardzija, all of whom I continue to admire personally and professionally.

There is a robust community of media scholars whose work inspires me, and whom I feel blessed to count as friends, particularly Ben Aslinger, Martina Baldwin, Miranda Banks, Deborah Barker, Melissa Click, Shelley Cobb, Neil Ewan, Emily Fox-Kales, Anna Froula, Leigh Goldstein, Joshua Green, Hannah Hamad, Nina Huntemann, Deb Jaramillo, Mary Celeste Kearney, Amanda Ann Klein, Christina Lane, Alice Leppert, Elana Levine, Moya Luckett, Linda Mizejewski, Elizabeth Nathanson, Andy Owens, Maria Pramaggiore, Sarah Projansky, Karen Ritzenhoff, Vicki Sturtevant, Yvonne Tasker, Pamela Thoma, Shilyh Warren, Brenda Weber, Julie Wilson, and Emily Chivers Yochim.

It is both convenient and telling that in order to cite the ways in which my work on wifedom has previously appeared in print, one name rises above all. Diane Negra, whom I met in 2004, has been, bar none, the biggest champion of my career, ideas, and publications since that time. From editing my work, to mentoring my career, to inviting me to coauthor with her, to conversing with me for hours on the state of feminism and contemporary media, Diane is not only a brilliant scholar, but also the gold standard for how to be a professionally generous mentor. On top of all that, she is a cherished friend.

The coda in chapter 1 borrows from "Escaping the Recession? The New Vitality of the Woman Worker," which appears in *Gendering the Recession: Media and Culture in an Age of Austerity*, published by Duke University Press in 2014, and edited by Diane Negra and Yvonne Tasker.

My discussion of Bethenny Frankel in chapter 3 borrows from a piece that Diane Negra and I coauthored, "After Ever After: Bethenny Frankel, Self-Branding, and the 'New Intimacy of Work,'" which can be found in *Cupcakes, Pinterest, Ladyporn: Feminized Popular Culture in the Early Twenty-First Century*, edited by Elana Levine and published in 2015 by the University of Illinois Press. I authored two articles on *The Good Wife*, both of which informed the discussion of political wifedom that appears in chapter 5. I examined technology, sexuality, and privacy on the show in a piece printed in *Feminist Media Studies* in 2014. I also contributed to a 2017 special issue of *Television and New Media* devoted to *The Good Wife*, and benefited from the advice of the issue's special editors, Taylor Nygaard and Jorie Lagerwey.

This book participates in New York University Press's Critical Cultural Communication Series, and I am grateful to editors Jonathan Gray, Nina Huntemann, and Aswin Punathambekar for valuing the manuscript and championing it to the press. I am especially appreciative of Nina, who advised me on reframing the introduction to better clarify the book's overriding themes. This conversation came at a time when I felt a bit lost in the project, and her perspicacious insight reminded me exactly what was at stake in the analysis. I have also borrowed her excellent wording for the description on the book's jacket. At the press, I want to recognize my editor Lisha Nadkarni, who smartly helped me to redraft the book proposal and provided assurances at every point in the publishing process thereafter. I am also deeply indebted to my three anonymous readers. Their critical and essential suggestions ran the gamut from addressing the manuscript at the macro and theoretical level to offering suggestions that were precise and exacting. The project is undeniably better for their having influenced it.

In its final stages, the book was read by freelance copyeditor extraordinaire Anne Keefe, who not only edited with a careful eye, but also so clearly "got" the book. Her lively marginal comments made me feel as if we had been lifelong friends, though we have in fact never met in person.

Turning finally to my gratitude for my family: to my dad, fellow docent Donald Leonard, whose abiding faith, and joking not-so-gentle reminders ("Suzy, how's the book coming?"), made it simply unimaginable that the book would not someday get done. To my mom, the incomparable and indomitable Anne Leonard, whose only business, it seemed, was to make me feel loved. To my brother Keith Leonard, whose caustic wit and keen eye keep my critical muscles flexed. Finally, and crucially, to my wonderful, kind, effervescent husband, Alan Billing. Supporting each other's passions and aspirations—our long-ago pledge—has a taken a number of disparate forms in the context of this book. From lending the manuscript his surprising talents as a copyeditor, to sparring with me over word definitions, to nurturing the other project that got birthed while this book was being written, our daughter Anabelle, he has given new meaning to the phrase "unflagging support." (He is also willing, on occasion, to don a disco outfit, which will make sense only if one has read chapter 1.) Alan, I can't thank you enough. To Anabelle, may your life know business and, much more importantly, pleasure.

NOTES

INTRODUCTION

1 Jamie Otis with Dibs Baer, *Wifey 101: Everything I Got Wrong after Finding Mr. Right* (New York: Jamie Otis, 2016), vii, ix.

2 Irin Carmon, "I Do, or Do I?" *Cosmopolitan*, September 2013.

3 Wendy Wang and Kim Parker, "Record Share of Americans Have Never Been Married," *Pew Research Center*, September 24, 2014, http://www.pewsocialtrends.org/.

4 Stephanie Coontz, "The Disestablishment of Marriage," *New York Times*, June 22, 2013.

5 Stephanie Harzewski, *Chick Lit and Postfeminism* (Charlottesville: University of Virginia Press, 2011), 180.

6 Angela McRobbie, *The Aftermath of Feminism: Gender, Culture, and Social Change* (London: Sage, 2009), 62, 145.

7 Stephanie Coontz, *Marriage, a History* (New York: Viking, 2005), 9.

8 Ibid., 4, 261–62.

9 Ibid., 261–62.

10 Elspeth Probyn, "Choosing Choice: Images of Sexuality and 'Choiceoisie' in Popular Culture," in *Negotiating at the Margins: The Gendered Discourses of Power and Resistance*, ed. Sue Fisher and Kathy Davis (New Brunswick, NJ: Rutgers University Press, 1993), 282.

11 Anthony Giddens, *The Transformation of Intimacy: Sexuality, Love and Eroticism in Modern Societies* (Cambridge, UK: Polity, 1992), 58.

12 Kristin Celello, *Making Marriage Work: A History of Marriage and Divorce in the Twentieth-Century United States* (Chapel Hill: University of North Carolina Press, 2012), 135–36.

13 Wendy Langford, *Revolutions of the Heart: Gender, Power and the Delusions of Love* (London: Routledge, 1999), 1, 152.

14 Shere Hite, *Women and Love: A Cultural Revolution in Progress* (London: Viking, 1988).

15 David R. Shumway, *Modern Love: Romance, Intimacy and the Marriage Crisis* (New York: New York University Press, 2003), 188.

16 Wendy Brown, "Neoliberalized Knowledge," *History of the Present* 1, no. 1 (2011): 118.

17 "The Decline of Marriage and Rise of New Families." *Pew Research Center*, November 18, 2010, http://www.pewsocialtrends.org/.

18 W. Bradford Wilcox, "Marriage Haves and Have-Nots," *New York Times*, July 3, 2011.

19 Wang and Parker, "Record Share of Americans Have Never Been Married."

20 Liza Mundy, "The Gay Guide to Wedded Bliss," *The Atlantic*, June 2013.

21 Black men face even bleaker prospects: due to death and incarceration, there are simply fewer of them, reported a 2015 article titled "1.5 Million Missing Black Men." This paucity of black men has specific implications for marital futures: "The black women left behind find that potential partners of the same race are scarce, while men, who face an abundant supply of potential mates, don't need to compete as hard to find one." Justin Wolfer, David Leonhard, and Kevin Quealy, "1.5 Million Missing Black Men," *New York Times*, April 20, 2015.

22 Anne Case and Sir Angus Deaton, "Rising Morbidity and Mortality in Midlife among White Non-Hispanic Americans in the 21st Century," *Proceedings of the National Academy of the Sciences* 112, no. 49 (2015), http://wws.princeton.edu/.

23 Comment by Sharon Sassler, "Something Old, Something New," *Innovation Hub*, WGBH, Boston, October 1, 2016, http://blogs.wgbh.org/innovation-hub/.

24 Quoted in Belinda Luscombe, "Who Needs Marriage? How an American Institution is Changing," *Time*, November 18, 2010, http://content.time.com/.

25 June Carbone and Naomi Cahn, *Marriage Markets: How Inequality Is Remaking the American Family* (Oxford, UK: Oxford University Press, 2014), 3.

26 Tyler Cowen, "The Marriages of Power Couples Reinforce Economic Inequality," *New York Times*, December 24, 2015.

27 Carbone and Cahn, *Marriage Markets*, 4, 15.

28 Eleanor Barkhorn, "Getting Married Later Is Great for College-Educated Women," *The Atlantic*, March 15, 2013, http://www.theatlantic.com/.

29 Catherine Rampell, "Marriage Is for Rich People," *New York Times*, February 6, 2012.

30 Jaye Cee Whitehead, "The Wrong Reasons for Same-Sex Marriage," *New York Times*, May 15, 2011.

31 Obergefell et al. v. Hodges, Director, Ohio Department of Health, 576 U.S. (2015), http://www.supremecourt.gov/.

32 J. Jack Halberstam, *Gaga Feminism: Sex, Gender, and the End of Normal* (Boston: Beacon Press, 2012), 102.

33 For a work that innovatively examines other pitfalls that have accompanied the legalization of gay marriage, see Katherine Franke, *Wedlocked: The Perils of Marriage Equality* (New York: New York University Press, 2015).

34 Catherine Rottenberg, "The Rise of Neoliberal Feminism," *Cultural Studies* 28, no. 3 (2014): 420.

35 Rosalind Gill, "Mediated Intimacy and Postfeminism: A Discourse Analytic Examination of Sex and Relationships Advice in a Women's Magazine," *Discourse and Communication* 3, no. 4 (2009): 354.

36 Imre Szeman, "Entrepreneurship as the New Common Sense," *South Atlantic Quarterly* 114, no. 3 (2015): 474.

37 Gill, "Mediated Intimacy and Postfeminism," 353.

38 Nancy Armstrong, "Some Call It Fiction: On the Politics of Domesticity," in *Feminisms: An Anthology of Literary Theory and Criticism*, ed. Robyn R. Warhol and Diane Price Herndl (New Brunswick, NJ: Rutgers University Press, 1997), 913.

39 Viviana A. Zelizer, *The Purchase of Intimacy* (Princeton, NJ: Princeton University Press, 2005), 11, 12, 28.

40 Annie Lowrey, "Are Park Avenue Wives Really Like Bonobos? The Book That's Infuriating the Ladies Who Lunch," *New York*, June 1, 2015.

41 Melissa Gregg, *Work's Intimacy* (Cambridge, UK: Polity Press, 2011), 18.

42 Gill, "Mediated Intimacy and Postfeminism," 365.

CHAPTER 1. ENTERPRISING WIVES

1 This chapter's epigraph is quoted in Anna Mazarakis, "Patton '77 Dispenses Advice for Female Students at Campus Lecture," *Daily Princetonian*, April 18, 2013; Susan Patton, "Advice for the Young Women of Princeton: The Daughters I Never Had," *Daily Princetonian*, March 29, 2013.

2 Patton, "Advice for the Young Women of Princeton."

3 Age always seems to work decisively against marriage-inclined women. As Rachel Greenwald writes in *Find a Husband after 35 (Using What I Learned at Harvard Business School)* (New York: Ballantine Books, 2003), "The post-35 dating world is like a typical supply and demand situation . . . where there is less supply (single men) than demand (single women wanting to meet single men)" (62).

4 Susan Patton, *Marry Smart: Advice for Finding THE ONE* (New York: Gallery Books, 2014).

5 Susan Patton, *Marry by Choice, Not by Chance: Advice for Finding the Right One at the Right Time* (New York: Gallery Books, 2014).

6 Sheryl Sandberg, *Lean In: Women, Work, and the Will to Lead* (New York: Knopf, 2013).

7 Patton, "Advice for the Young Women of Princeton."

8 Sandberg, *Lean In*, 110.

9 Sarah Banet-Weiser, *Authentic™: The Politics of Ambivalence in a Brand Culture* (New York: New York University Press, 2012), 7.

10 Andrew J. Cherlin, "In the Season of Marriage, a Question: Why Bother?" *New York Times*, April 27, 2013.

11 Eli J. Finkel et al., "Online Dating: A Critical Analysis From the Perspective of Psychological Science," *Psychological Science in the Public Interest* 13, no. 1 (2012): 13.

12 A telling example of online dating's having shed its social stigma came in 2002 when Ellen Fein and Sherrie Schneider, authors of the 1995 sensation *The Rules: Time-Tested Secrets for Capturing the Heart of Mr. Right* (New York: Grand Central Publishing), extended their franchise to encompass the online dating realm, and coauthored *The Rules for Online Dating: Capturing the Heart of Mr. Right in Cyberspace* (New York: Pocket Books, 2002). The publication represented a rather

abrupt about-face for the authors who in *The Rules II* (New York: Grand Central Publishing, 1997) openly disparaged online dating.

13 Dan Slater, *Love in the Time of Algorithms: What Technology Does to Meeting and Mating* (New York: Current, 2013), 6, 179.

14 Brooke Lea Foster, "The Tinder Dating Pool Isn't Completely Shallow," *New York Times*, March 26, 2016.

15 Gary S. Becker, "A Theory of Marriage: Part I," *Journal of Political Economy* 81, no. 4 (1973): 814–15.

16 Aaron Ahuvia and Mara Adelman, "Market Metaphors for Meeting Mates," *Research in Consumer Behavior* 6 (1993): 63.

17 Gill, "Mediated Intimacy and Postfeminism," 351–52.

18 Pierre Bourdieu, "Pierre Bourdieu on Marriage Strategies," *Population and Development Review* 28, no. 3 (2002): 549.

19 Catherine Hakim, *Erotic Capital: The Power of Attraction in the Boardroom and the Bedroom* (New York: Basic Books, 2011), 117.

20 Andrew T. Fiore and Judith S. Donath, "Homophily in Online Dating: When Do You Like Someone Like Yourself?" *CHI* (April 2005): 1.

21 Patton, "Advice for the Young Women of Princeton."

22 Catherine Rampell, "Women and Marriage at Princeton," *New York Times*, April 1, 2013.

23 Amy Robach and Deborah Camiel, "Love @ First Byte: The Secret Science of Online Dating," *CNBC*, February 8, 2012, http://www.nbcnews.com/.

24 "Woman Seeks Rich Husband, Banker Says Crappy Deal," *Reuters*, October 10, 2007, http://www.reuters.com/.

25 Posted by MyChocolateDiet, "J.P. Morgan to a Pretty Girl Seeking a Rich Husband," *My Fitness Pal* message board, n.d., http://www.myfitnesspal.com/.

26 Bonnie Rochman, "Love Isn't Color Blind: White Online Daters Spurn Blacks," *Time*, February 22, 2011.

27 Ted Striphas, "Algorithmic Culture," *European Journal of Cultural Studies* 18, nos. 4–5 (2015): 395.

28 Slater, *Love in the Time of Algorithms*, 137–38.

29 Rebecca Heino, Nicole B. Ellison, and Jennifer Gibbs, "Relationshopping: Investigating the Market Metaphor in Online Dating," *Journal of Social and Personal Relationships* 27, no. 4 (2010): 434–38.

30 Banet-Weiser, *Authentic™*, 9.

31 Greenwald, *Find a Husband after 35*, 87, 88, 93.

32 Damona Hoffman, *Spin Your Web: How to Brand Yourself for Successful Online Dating* (Cardiff, CA: Waterfront Digital, 2013), 13, 16.

33 Greenwald, *Find a Husband after 35*, 114.

34 Amy Webb, *Data, a Love Story: How I Gamed Online Dating to Meet My Match* (New York: Dutton, 2013).

35 Amy Webb, "How I Hacked Online Dating," *TED*, April 2013, http://www.ted.com/.

36 Webb, *Data, a Love Story*, 202.

37 Alison Hearn, "Structuring Feeling: Web 2.0, Online Ranking and Rating, and the Digital Reputation Economy," *Ephemera* 10, nos. 3–4 (2010): 422.

38 Laurie Davis, *Love @ First Click: The Ultimate Guide to Online Dating* (New York: Atria Books, 2013), 42.

39 Greenwald, *Find a Husband after 35*, 126.

40 Erika Ettin, *Love at First Site: Tales and Tips for Online Dating Success from a Modern-Day Matchmaker* (Austin: River Grove Books, 2014), 82, 166.

41 Amy Spencer, *Meeting Your Half-Orange: An Utterly Upbeat Guide to Using Dating Optimism to Find Your Perfect Match* (Philadelphia: Running Press, 2010), 38, 132.

42 Barbara Ehrenreich, *Bright-Sided: How Positive Thinking Is Undermining America* (New York: Metropolitan Books, 2009), 3.

43 Gregg, *Work's Intimacy*, 10.

44 Hearn, "Structuring Feeling," 427.

45 Greenwald, *Find a Husband after 35*, 87.

46 Webb, *Data, a Love Story*, 213.

47 Davis, *Love @ First Click*, 46.

48 In Gillian Flynn's dark thriller *Gone Girl* (New York: Orion, 2012), the diabolical and murderous Amy offers a brilliant send-up of the need for women to adopt such postures in order to be what she calls a "cool girl."

49 Webb, *Data, a Love Story*, 187, 288.

50 Diane Negra, *What a Girl Wants? Fantasizing the Reclamation of Self in Postfeminism* (New York: Routledge, 2009).

51 McRobbie, *Aftermath of Feminism*, 57.

52 Banet-Weiser, *Authentic™*, 61.

53 Webb, *Data, a Love Story*, 163.

54 Alison Hearn, "Meat, Mask, Burden: Probing the Contours of the Branded Self," *Journal of Consumer Culture* 8, no. 2 (2008): 201.

55 Szeman, "Entrepreneurship as the New Common Sense," 483.

56 Interview with Koereyelle DuBose, "Single Wives Club: The Brand, the Organization, the Life and Style," *YouTube*, October 2, 2014, http://www.youtube.com/.

57 Lauren Berlant, *Cruel Optimism* (Durham, NC: Duke University Press, 2011), 24–48.

58 Finkel et al., "Online Dating," 50.

59 Banet-Weiser, *Authentic™*, 80.

60 Stig Hjarvard, *The Mediatization of Culture and Society* (London: Routledge, 2013), 150–51.

61 Hakim, *Erotic Capital*, 1–2, 15. Hakim is an avowed skeptic of feminism, believing that radical feminists have dissuaded women from using erotic capital, when it is actually a highly viable metric for determining success in social contexts. While I disagree with this premise, I do find value in her belief that erotic capital can have tangible benefits, especially as it relates to online dating.

62 Ettin, *Love at First Site*, 16.

63 Davis, *Love @ First Click*, 6, 9.

64 Eva Illouz, *Cold Intimacies: The Making of Emotional Capitalism* (Cambridge, UK: Polity Press, 2007), 32.

65 Ettin, *Love at First Site*, 55.

66 Illouz, *Cold Intimacies*, 34, 36.

67 I thank Anne Keefe for this point, and for recognizing its irony.

68 Brenda R. Weber, *Makeover TV: Selfhood, Citizenship, and Celebrity* (Durham, NC: Duke University Press, 2009).

69 Beverley Skeggs, "The Value of Relationships: Affective Scenes and Emotional Performances," *Feminist Legal Studies* 18, no. 1 (2010): 43.

70 Webb, *Data, a Love Story*, 284.

71 Gill, "Mediated Intimacy and Postfeminism," 353.

72 Illouz, *Cold Intimacies*, 73.

73 Skeggs, "Value of Relationships," 43.

74 Adam Arvidsson, "'Quality Singles': Internet Dating and the Work of Fantasy," *New Media and Society* 8, no. 4 (2006): 680–81.

75 Finkel et al., "Online Dating," 22. eHarmony historically disallowed users to seek partners of the same sex, though they lost a 2009 lawsuit accusing this practice of being discriminatory. As a part of the settlement, the company created Compatible Partners, a gay-only dating site. As a result of another suit in 2010, the company was forced to merge Compatible Partners with eHarmony, so that users could not be charged twice for using both.

76 Ettin, *Love at First Site*, 77.

77 For a brief gesture to the idea that categorization of the self began with online dating sites, see Nancy Baym, *Personal Connections in the Digital Age* (Malden, MA: Polity, 2010), 110.

78 Davis, *Love @ First Click*, 39, 64.

79 See post by "RealDeal," review of *Love @ First Click: The Ultimate Guide to Online Dating*, Amazon, n.d., http://www.amazon.com/.

80 Harzewski, *Chick Lit and Postfeminism*, 155.

81 Arvidsson, "Quality Singles."

82 Kate Aurigemma, "Performing Class Online: An Analysis of Online Dating Profiles," May 9, 2012, unpublished seminar paper.

83 Greenwald, *Find a Husband after 35*, 69.

84 Hoffman, *Spin Your Web*, 33, 32.

85 Moira Weigel, *Labor of Love* (New York: Farrar, Straus and Giroux, 2016).

86 Arvidsson, "Quality Singles," 686.

87 Lori Gottlieb, "How Do I Love Thee?" *The Atlantic*, March 2006.

88 Lori Gottlieb, "Marry Him!" *The Atlantic*, March 2008; Lori Gottlieb, *Marry Him: The Case for Setting for Mr. Good Enough* (New York: Dutton, 2010).

89 Gottlieb, "Marry Him!"

90 Anthea Taylor, *Single Women in Popular Culture: The Limits of Postfeminism* (Basingstoke, UK: Palgrave Macmillan, 2012), 15.

91 Negra, *What a Girl Wants?* 47.

92 Suzanne Leonard, "Escaping the Recession? The New Vitality of the Woman Worker," in *Gendering the Recession: Media and Culture in an Age of Austerity*, ed. Diane Negra and Yvonne Tasker (Durham, NC: Duke University Press, 2014), 31–58.

93 For a resounding rejoinder to the prediction that new economies will mean the "end of men," see Caryl Rivers and Rosalind Barnett, *The New Soft War on Women: How the Myth of Female Ascendance Is Hurting Women, Men—and Our Economy* (New York: Tarcher/Penguin, 2013).

94 Richard Thaler, "Breadwinning Wives and Nervous Husbands," *New York Times*, June 1, 2013.

95 Ralph Richard Banks, *Is Marriage for White People?* (New York: Penguin, 2011), 92.

96 Sanja Jagesic, "Race and Relationship Advice: Effects of Marriage Market Differences on Cultural Expectations of Behavior," *Feminist Media Studies* 14, no. 1 (2014): 85.

97 Banks, *Is Marriage for White People?* 48.

98 Kate Bolick, "All the Single Ladies," *The Atlantic*, November 2011, 122.

99 Wang and Parker, "Record Share of Americans Have Never Been Married."

CHAPTER 2. ALMOST WIVES

1 *ABC News* even ran a decidedly nonobjective story about the series; emerging from their "Medical Unit," the article featured various plastic surgeons critiquing *Bridalplasty*'s questionable medical ethics. See Courtney Hutchison, "*Bridalplasty*: Plastic Surgery as a TV Prize?" *ABC News*, September 20, 2010.

2 Laurie Ouellette and James Hay, *Better Living through Reality TV: Television and Post-Welfare Citizenship* (Malden, MA: Blackwell, 2008), 2.

3 This term refers to an intimate but nonsexual relationship between two men. For an investigation of the bromance's origins and rising popularity in twenty-first-century media culture, see Michael DeAngelis, ed., *Reading the Bromance: Homosocial Relationships in Film and Television* (Detroit: Wayne State University Press, 2014).

4 Tatiana Siegel, "R.I.P. Romantic Comedies: Why Harry Wouldn't Meet Sally in 2013," *Hollywood Reporter*, October 4, 2013.

5 Megan Garber, "When Harry Met eHarmony," *The Atlantic*, July 9, 2014.

6 For a capacious discussion of the ways that online dating is framed, discussed, and experienced in American and British television, see Lauren Rosewarne, *Intimacy on the Internet: Media Representation of Online Connections* (New York: Routledge, 2016).

7 Thanks to dating shows' penchant for broadcasting contestants in boozy situations where clothes are scant and sexuality tends to the polyamorous, Jonathan Gray credits dating shows with "sexing up reality television." See Gray, "Cinderella Burps: Gender, Performativity, and the Dating Show," in *Reality TV: Remaking*

Television Culture, 2nd ed., ed. Susan Murray and Laurie Ouellette (New York: New York University Press, 2009), 262.

8 For readings of *The Bachelor* that charge the show with regressively enforcing antiquated gender politics, see Gust Yep and Ariana Ochoa Camacho, "The Normalization of Heterogendered Relations in *The Bachelor*," *Feminist Media Studies* 4, no. 3 (2004): 338–41; and Andrea M. McClanahan, "Must Marry TV: The Role of the Heterosexual Imaginary in *The Bachelor*," in *Critical Thinking about Sex, Love, and Romance in the Mass Media*, ed. Mary-Lou Galician and Debra L. Merskin (New York: Routledge, 2006), 303–18. For readings attentive to the more outlandishly manufactured quality of reality dating shows in general, see Judith Halberstam, "Pimp My Bride: Reality TV Gives Marriage an Extreme Makeover," *The Nation*, July 5, 2004; and Gray, "Cinderella Burps." For an offering that mediates between these poles, see Misha Kavka, "The Queering of Reality TV," *Feminist Media Studies* 4, no. 2 (2004): 220–23.

9 Suzanne Leonard, "Marriage Envy," in special issue on envy edited by Jane Gallop, *Women's Studies Quarterly* 34, nos. 3–4 (2006): 43–64.

10 Elisabeth Beck-Gernsheim, "On the Way to a Post-Familial Family: From a Community of Need to Elective Affinities," *Theory, Culture and Society* 15, no. 3 (1998): 53–70.

11 Quoted in Rachel E. Dubrofsky, *The Surveillance of Women on Reality Television: Watching "The Bachelor" and "The Bachelorette"* (Lanham, MD: Lexington Books, 2011), 110. The bias toward attractive women predictably rankles feminist commentators; as Yep and Camacho write, the show "reinforces current US standards of female beauty and objectification of the woman's body." "Normalization of Heterogendered Relations in *The Bachelor*," 339.

12 Dubrofsky, *Surveillance of Women on Reality Television*, 125.

13 Samuel K. Bonsu, Aron Darmody, and Marie-Agnès Parmentier, "Arrested Emotions in Reality Television," *Consumption Markets and Culture* 13, no. 1 (2010): 99.

14 Misha Kavka, *Reality Television, Affect and Intimacy: Reality Matters* (London: Palgrave Macmillan, 2008), 109–10.

15 Amanda Hess, "A *Bachelorette* Composer Reveals How He Drums Up Drama and Romance on Reality TV," *Slate*, May 23, 2014, http://www.slate.com/.

16 Dubrofsky, *Surveillance of Women on Reality Television*, 54, 53.

17 Susan Ostrov Weisser, *The Glass Slipper: Women and Love Stories* (New Brunswick, NJ: Rutgers University Press, 2013), 188.

18 Dubrofsky, *Surveillance of Women on Reality Television*, 131–32.

19 Arlie Hochschild, *The Managed Heart: Commercialization of Human Feeling* (Berkeley: University of California Press, 1983).

20 Gregg, *Work's Intimacy*, 10.

21 Spencer E. Cahill, "Emotional Capital and Professional Socialization: The Case of Mortuary Science Students (and Me)," *Social Psychology Quarterly* 62, no. 2 (1999): 101–16.

22 Spencer, *Meeting Your Half-Orange*, 126.

23 In an *Entertainment Weekly* spread devoted to the ninth season's contestants of *The Bachelorette*, host Chris Harrison previews six suitors and twice raises questions about their seriousness. "*The Bachelorette*: Meet the New Guys," *Entertainment Weekly*, May 24, 2013.

24 Brenda R. Weber, "Trash Talk: Gender as an Analytic on Reality Television," in *Reality Gendervision: Sexuality and Gender on Transatlantic Reality Television*, ed. Weber (Durham, NC: Duke University Press, 2014), 19.

25 Yanyi Luo and Kate Brennan, "I Didn't Come Here to Make Friends," *The Bachelor Interns*, June 12, 2016, http://www.thebachelorinterns.com/.

26 Allie Jones, "How *Bachelor* Contestants Cash In After the Show Is Over," *New York*, March 13, 2017.

27 Rachel E. Dubrofsky and Antoine Hardy, "Performing Race in *Flavor of Love* and *The Bachelor*," *Critical Studies in Media Communication* 25, no. 4 (2008): 375.

28 Jon Kraszewski, "Branding, Nostalgia, and the Politics of Race on VH1's *Flavor of Love*," *Quarterly Review of Film and Video* 31, no. 3 (2014): 250–51.

29 Eva Illouz, *Consuming the Romantic Utopia: Love and the Cultural Contradictions of Capitalism* (Berkeley: University of California Press, 1998).

30 Amy Chozick and Bill Carter, "After Rough Patch, 'The Bachelor' Wins Back Viewers," *New York Times*, March 10, 2013.

31 Weisser, *Glass Slipper*, 188.

32 For a discussion of Bravo's treatment of female entrepreneurs, see Jorie Lagerwey, *Postfeminist Celebrity and Motherhood: Brand Mom* (New York: Routledge, 2017).

33 Lindsay Giggey, "'Maybe Romance Will Crop Up': Product Placement on *The Millionaire Matchmaker*," *In Media Res*, May 10, 2011, http://mediacommons. futureofthebook.org/.

34 Patti Stanger with Lisa Johnson Mandell, *Become Your Own Matchmaker: Eight Easy Steps for Attracting Your Perfect Mate* (New York: Atria Books, 2009).

35 Amanda Fortini, "The Mating Game," *New York Times*, October 22, 2010.

36 Ibid.

37 Weber, *Makeover TV*, 75.

38 Stanger, *Become Your Own Matchmaker*, v, 180–89.

39 Suzanne Leonard, "The Americanization of Emma Bovary: From Feminist Icon to Desperate Housewife," *Signs: Journal of Women in Culture and Society* 38, no. 3 (2013): 647–69.

40 Erika Engstrom, *The Bride Factory: Mass Media Portrayals of Women and Weddings* (New York: Peter Lang, 2012), 173.

41 Katherine E. Morrissey, "Rise of Bridezilla: Reveling in Love's Discontents" (paper presented at the annual meeting for the Society of Cinema and Media Studies, Seattle, March 19–23, 2014).

42 Gwendolyn Audrey Foster, *Class-Passing: Social Mobility in Film and Popular Culture* (Carbondale: Southern Illinois University Press, 2005), 74.

43 Elizabeth Freeman, *The Wedding Complex: Forms of Belonging in Modern American Culture* (Durham, NC: Duke University Press, 2002), 4.

44 Tiara Sukhan, "Bootcamp, Brides, and BMI: Biopedagogical Narratives of Health and Belonging on Canadian Size-Transformation Television," *Television and New Media* 14, no. 3 (2012): 202.

45 The show is based on and credits the exercise plan developed by nutritionist and personal trainer Cynthia Conde, who developed the military-style workout in 2001 for her celebrity clients.

46 Katherine Sender, *The Makeover: Reality Television and Reflexive Audiences* (New York: New York University Press, 2012), 91.

47 Banet-Weiser, *Authentic^{TM}*.

48 Sender, *The Makeover*, 135.

49 Engstrom, *Bride Factory*, 165.

50 Sukhan, "Bootcamp, Brides, and BMI," 204.

51 Beverley Skeggs and Helen Wood, "The Labour of Transformation and Circuits of Value 'around' Reality Television," *Continuum: Journal of Media and Cultural Studies* 22, no. 4 (2008): 560.

52 Alison Winch and Anna Webster, "Here Comes the Brand: Wedding Media and the Management of Transformation," *Continuum: Journal of Media and Cultural Studies* 26, no. 1 (2012): 52.

53 Skeggs, "Value of Relationships," 48.

CHAPTER 3. RETURN OF THE HOUSEWIFE

1 This chapter's epigraph is drawn from Sharon Sharp, "Disciplining the Housewife in *Desperate Housewives* and Domestic Reality Television," in *Reading "Desperate Housewives": Beyond the White Picket Fence*, ed. Janet McCabe and Kim Akass (New York: I. B. Tauris, 2006), 120; Meghan Casserly, "Are Housewives to Blame for the Plight of Working Women?" *Forbes*, June 7, 2012, http://www.forbes.com/.

2 Casserly, "Are Housewives to Blame for the Plight of Working Women?"

3 Stephanie Coontz, *The Way We Never Were: American Families and the Nostalgia Trap* (New York: Basic Books, 1992), 23, 27, 37.

4 Betty Friedan, *The Feminine Mystique* (1963; repr., New York: Norton, 2001), 422.

5 Ibid., 120.

6 As Lesley Johnson and Justine Lloyd argue in *Sentenced to Everyday Life: Feminism and the Housewife* (New York: Berg, 2004), the oppressed housewife as an image furnished second-wave feminists with a figure against which to define themselves, and problematizing the "happy housewife" ideal served as a motivating impetus for the movement.

7 Lynn Spigel, *Make Room for TV: Television and the Family Ideal in Postwar America* (Chicago: University of Chicago Press, 1992), 2–3.

8 Helen Wood, Beverley Skeggs, and Nancy Thumim, "'It's Just Sad': Affect, Judgement and Emotional Labour in 'Reality' Television Viewing," in *Feminism, Domesticity and Popular Culture*, ed. Stacy Gillis and Joanne Hollows (New York: Routledge, 2009), 136.

9 Nina C. Leibman, *Living Room Lectures: The Fifties Family in Film and Television* (Austin: University of Texas Press, 1995), 187, 193.

10 Mary Beth Haralovich, "Sitcoms and Suburbs: Positioning the 1950s Homemaker," *Quarterly Review of Film and Video* 11, no. 1 (1989): 61.

11 Elaine Tyler May, *Homeward Bound: American Families in the Cold War Era* (New York: Basic Books, 1988), 167.

12 Elizabeth Nathanson, "As Easy as Pie: Cooking Shows, Domestic Efficiency, and Postfeminist Temporality," *Television and New Media* 10, no. 4 (2009): 321.

13 Stacy Gillis and Joanne Hollows, "Introduction," in *Feminism, Domesticity and Popular Culture*, ed. Gillis and Hollows (New York: Routledge, 2009), 6.

14 Marsha F. Cassidy, "Sob Stories, Merriment, and Surprises: The 1950s Audience Participation Show on Network Television and Women's Daytime Reception," *Velvet Light Trap* 42 (Fall 1998): 48.

15 Amber Watts, "Melancholy, Merit, and Merchandise: The Postwar Audience Participation Show," in *Reality TV: Remaking Television Culture*, ed. Susan Murray and Laurie Ouellette (New York: New York University Press, 2004), 315.

16 Andrea Press, "Gender and Television in Hollywood's Golden Age and Beyond," *Annals of the Academy of Political and Social Science* 625 (September 2009): 140.

17 Haralovich, "Sitcoms and Suburbs," 61.

18 For primers on postfeminism's tendency to privilege white, middle-class subjects, see Diane Negra and Yvonne Tasker, eds., *Interrogating Postfeminism: Gender and the Politics of Popular Culture* (Durham, NC: Duke University Press, 2007); Rosalind Gill, "Postfeminist Media Culture: Elements of a Sensibility," *European Journal of Cultural Studies* 10, no. 2 (2009): 147–66; and Jess Butler, "For White Girls Only? Postfeminism and the Politics of Inclusion," *Feminist Formations* 25, no. 1 (2013): 35–58.

19 Charlotte Brunsdon, *The Feminist, the Housewife and the Soap Opera* (Oxford, UK: Clarendon Press, 2000), 216.

20 Rosalind Gill, "Review of *Sentenced to Everyday Life: Feminism and the Housewife* by Lesley Johnson and Justine Lloyd, and *Mediating the Family: Gender, Culture and Representation* by Estella Tincknell," *International Journal of Cultural Studies* 8, no. 4 (2005): 505.

21 bell hooks, *Ain't I a Woman: Black Women and Feminism* (Boston: South End Press, 1981), 146.

22 Judy Dutton, "Meet the New Housewife Wannabes," *Cosmopolitan*, June 2000.

23 Sarah Projansky, *Watching Rape: Film and Television in Postfeminist Culture* (New York: New York University Press, 2001), 67.

24 Elspeth Probyn, "New Traditionalism and Post-Feminism: TV Does the Home" *Screen* 31, no. 2 (1990): 52.

25 Negra, *What a Girl Wants?* 72.

26 Brunsdon, *The Feminist, the Housewife and the Soap Opera*, 216.

27 Over a decade after the publication of the *Cosmopolitan* article, media culture continued to retain its obsessive focus on housewives and frame this identity in

the context of feminism. The tagline to a 2013 article in *New York* magazine was "Feminists who say they're having it all by choosing to stay home." See Lisa Miller, "The Retro Wife," *New York*, March 17, 2013.

28 Bernard Weinraub, "How Desperate Women Saved Desperate Writer," *New York Times*, October 23, 2004.

29 Catherine Orenstein, "Housewife Wars," *Ms. Magazine*, Spring 2005.

30 Tanner Stransky, "Housewives Confidential," *Entertainment Weekly*, March 30, 2012, 33.

31 Jennifer L. Pozner and Jessica Seigel, "Desperately Debating Housewives," *Ms. Magazine*, Spring 2005.

32 The show likewise resurrected the careers of four actresses over forty, a consequential intervention given Hollywood's historic marginalization of aging women.

33 Weinraub, "How Desperate Women Saved Desperate Writer."

34 See Lisa Hill, "Gender and Genre: Situating *Desperate Housewives*," *Journal of Popular Film and Television* 38, no. 4 (2010): 162–69; and Rosalind Coward, "Still Desperate: Popular Television and the Female Zeitgeist," in *Reading "Desperate Housewives": Beyond the White Picket Fence*, ed. Janet McCabe and Kim Akass (New York: I. B. Tauris, 2006), 31–41.

35 With its salacious, sexually provocative, and borderline campy tone, *Desperate Housewives* helped set a brand identity for ABC that proved remarkably resilient, as seen in the success of prime-time dramas like *Grey's Anatomy* (2005–), *Revenge* (2011–15), *Scandal* (2012–18), and *How to Get Away With Murder* (2014–).

36 Janet McCabe and Kim Akass, "Introduction," in *Reading "Desperate Housewives": Beyond the White Picket Fence*, ed. McCabe and Akass (New York: I. B. Tauris, 2006), 13.

37 The comparison to *The Stepford Wives* is apt on a number of levels. In addition to gesturing to how men bear responsibility for turning their wives into empty simulacra of domestic contentment, *Desperate Housewives* blatantly invokes the film when Bree's son accuses her of "running for the mayor of Stepford."

38 Anna Marie Bautista, "Desperation and Domesticity: Reconfiguring the 'Happy Housewife' in *Desperate Housewives*," in *Reading "Desperate Housewives": Beyond the White Picket Fence*, ed. Janet McCabe and Kim Akass (New York: I. B. Tauris, 2006), 164.

39 Ibid., 160.

40 Leonard, "Americanization of Emma Bovary."

41 Pozner and Seigel, "Desperately Debating Housewives."

42 Sharp, "Disciplining the Housewife in *Desperate Housewives* and Domestic Reality Television," 122.

43 Janet McCabe, "What Is It with That Hair? Bree Van de Kamp and Policing Contemporary Femininity," in *Reading "Desperate Housewives": Beyond the White Picket Fence*, ed. Janet McCabe and Kim Akass (New York: I. B. Tauris, 2006), 79.

44 Bautista, "Desperation and Domesticity," 162.

45 Susan J. Douglas and Meredith W. Michaels, *The Mommy Myth: The Idealization of Motherhood and How It Has Undermined All Women* (New York: Simon and Schuster, 2004), 11.

46 Niall Richardson, "As Kamp as Bree: The Politics of Camp Reconsidered by *Desperate Housewives*," *Feminist Media Studies* 6, no. 2 (2006): 158. From reality television shows such as *Wife Swap* (2004–13) and *Supernanny* (2004–13), to films such as *13 Going on 30* (2004), *The Stepford Wives* (2004), and *Raising Helen* (2004), a neoliberal insistence on the hagiographic importance of mothering saturated popular culture during this period. See Negra, *What a Girl Wants?* for an investigation of this phenomenon.

47 Quoted in Hill, "Gender and Genre," 166.

48 Ann Oldenburg, "From Domestic to 'Desperate,'" *USA Today*, September 30, 2004.

49 Douglas and Michaels, *Mommy Myth*, 12.

50 Stephanie Genz, "'I am Not a Housewife, but . . .': Postfeminism and the Revival of Domesticity," in *Feminism, Domesticity and Popular Culture*, ed. Stacy Gillis and Joanne Hollows (New York: Routledge, 2009), 53–54.

51 McCabe, "What Is It with That Hair?" 79.

52 Quoted in John Kenneth Muir, *TV Year: Volume I, The Prime Time 2005–2006 Season* (New York: Applause Books, 2007), 112.

53 Stransky, "Housewives Confidential," 45.

54 These spin-offs include *Date My Ex: Jo and Slade* (2008), *Bethenny Getting Married?* (2010), *Bethenny Ever After* (2011–12), *Don't Be Tardy* (2012–), *The Kandi Factory* (2013), *Tamra's OC Wedding* (2013), *Vanderpump Rules* (2013–), *I Dream of NeNe: The Wedding* (2013), *Kandi's Wedding* (2014), *Manzo'd with Children* (2014–16), *Kandi's Ski Trip* (2015), *Teresa Checks In* (2015), and *Vanderpump Rules After Show* (2015–16).

55 Carina Chocano, "Housewives, Rebranded," *New York Times*, November 18, 2011.

56 Leslie Bruce, "The Guiltiest Pleasure on Television," *Hollywood Reporter*, January 13, 2012.

57 Martina Baldwin, "Buzz by Bravo: A Trendsetting Niche Network's Place within Contemporary Television" (PhD diss., University of Illinois at Urbana–Champaign, 2016), 97.

58 Ibid., 60.

59 Suzanne Leonard and Diane Negra, "After Ever After: Bethenny Frankel, Self-Branding, and the 'New Intimacy of Work,'" in *Cupcakes, Pinterest, Ladyporn: Feminized Popular Culture in the Early 21st Century*, ed. Elana Levine (Champaign: University of Illinois Press, 2015), 196–214.

60 Lizzie Widdicombe, "Perfect Pitching," *New Yorker*, September 21, 2015.

61 Madeline Berg, "Skinnygirl, Fat Wallet: How Bethenny Frankel Earns More Than Any Other Real Housewife," *Forbes*, November 16, 2016, http://www.forbes.com/.

62 Emma Lieber, "Realism's Housewives," *New England Review* 33, no. 4 (2013): 129.

63 Julie A. Wilson, "Reality Television Celebrity: Star Consumption and Self-Production in Media Culture," in *A Companion to Reality Television*, ed. Laurie Ouellette (Malden, MA: Wiley Blackwell, 2014), 430.

64 Frankel has not achieved the same level of success outside reality television. Frankel briefly helmed *Bethenny* (2014), a network talk show canceled in part, I would suggest, because Frankel's scrappy, sharp-tongued New York persona did not translate across the nation's many nonurban centers.

65 Kavita Ilona Nayar, "You Didn't Build That: Audience Reception of a Reality Television Star's Transformation from a Real Housewife to a Real Brand," *Journal of Popular Culture* 48, no. 1 (2015): 3–16.

66 Ibid., 8.

67 Jacquelyn Arcy, "Affective Enterprising: Branding the Self Through Emotional Excess," in *The Fantasy of Reality: Critical Essays on "The Real Housewives,"* ed. Rachel Silverman (New York: Peter Lang, 2015), 75, 82, 84.

68 Widdicombe, "Perfect Pitching."

69 Alison Hearn, "Producing 'Reality': Branded Content, Branded Selves, Precarious Futures," in *A Companion to Reality Television*, ed. Laurie Ouellette (Malden, MA: Wiley Blackwell, 2014), 438.

70 Youyoung Lee, "*The Real Housewives* of Bankruptcies, Businesses, and Divorces by the Numbers," *Huffington Post*, January 25, 2013, http://www.huffingtonpost.com/.

71 June Deery, "Mapping Commercialization in Reality Television," in *A Companion to Reality Television*, ed. Laurie Ouellette (Malden, MA: Wiley Blackwell, 2014), 19.

72 Chocano, "Housewives, Rebranded."

73 Jessica Grose, "Happy Housewives," *Slate*, November 18, 2010, http://www.slate.com/.

CHAPTER 4. FROM BASKETBALL WIVES TO EXTREME COUGAR WIVES

1 Lauren Squires, "Class and Productive Avoidance in *The Real Housewives* Reunions," *Discourse, Context, and Media* 6 (2014): 37–38.

2 Lauren Berlant, *The Female Complaint* (Durham, NC: Duke University Press, 2008), 5, 19.

3 Sender, *The Makeover*, 44.

4 Skeggs, "Value of Relationships," 30.

5 Lieber, "Realism's Housewives," 122.

6 Hearn, "Producing 'Reality,'" 445.

7 Hearn, "Producing 'Reality,'" 445, 448.

8 For an investigation of segmentation in cable markets, see Joseph Turow, *Breaking Up America: Advertisers and the New Media World* (Chicago: University of Chicago Press, 1997); Sarah Banet-Weiser, Cynthia Chris and Anthony Freitas, eds., *Cable Visions: Television Beyond Broadcasting* (New York: New York University Press, 2007); Catherine Johnson, *Branding Television* (London: Routledge,

2011); and Amanda Lotz, *The Television Will Be Revolutionized* (New York: New York University Press, 2014).

9 Laura Grindstaff, "Just Be Yourself—Only More So: Ordinary Celebrity in the Era of Self-Service Television," in *Real Worlds: The Global Politics of Reality Television*, ed. Marwan M. Kraidy and Katherine Sender (Routledge: New York, 2011), 45.

10 The Lifetime show *UnReal* (2015–) similarly focuses on the conditions of production for a *Bachelor*-esque reality show and coldly illustrates the deeply manipulative role that producers play in orchestrating scenarios and events.

11 Grindstaff, "Just Be Yourself," 51.

12 Jane Feuer, "'Quality' Reality and the Bravo Media Reality Series," *Camera Obscura* 30, no. 1 88 (2015): 191.

13 Baldwin, "Buzz by Bravo," 188.

14 Terry Nelson, "Exploiting and Capitalizing on Unique Black Femininity: An Entrepreneurial Perspective," in *Real Sister: Stereotypes, Respectability and Black Women in Reality TV*, ed. Jervette R. Ward (New Brunswick, NJ: Rutgers University Press, 2015), 170.

15 Bruce, "Guiltiest Pleasure on Television."

16 Kristen J. Warner, "They Gon' Think You Loud Regardless: Ratchetness, Reality Television, and Black Womanhood," *Camera Obscura* 30, no. 1 88 (2015): 134.

17 Jacquelyn Arcy, "Real Housework: Branding Emotional Labor in *The Real Housewives of New York City*," *In Media Res*, March 14, 2013, http://mediacommons.futureofthebook.org/.

18 Ruth Wollersheim, "Retrograde Returns of the American Housewife: Reimagining an Old Character in a New Millennium" (PhD diss., University of Wisconsin–Milwaukee, 2015), 132.

19 "Bravo Spec Sheet," app. B of Baldwin, "Buzz by Bravo."

20 Ironically, Bravo became so successful that it eventually eclipsed its parent company. By 2010, Bravo was worth five times more than NBC. Peter Lauria, "The 25 Most Valuable Cable Channels," *Daily Beast*, September 20, 2010, http://www.thedailybeast.com/.

21 Daisy Whitney, "Bravo Stretches, Adds Viewers and Advertisers," *Advertising Age*, June 9, 2003.

22 Katherine Sender, "Dualcasting: Bravo's Gay Programming and the Quest for Women Audiences," in *Cable Visions: Television Beyond Broadcasting*, ed. Sarah Banet-Weiser, Cynthia Chris, and Anthony Freitas (New York: New York University Press, 2007), 310–13.

23 "About Bravo Media," *NBCUniversal*, n.d., http://www.nbcuniversal.com/.

24 Nicole Cox and Jennifer Proffitt, "The Housewives' Guide to Better Living: Promoting Consumption on Bravo's *The Real Housewives*," *Communication, Culture and Critique* 5, no. 2 (2012): 295–312.

25 Pier Dominguez, "'I'm Very Rich, Bitch!': The Melodramatic Money Shot and the Excess of Racialized Gendered Affect in the *Real Housewives* Docusoaps," *Camera Obscura* 30, no. 1 88 (2015): 187.

26 Vicki Mayer, "Housewives in Crisis, Economic That Is," *Flow*, January 10, 2010, http://blog.commarts.wisc.edu/.

27 Stephanie Clifford, "We'll Make You a Star (If the Web Agrees)," *New York Times*, June 5, 2010.

28 Jorie Lagerwey, "*Kell on Earth*: Kelly Kutrone and the Rare Failure of Brand Bravo," *Flow*, June 2013, http://www.flowjournal.org/.

29 Feuer, "'Quality' Reality and the Bravo Media Reality Series," 187.

30 Peter Bjelskou, "The Real Entrepreneurs of New York City: Selling Elegance and Class in the Marketplace," in *The Fantasy of Reality: Critical Essays on "The Real Housewives*," ed. Rachel Silverman (New York: Peter Lang, 2015), 94.

31 Mike Vulpo, "I Went 24 Hours Using Only *Real Housewives* Products and Life Became a Lot More Fabulous," *E! News*, July 20, 2015, http://www.eonline.com/.

32 "Bravo Exec on the Art of Creating 'Reality,'" *National Public Radio*, August 12, 2009, http://www.npr.org/.

33 Jorie Lagerwey, *Postfeminist Celebrity and Motherhood: Brand Mom* (New York: Routledge, 2016), 53.

34 Michael J. Lee and Leigh Moscowitz, "The 'Rich Bitch': Class and Gender on *The Real Housewives of New York City*," *Feminist Media Studies* 13, no. 1 (2013): 79.

35 Dominguez, "I'm Very Rich, Bitch!" 158–59.

36 For a discussion of Bravo's use of cross-promotion, see Erin Copple Smith, "'Affluencers' by Bravo: Defining an Audience through Cross Promotion," *Popular Communication* 10, no. 4 (2012): 286–301.

37 Baldwin, "Buzz by Bravo."

38 Catherine R. Squires, "The Conundrum of Race and Reality Television," in *A Companion to Reality Television*, ed. Laurie Ouellette (Malden, MA: Wiley Blackwell, 2014), 268.

39 As Alison Hearn argues in "Producing 'Reality,'" branded formats dominate reality television show production: "Like a recipe for a program, a format can include a program bible, production guidelines, requisite soundtracks, set-design instructions, and graphic elements that are then filled with local content" (443).

40 I borrow this argument in part from Dominguez, who notes in "I'm Very Rich, Bitch!" that Bravo has "included white cast members in programs with primarily black casts to help maintain the white racial imaginary of its viewers" (171).

41 Racquel Gates, "Keepin' It Reality Television," in *Watching While Black: Centering the Television of Black Audiences*, ed. Beretta E. Smith-Shomade (New Brunswick, NJ: Rutgers University Press, 2012), 141.

42 Squires, "Conundrum of Race and Reality Television," 269.

43 Wollersheim, "Retrograde Returns of the American Housewife," 157.

44 In the reality show *Newlyweds* (2003–5), singer Jessica Simpson guilelessly asked her then husband, Nick Lachey, "Is this chicken, what I have, or is this fish? I know it's tuna, but it says 'Chicken of the Sea.'" The comment predictably subjected Simpson to significant ridicule.

45 Gretta Moody, "Real Black, Real Money: African American Audiences on *The Real Housewives of Atlanta*," in *How Television Shapes Our Worldview: Media Representations of Social Trends*, ed. Deborah Macey, Kathleen Ryan, and Noah Springer (New York: Lexington Books, 2014), 277, 283–84.

46 See Nicole Cox, "Race (Re)visited: It's a (Mostly) White World," in *The Fantasy of Reality: Critical Essays on "The Real Housewives*," ed. Rachel Silverman (New York: Peter Lang, 2015), 43–58.

47 Cynthia Davis, "The Semiotics of Fashion and Urban Success in *The Real Housewives of Atlanta*," in *Real Sister: Stereotypes, Respectability, and Black Women in Reality TV*, ed. Jervette R. Ward (New Brunswick, NJ: Rutgers University Press, 2015), 72–73.

48 Robin M. Boylorn, "'Brains, Booty, and All Bizness': Identity Politics, Ratchet Respectability, and *The Real Housewives of Atlanta*," in *The Fantasy of Reality: Critical Essays on The Real Housewives*, ed. Rachel Silverman (New York: Peter Lang, 2015), 34.

49 Quoted in Warner, "They Gon' Think You Loud Regardless," 146–47.

50 For a link to the video, see "Nene Leakes: 'RHOA' Is So Popular Because We're Brown!" November 9, 2012, http://bossip.com/.

51 Nina Cartier, "Black Women On-Screen as Future Texts: A New Look at Black Pop Culture Representations," *Cinema Journal* 53, no. 4 (2014): 150.

52 Dominguez, "I'm Very Rich, Bitch!" 181n33, 170.

53 Jennifer Fuller, "Branding Blackness on US Cable Television," *Media, Culture and Society* 32, no. 2 (2010): 287.

54 Sherri Williams and Lynessa Williams, "#BlackSocialTV: How Black Viewers Are Dominating on Two Screens," *The List*, May 5, 2014, http://medium.com/.

55 Andy Cohen, *Most Talkative: Stories from the Front Lines of Pop Culture* (New York: Henry Holt, 2012), 196.

56 Kraszewski, "Branding, Nostalgia, and the Politics of Race on VH1's *Flavor of Love*," 243, 245.

57 Fuller, "Branding Blackness on US Cable Television," 289.

58 Dubrofsky and Hardy, "Performing Race in *Flavor of Love* and *The Bachelor*," 376.

59 Berlant, *Female Complaint*, 13, 15, 16.

60 Racquel Gates, "You Can't Turn a Ho into a Housewife: *Basketball Wives* and the Politics of Wifedom," *In Media Res*, September 26, 2011, http://mediacommons.futureofthebook.org/.

61 Jagesic, "Race and Relationship Advice," 87.

62 Racquel Gates, "Activating the Negative Image," *Television and New Media* 16, no. 7 (2015): 622.

63 Jeannine Amber, "Real World," *Essence*, January 2013.

64 Warner, "They Gon' Think You Loud Regardless," 143–44.

65 Gates, "Activating the Negative Image," 623.

66 Racquel Gates speculates that the popularity of shows like *Basketball Wives* and the cultural visibility of their female stars likely helped to convince larger,

mainstream networks like Fox that there were lucrative black television audiences eager for programming, which resulted in black-focused hits like the music melodrama *Empire* (2015–). Forum post, *Console-ing Passions*, June 2016.

67 Amber, "Real World."

68 Gates, "Activating the Negative Image," 623.

69 Erica B. Edwards, "'It's Irrelevant to Me!' Young Black Women Talk Back to VH1's *Love and Hip Hop New York*," *Journal of Black Studies* 47, no. 3 (2016): 288.

70 Mary Billard, "Silent Partners No Longer," *New York Times*, March 29, 2012.

71 Ibid.

72 David Knowles, "VH1's 'Mob Wives' Could Challenge the 'Housewives' Franchise," *Hollywood Reporter*, April 15, 2011.

73 Lauren Steussey, "*Mob Wives* Creator Had Her Reasons: 'I Set These Women Free,'" January 12, 2016, http://www.silive.com/.

74 Misha Kavka, "Truly, Madly, Queerly: Extending the Camp Canon" (paper presented at the annual meeting for the Society of Cinema and Media Studies, Atlanta, March 31–April 3, 2016).

75 Misha Kavka, "A Matter of Feeling: Mediated Affect in Reality Television," in *A Companion to Reality Television*, ed. Laurie Ouellette (Malden, MA: Wiley Blackwell, 2014), 462, 464.

76 Moya Luckett, "Playmates and Polygamists: Feminine Textuality in *Big Love*, *Sister Wives*, and *The Girls Next Door*," *Feminist Media Studies* 14, no. 4 (2014): 566.

77 Brenda R. Weber, "The Epistemology of the (Televised, Polygamous) Closet: Progressive Polygamy, Spiritual Neoliberalism, and the Will to Visibility," *Television and New Media* 17, no. 5 (2016): 382.

78 Luckett, "Playmates and Polygamists," 568–69.

79 Squires, "Conundrum of Race and Reality Television," 268.

CHAPTER 5. GOOD WIVES

1 The plight of America's wronged wives was explored in a 2014 Broadway play, *Tail! Spin!* where *Saturday Night Live* veteran Rachel Dratch channels notables such as Jenny Sanford and Huma Abedin. The play's dialogue is assembled from interviews, public statements, and the often-off-color communications between straying husbands and their paramours.

2 "Wives of Spitzer, Weiner Scrutinized in NYC Races," *Associated Press*, July 21, 2013.

3 Sharon Cotliar, Kristen Mascia, and Sandra Sobieraj Westfall, "Real Life 'Good Wives' Blindsided and Betrayed," *People*, November 9, 2009.

4 The iconic picture of Diane and Hillary on what appears to be a political stage appeared numerous times in the series.

5 Dina Matos McGreevey, *Silent Partner: A Memoir of My Marriage* (New York: Hyperion, 2007), 238–39.

6 Weiner's scandal has been a media favorite, perhaps in no small part because the crass associations his last name invokes inevitably court jest. A 2013 episode

of *Law and Order: SVU* (1999–), for example, featured a mayoral candidate who favored racy correspondence with underage women, using the pseudonym "Enrique Trouble." During the same period, *Scandal*'s aptly titled episode "Say Hello to My Little Friend" outlined a senator's troubles after one of the myriad women he has been sexting is murdered. Even the otherwise fairly highbrow Showtime series *Homeland* (2011–) spoofed Weiner's troubles, naming a congressman who loses his seat for being caught with his pants down Richard "Dick" Johnson.

7 For an article which makes repeated reference to Abedin's intimacy with the Clintons, see Michael Grynbaum, Michael Barbaro, and Amy Chozick, "A Wife with Powerful Ties Is an Unexpected Architect of a New York Comeback," *New York Times*, May 23, 2013.

8 Media theorist Mark Andrejevic importantly credits the Lewinsky scandal with having "highlighted the split that characterized the reception of news *as* entertainment." See *Reality TV: The Work of Being Watched* (Lanham, MD: Rowman and Littlefield, 2004), 73. Matt Bai's *All the Truth Is Out: The Week Politics Went Tabloid* (New York: Knopf, 2014), however, dates the sea change in political reporting to a different sex scandal, the 1987 Gary Hart affair. The Democratic presidential hopeful's career careened off course thanks to pictures taken of his extramarital dalliance aboard the all-too-fittingly named *Monkey Business* yacht, a scandal Bai credits with turning unprecedented attention to the personal character of political candidates.

9 For a reading of how the *National Enquirer* earned its journalistic stripes thanks to its relentless investigation of John Edwards' affair, and its discovery of the hyperbolically extreme measures the politician was taking to cover it up, see Howard Kurtz, "Tabloid Takedown," *Playboy*, February 2005.

10 Jonathan Van Meter, "Anthony Weiner and Huma Abedin's Post-Scandal Playbook," *New York Times Magazine*, April 10, 2013.

11 Hillary Clinton, *Living History* (New York: Scribner, 2003), 501.

12 Rebecca Johnson, "The Survivor: Silda Spitzer," *Vogue*, March 2009.

13 Though the network had plans to extend the series into a full-season show, this project never materialized and *Political Animals* ended after six episodes.

14 Confirming the central role that Clinton played in inspiring television dramas, on October 17, 2013, the *New York Times* ran an article titled "Hillary Rodham Clinton Meets Her TV Counterparts" about Clinton's presence at a fund-raiser also attended by Julianna Margulies and Sigourney Weaver.

15 Quoted in Breia Brissey, "*The Good Wife* Is the Best Show on TV . . . Again," *Entertainment Weekly*, November 8, 2013.

16 David Stout, "Testing of a President: The Other Woman; Flowers Acknowledges Earning $500,000 from Scandal," *New York Times*, March 21, 1998.

17 For an overview of these developments in celebrity culture, see Graeme Turner, *Understanding Celebrity* (London: Sage, 2004); Turner, *Ordinary People and the Media* (London: Sage, 2010); and Su Holmes and Sean Redmond, eds., *New Directions in Celebrity Culture* (London: Routledge, 2006).

18 Further evidence of the staying power of the Lewinsky story appeared in 2013, when chick lit authors Emma McLaughlin and Nicola Kraus released *The First Affair*, an imaginative re-creation wherein the first-person narrator is a young White House intern who has an affair with a sitting president. Featuring a smoldering relationship characterized by oral sex, a stained dress, and inventive uses of a hairbrush, the book's evocation of the real-life scandal is unmistakable. Emma McLaughlin and Nicola Kraus, *The First Affair* (New York: Atria Books, 2013).

19 Monica Lewinsky, "Shame and Survival," *Vanity Fair*, June 2014.

20 Rielle Hunter, *What Really Happened: John Edwards, Our Daughter, and Me* (New York: Benbella Books, 2012). Hunter's widely panned book was released weeks after the conclusion of a sensationalized trial wherein Edwards was accused of using campaign donations to hide the affair from his wife, Elizabeth. He was eventually acquitted of one of the charges, and the jury was hung on the rest of the counts. A mistrial was declared, but Edwards was never retried.

21 Chris Rojek calls such figures "cele-toids" in order to underscore the tabloid aspects of their celebrity. Rojek, *Celebrity* (London: Reaktion Books, 2001), 20–21.

22 AshleyMadison.com is the popular online dating site designed to facilitate connections between users in search of extramarital affairs.

23 "Hillary Clinton Reveals Anguish over Lewinsky Saga," *Bangladesh News*, January 22, 2008.

24 Clinton, *Living History*, 468.

25 The idea that it is empowering for women to tell their own stories in a first-person voice has a long history in feminist literary criticism. See, for example, Joanne S. Frye, *Living Stories, Telling Lives: Women and the Novel in Contemporary Experience* (Ann Arbor: University of Michigan Press, 1986); Rita Felski, *Beyond Feminist Aesthetics: Feminist Literature and Social Change* (Cambridge, MA: Harvard University Press, 1989); and Gayle Greene, *Changing the Story: Feminist Fiction and the Tradition* (Bloomington: Indiana University Press, 1991).

26 In 2010, *Ms. Magazine* called *The Good Wife* "one of the most feminist shows currently on television." Aviva Dove-Viebahn, "Stand by Your Man?" *Ms. Magazine*, Spring 2010.

27 Tatiana Siegel, "Scandals Juicy, but Market Dry," *Variety*, May 30–June 5, 2011.

28 Tatiana Baez, "Huma Abedin Tells All: Weiner's Estranged Wife Reportedly Seeks Book Deal for $2 Million," *Salon*, April 14, 2017, http://www.salon.com/.

29 Berlant, *Female Complaint*, 2. A series of similarly painful memoirs from less public figures emerged during a coterminous period, a cohort that attests further to the prevalence of the female complaint genre. See Julie Metz, *Perfection: A Memoir of Betrayal and Renewal* (New York: Voice, 2009); Laura Munson, *This Is Not the Story You Think It Is: A Season of Unlikely Happiness* (New York: Amy Einhorn Books, 2010); Rachel Cusk, *Aftermath: On Marriage and Separation* (New York: Farrar, Straus and Giroux, 2012); and Jen Waite, *A Beautiful, Terrible Thing: A Memoir of Marriage and Betrayal* (New York: Plume, 2017).

30 Berlant, *Female Complaint*, 2.

31 Nathan Rambukkana, *Fraught Intimacies: Non/Monogamy in the Public Sphere* (Vancouver: University of British Columbia Press, 2015).

32 Katharine Q. Seelye, "A New Twist to Wives' Playbook for Sex Scandals," *New York Times*, June 18, 2011.

33 Jenny Sanford, *Staying True* (New York: Ballantine, 2010), 180.

34 Ibid., 78, 182, 112–14.

35 Ibid., 123.

36 Matos McGreevey, *Silent Partner*, 3, 23, 28, 134.

37 Elizabeth Edwards, *Resilience* (New York: Broadway Books, 2009), 137–38.

38 Jenny Sanford is nevertheless an exception to this statement. She describes her contributions to her husband's campaign as follows: "This work was really about achieving Mark's dream and not my own." However, she did find his political aspirations "worthy" (*Staying True*, 51).

39 Edwards, *Resilience*, 204, 218.

40 Michelle Cottle, "The Real Running Mates," *Newsweek*, May 23–30, 2011.

41 Matos McGreevey, *Silent Partner*, 233.

42 Cottle, "Real Running Mates," 56.

43 Karen Tumulty and Jason Horowitz, "Huma Abedin Steps into High-Profile Role as Anthony Weiner's Chief Defender," *Washington Post*, July 24, 2013.

44 Edwards, *Resilience*, 222–23.

45 Gayle Haggard with Angela Hunt, *Why I Stayed: The Choices I Made in My Darkest Hour* (Carol Stream, IL: Tyndale House Publishers, 2010), 236.

46 The term Super Tuesday refers to the day in presidential primary season when the most U.S. states hold elections and caucuses. It can be a turning point in contentious primary cycles, meaning that the winner of Super Tuesday typically goes on to secure the party's nomination.

47 Steve Kornaki, "When Maria Shriver Stood by Her Man," *Salon*, May 17, 2011, http://www.salon.com/.

48 Eric Bradner, "Melania Trump: Donald Trump Was 'Egged On' into 'Boy Talk,'" *CNN*, October 18, 2016, http://www.cnn.com/.

49 Sandra Sobieraj Westfall, "Anthony Weiner, 'I Feel Like a Different Person,'" *People*, July 30, 2012.

50 Mark Jacobson, "Huma? Hey, Honey? Was I Happy before I Started Running for Mayor?" *New York*, July 14, 2013.

51 Westfall, "Anthony Weiner, 'I Feel Like a Different Person,'" 60.

52 Jonathan Van Meter, "Anthony Weiner and Huma Abedin's Post-Scandal Playbook," *New York Times Magazine*, April 10, 2013.

53 A *People* magazine article titled "Why Huma Stayed" postulates, "In the end it wasn't politics that kept her with him. It was their son." *People*, August 12, 2013.

54 Westfall, "Anthony Weiner, 'I Feel Like a Different Person,'" 60.

55 Van Meter, "Anthony Weiner and Huma Abedin's Post-Scandal Playbook."

56 Ibid.

57 Grynbaum, Barbaro, and Chozick, "A Wife with Powerful Ties Is an Unexpected Architect of a New York Comeback."

58 Huma Abedin, "The Good Wife," *Harper's Bazaar*, September 2013.

59 Rebecca Johnson, "Hillary's Secret Weapon: Huma Abedin," *Vogue*, August 1, 2007.

60 Hinda Mandell, "Stand by Your Man Revisited: Political Wives and Scandal," in *Media Depictions of Brides, Wives, and Mothers*, ed. Alena Amato Ruggerio (New York: Lexington Books, 2012), 143–54.

61 Mark Leibovich, "Anthony Weiner Says His Wife Never Agreed to That Documentary," *New York Times*, August 19, 2016.

62 Nathan Heller, "Huma Abedin on Her Job, Family, and the Campaign of a Lifetime," *Vogue*, August 17, 2016.

INDEX

Note: Page numbers in *italics* indicate photographs.

ABOUT THE AUTHOR

Suzanne Leonard is Associate Professor of English at Simmons College and co-coordinator of the college's interdisciplinary minor in cinema and media studies. She is the author of *Fatal Attraction* (2009) and co-editor of *Fifty Hollywood Directors* (2015).